Lecture Notes in Computer Science 8338

Commenced Publication in 1973
Founding and Former Series Editors:
Gerhard Goos, Juris Hartmanis, and Jan van Leeuwen

T0224796

John Barnes

Ada 2012 Rationale

The Language
The Standard Libraries

 Springer

Author

John Barnes
John Barnes Informatics
11 Albert Road, Caversham, Reading RG4 7AN, UK
E-mail: jgpb@jbinfo.demon.co.uk

ISSN 0302-9743   e-ISSN 1611-3349
ISBN 978-3-642-45209-3   e-ISBN 978-3-642-45210-9
DOI 10.1007/978-3-642-45210-9
Springer Heidelberg New York Dordrecht London

Library of Congress Control Number: 2013954445

CR Subject Classification (1998): D.3, D.4, D.1, D.2

LNCS Sublibrary: SL 2 – Programming and Software Engineering

Typeset by John Barnes Informatics.
Camera-ready by author, data conversion by Markus Richter, Heidelberg

Printed on acid-free paper

Springer is part of Springer Science+Business Media (www.springer.com)

Foreword

Programming languages and their user and implementer communities are living organisms, which – as time goes by – either decay and perish in obsolescence or evolve in a dynamic combination of wisdom that comes with age and freshness that comes with vision.

Almost six years after writing the foreword to the Rationale for Ada 2005, I look with marvel at Ada 2012, at how it has come about, at the extent of innovation that it carries, and at the competence, dedication, rigour, perseverance and solidity of the community that has worked to make it happen.

Ada 2005 was in many ways a beautiful programming language, perhaps more intellectually than aesthetically, as in the Ada style of things. It brought the promises of Ada 95 to maturation and added great features in a number of its key areas of strength. The technology gap was important for some vendors however, and the user community had to invest considerable resources in digesting the novelty that it brought about. Ada 2005 attracted attention to itself from outside its niche market and gained respect from those knowledgeable in object orientation, real-time and systems programming and container libraries. So one may wonder what caused the Ada 2012 project to start at all, aside from the normative obligation entailed by ISO governance, to confirm, withdraw or amend every individual standard at five year intervals.

The term that comes to mind to explain the Ada 2012 project is "vision". Ada has always been strong in application domains where safety and criticality concerns are paramount. For as much as those domains are intrinsically conservative and not inclined to giant leaps, their needs, however, are not static and, as of late, have begun to evolve more rapidly than in the past, to keep pace with internal and external changes. New needs emerged, which required fresh attention and timely response. It takes vision to see those needs coming and even more so to devise a response to them that meets the user requirement, can be satisfactorily developed by language implementers, and fits in with the language structure, style and use.

One major emerging need was for specification contracts to protect the program from incorrect composition at run time. For programs to be robust, safely reusable and long lasting, you want expressive contracts to be attached to specifications – contracts that talk to the programmer and not only to the compiler – so that a solid and semantically rich understanding can be established between the user of the program component, be it a procedure or a type, and its implementer. The Ada 2012 response to this challenge was to introduce pre- and post-conditions for subprograms, invariants for types and predicates for subtypes. This was a bold move that made Ada the first mainstream programming language to offer those features as part of an ISO standard.

The other main need was to allow Ada programs to run, with adequate guarantees of time predictability, on multicore and multithreaded architectures. The Ada response to this need has been solid so that users can build on it safely and effectively but also cautious: multicore architectures and parallel programming are very complex beasts, which defeat intuition, break composability and threaten predictability. Much more research is needed to learn how to master all aspects of them before relevant solutions become mature enough to make it into industrial technology such as Ada.

While working on those two momentous challenges, as directed by WG9, the body within ISO/IEC JTC1/SC22 which has responsibility for the maintenance of the Ada standard, the ARG (the body of technical experts that actually does the language standard maintenance work) of course also considered corrective and adaptive maintenance needs arising from user and implementation experience with Ada 2005. In the end, the amount of work that went into the Ada 2012 project and the extent of changes that resulted from it were larger than anticipated: evidence that there is energy that can be drawn from in the Ada community.

It is a pleasure for me to invite the reader to read and enjoy this Rationale for Ada 2012, under the knowledgeable hand, deft guidance, and witty style of its author, John Barnes, who continues to surprise me with how vast, profound, and complete is his understanding of the language, no matter how large it grows. It is especially instructive for me to appreciate how humbling it is to parallel my standing to his, in all matters of Ada authority.

Producing this book as an LNCS volume is a financial burden that Ada-Europe would not have been able to sustain alone. On behalf of Ada-Europe, I am grateful to all those who supported the production project. Particularly prominent, in fact, and indeed vital, in that respect has been the role of AdaCore, which I want to acknowledge both personally and institutionally.

Much as happened with the Rationale for Ada 2005, the readers of the Ada User Journal, the quarterly publication of Ada-Europe, were able to get first-hand incremental instalments of the Rationale for Ada 2012. Having stepped from the role of editor-in-chief of the Ada User Journal to that of President of Ada-Europe I have perhaps gained in status but lost the privilege of being the first reader of those instalments. An LNCS volume entirely devoted to the Rationale for Ada 2012 is a great achievement, as a prestigious venue in itself, and as the continuation of the Ada presence in a lead vehicle for the publication of advances in computer science.

It is most likely that writing this Foreword closes the bracket that inaugurated my service as President of Ada-Europe by writing the Foreword to the 2005 edition of the Rationale. I am taking this as a wish that Ada 2012 will have a sufficiently long and successful life to see me safely go before a new Foreword will have to be written.

Dear reader: I am delighted that I can again present to your doorstep, or to a library near you, a book of this value; I promise you that it will be worth your reading.

Tullio Vardanega
Ada-Europe, President
Padua
Italy
September 2013

Preface

Welcome to Ada 2012. This Rationale should enable those familiar with Ada 2005 to gain a basic understanding of the new features introduced into Ada 2012 and the reasons for the changes from Ada 2005.

This document starts with an introduction which provides an overview of the changes. There are then a number of major chapters looking at seven key areas (contracts, expressions, structure and visibility, tasking, general stuff, predefined library and containers) and finally an epilogue largely concerned with compatibility issues.

Earlier versions of individual chapters were previously published in the Ada User Journal as a number of separate papers in the issues from September 2011 until September 2013.

I need to thank all those who have helped in the preparation of this document. First I must acknowledge the help of AdaCore and Ada-Europe for financial support for attending various meetings. And then I must thank those who have helped in various ways. There are almost too many to name, but I must give thanks to Randy Brukardt, Ed Schonberg and Tucker Taft of the ARG, to Jeff Cousins, Alan Burns and other colleagues on the UK Ada Panel (BSI/IST/5/–/9), to Joyce Tokar of WG9, and to Tullio Vardanega, Luis Miguel Pinho and Patricia López Martínez of Ada-Europe.

I must especially thank Randy for his diligence and patience in reviewing various drafts of the individual papers and putting me back on track when I got lost. In addition, I must thank Randy for his efforts in creating a version of this Rationale for the web and especially for creating an extremely valuable index which is incorporated here.

Writing this rationale has been a learning experience for me and I trust that readers will also find the material useful in learning about Ada 2012. An integrated description of Ada 2012 as a whole including some further examples will be found in a forthcoming version of my textbook.

Finally, for the full details, please consult the Ada 2012 Reference Manual or the version known as the Annotated Ada Reference Manual which contains much additional commentary. These will be found online on the AdaIC website at http://www.adaic.org/ada-resources/standards/ada12.

Moreover, the Ada 2012 Reference Manual is also published as LNCS 8339 in the same style as this Rationale.

John Barnes
Caversham
England
October 2013

Contents

Foreword v

Preface vii

1 Introduction 1

1.1 Revision process 1
1.2 Scope of revision 1
1.3 Overview of changes 3
    1.3.1 Contracts 4
    1.3.2 Expressions 9
    1.3.3 Structure and visibility 15
    1.3.4 Tasking and real-time facilities 18
    1.3.5 General improvements 21
    1.3.6 Standard library 25
1.4 Conclusions 30

2 Contracts and Aspects 33

2.1 Overview of changes 33
2.2 Aspect specifications 34
2.3 Preconditions and postconditions 42
2.4 Type invariants 51
2.5 Subtype predicates 56
2.6 Default initial values 61
2.7 Storage occupancy checks 63

3 Expressions 65

3.1 Overview of changes 65
3.2 If expressions 66
3.3 Case expressions 70
3.4 Quantified expressions 71
3.5 Expression functions 73
3.6 Membership tests 77
3.7 Qualified expressions 80

4 Structure and Visibility 83

4.1 Overview of changes 83
4.2 Subprogram parameters 84
4.3 Incomplete types 88
4.4 Discriminants 92

| 4.5 | Use clauses | 92 |
| 4.6 | Extended return statements | 95 |

5   Tasking and Real-Time   99

5.1	Overview of changes	99
5.2	Scheduling	100
5.3	Multiprocessors	103
5.4	Interrupt timers and budgets	108
5.5	Volatile	109
5.6	Synchronized interfaces and requeue	110

6   Iterators, Pools, etc.   115

6.1	Overview of changes	115
6.2	Position of pragmas and labels	116
6.3	Iteration	120
6.4	Access types and storage pools	132
6.5	Restrictions	139
6.6	Miscellanea	143

7   Predefined Library   147

7.1	Overview of changes	147
7.2	Strings and characters	148
7.3	Directories	152
7.4	Locale	155
7.5	Hashing and comparison	156
7.6	Miscellanea	156

8   Containers   159

8.1	Overview of changes	159
8.2	Bounded and unbounded containers	159
8.3	Iterating and updating containers	164
8.4	Multiway tree containers	168
8.5	The holder container	178
8.6	Queue containers	180
8.7	Sorting	187
8.8	Streaming	189

9   Epilogue   191

9.1	Compatibility	191
	9.1.1 Incompatibilities with Ada 2005	191
	9.1.2 Inconsistencies with Ada 2005	193
9.2	Retrospective changes to Ada 2005	193
	9.2.1 Incompatibilities with original Ada 2005	194
	9.2.2 Inconsistencies with original Ada 2005	194

9.3   Unfinished topics from Ada 2005   195
           9.3.1 Aggregates for private types   195
           9.3.2 Partial generic instantiation   196
           9.3.3 Support for IEEE 559: 1989   196
           9.3.4 Defaults for generic parameters   196
           9.3.5 Pre/post conditions for subprograms   197
           9.3.6 Type and package invariants   197
           9.3.7 Exceptions as types   197
           9.3.8 Sockets operations   197
           9.3.9 In out parameters for functions   197
           9.3.10 Application defined scheduling   198
9.4   Unfinished topics for Ada 2012   198
           9.4.1 Integrated packages   198
           9.4.2 Cyclic fixed point   198
           9.4.3 Global annotations   199
           9.4.4 Shorthand for assignments   199
9.5   Postscript   199

References   205

Index   207

1 Introduction

This first chapter covers the background to the development of Ada 2012 and gives a brief overview of the main changes from Ada 2005. Other chapters then look at the changes in more detail.

1.1 Revision process

Ada has evolved over a number of years and, especially for those unfamiliar with the background, it is convenient to summarize the processes involved. The first version was Ada 83 and this was developed by a team led by the late Jean Ichbiah and funded by the USDoD. The development of Ada 95 from Ada 83 was an extensive process also funded by the USDoD. Formal requirements were established after comprehensive surveys of user needs and competitive proposals were then submitted resulting in the selection of Intermetrics as the developer under the leadership of Tucker Taft. Then came Ada 2005 and this was developed on a more modest scale. The work was almost entirely done by voluntary effort with support from within the industry itself through bodies such as the Ada Resource Association and Ada-Europe.

After some experience with Ada 2005 it became clear that some further evolution was appropriate. Adding new features as in Ada 2005 always brings some surprises regarding their use and further polishing is almost inevitable. Accordingly, it was decided that a further revision should be made with a goal of completion in 2012.

As in the case of Ada 2005, the development was performed under the guidance of ISO/IEC JTC1/SC22 WG9 (hereinafter just called WG9). Previously chaired by Jim Moore, it is now under the chairmanship of Joyce Tokar. This committee has included national representatives of many nations including Belgium, Canada, France, Germany, Italy, Japan, Spain, Sweden, Switzerland, the UK and the USA. WG9 developed guidelines [1] for a revision to Ada 2005 which were then used by the Ada Rapporteur Group (the ARG) in drafting the revised standard.

The ARG is a team of experts nominated by the national bodies represented on WG9 and the two liaison organizations, ACM SIGAda and Ada-Europe. In the case of Ada 2005, the ARG was originally led by Erhard Plödereder and then by Pascal Leroy. For Ada 2012, it was led by Ed Schonberg. The editor, who at the end of the day actually writes the words of the standard, continues to be the indefatigable Randy Brukardt.

Suggestions for the revised standard have come from a number of sources such as individuals on the ARG, national bodies on WG9, users and implementers via email discussions on Ada-Comment and so on. Also several issues were left over from the development of Ada 2005.

The revision process was completed early in 2012 and the new standard was approved late in 2012 thanks to a revised fast track mechanism.

1.2 Scope of revision

The changes from Ada 95 to Ada 2005 were significant (although not so large as the changes from Ada 83 to Ada 95). The main additions were

- in the OO area, multiple inheritance using interfaces and the ability to make calls using prefixed notation,

- more flexible access types with anonymous types, more control over null and constant, and downward closures via access to subprogram types,

- enhanced structure and visibility control by the introduction of limited with and private with clauses and by an extended form of return statement,

- in the real-time area, the Ravenscar profile [2], various new scheduling polices, timers and execution time budget control,

- some minor improvements to exception handling, numerics (especially fixed point) and some further pragmas such as Assert,

- various extensions to the standard library such as the introduction of operations on vectors and matrices, further operations on times and dates, and operations on wide wide characters; and especially:

- a comprehensive library for the manipulation of containers of various kinds.

The changes from Ada 2005 to Ada 2012 were intended to be relatively modest and largely to lead on from the experience of the additions introduced in Ada 2005. But one thing led to another and in fact the changes are of a similar order to those from Ada 95 to Ada 2005.

From the point of view of the ISO standard, Ada 2005 is the Ada 95 standard modified by two documents. First there was a Corrigendum issued in 2001 [3] and then an Amendment issued in 2005 [4]. In principle the poor user thus has to study these three documents in parallel to understand Ada 2005. However, they were informally incorporated into the Ada 2005 Reference Manual [5].

In the case of Ada 2012, this process of developing a further formal amendment would then lead to the need to consult four documents which would be madness and so this time we have simply a new Edition based formally on a single Revision.

The scope of this Revision is guided by a document issued by WG9 to the ARG in October 2008 [1]. The essence was that the ARG was requested to pay particular attention to

A   Improvements that will maintain or improve Ada's advantages, especially in those user domains where safety and criticality are prime concerns. Within this area it cites improving the use and functionality of containers, the ability to write and enforce contracts for Ada entities (for instance, via preconditions) and the capabilities of Ada on multicore and multithreaded architectures.

B   Improvements that will remedy shortcomings in Ada. It cites in particular the safety, use, and functionality of access types and dynamic storage management.

So the ARG was asked to improve both OO and real-time with a strong emphasis on real-time and high integrity features. Moreover, "design by contract" features should be added whereas for the previous amendment they were rejected on the grounds that they would not be static.

The ARG was also asked to consider the following factors in selecting features for inclusion:

- Implementability. Can the feature be implemented at reasonable cost?

- Need. Do users actually need it?

- Language stability. Would it appear disturbing to current users?

- Competition and popularity. Does it help to improve the perception of Ada and make it more competitive?

- Interoperability. Does it ease problems of interfacing with other languages and systems?

- Language consistency. Is it syntactically and semantically consistent with the language's current structure and design philosophy?

As before, an important further statement is that "In order to produce a technically superior result, it is permitted to compromise backwards compatibility when the impact on users is judged to be acceptable." In other words don't be paranoid about compatibility.

Finally, there is a warning about secondary standards. Its essence is don't use secondary standards if you can get the material into the RM itself.

The guidelines conclude with the target schedule. This includes WG9 approval of the scope of the amendment in June 2010 which was achieved and submission to ISO/IEC JTC1 in late 2011.

1.3   Overview of changes

It would be tedious to give a section by section review of the changes as seen by the Reference Manual language lawyer. Instead, the changes will be presented by areas as seen by the user. There can be considered to be six areas:

1   Introduction of dynamic contracts. These can be seen to lead on from the introduction of the Assert pragma in Ada 2005. New syntax (using **with** again) introduces aspect specifications which enable certain properties of entities to be stated where they are declared rather than later using representation clauses. This is put to good use in introducing pre- and postconditions for subprograms and similar assertions for types and subtypes.

2   More flexible expressions. The introduction of preconditions and so on increases the need for more powerful forms of expressions. Accordingly, if expressions, case expressions, quantified expressions and expression functions are all added. A related change is that membership tests are generalized.

3   Structure and visibility control. Functions are now permitted to have **out** and **in out** parameters, and rules are introduced to minimize the risk of inadvertent dependence on order of evaluation of parameters and other entities such as aggregates. More flexibility is permitted with incomplete types and another form of use clause is introduced. There are minor enhancements to extended return statements.

4   Tasking and real-time improvements. Almost all of the changes are in the Real-Time Systems annex. New packages are added for the control of tasks and budgeting on multiprocessor systems, and the monitoring of time spent in interrupts. There are also additional facilities for non-preemptive dispatching, task barriers and suspension objects.

5   Improvements to other general areas. More flexibility is allowed in the position of labels, pragmas, and null statements. A number of corrections are made to the accessibility rules, improvements are made to conversions of access types, and further control over storage pools is added. The composability of equality is now the same for both tagged and untagged record types.

6   Extensions to the standard library. Variants on the existing container packages are introduced to handle bounded containers more efficiently. Additional containers are added for a simple holder, multiway trees and queues. Moreover, a number of general features have been added to make containers and other such reusable libraries easier to use. Minor additions cover directories, locale capabilities, string encoding and further operations on wide and wide wide characters.

The reader might feel that the changes are quite extensive but each has an important role to play in making Ada more useful. Indeed the solution of one problem often leads to auxiliary requirements. The desire to introduce stronger description of contracts led to the search for good syntax which led to aspect specifications. And these strengthened the need for more flexible forms of expressions and so on. Some changes were driven by outside considerations such as multiprocessors and others stem from what now seem to be obvious but minor flaws in Ada 2005.

A number of potential changes were rejected as really unnecessary. For example, the author was at one time enthused by a desire for fixed point cyclic types. But it proved foolish without base 60 hardware to match our inheritance of arithmetic in a Babylonian style for angles.

Before looking at the six areas in a little more detail it is perhaps worth saying a few words about compatibility with Ada 2005. The guidelines gave the ARG freedom to be sensible in this area. Of course, the worst incompatibilities are those where a valid program in Ada 2005 continues to be valid in Ada 2012 but does something different. It is believed that incompatibilities of this nature will be most unlikely to arise in practice.

However, incompatibilities whereby a valid Ada 2005 program fails to compile in Ada 2012 are tolerable provided they are infrequent. A few such incompatibilities are possible. The most obvious cause is the introduction of one more reserved word, namely **some**, which is used in quantified expressions to match **all**. Thus if an existing Ada 2005 program uses **some** as an identifier then it will need modification. Once again, the introduction of a new category of unreserved keywords was considered but was eventually rejected as confusing.

1.3.1 Contracts

One of the important issues highlighted by WG9 for the Amendment was the introduction of material for enforcing contracts such as preconditions and postconditions. As a simple example consider a stack with procedures Push and Pop. An obvious precondition for Pop is that the stack must not be empty. If we have a function Is_Empty for testing the state of the stack then a call of Is_Empty would provide the basis for an appropriate precondition.

The question now is to find a good way to associate the expression **not** Is_Empty with the specification of the procedure Pop. Note that it is the specification that matters since it is the specification that provides the essence of the contract between the caller of the procedure Pop and the writer of its body. The contract provided by a traditional Ada subprogram specification is rather weak – essentially it just provides enough information for the compiler to generate the correct code for the calls but says nothing about the semantic behaviour of the associated body.

The traditional way to add information of this kind in Ada is via a pragma or by giving some kind of aspect clause. However, there were problems with this approach. One is that there is no convenient way to distinguish between several overloaded subprograms and another is that such information is given later on because of interactions with freezing and linear elaboration rules.

Accordingly, it was decided that a radical new approach should be devised and this led to the introduction of aspect specifications which are given with the item to which they relate using the reserved word **with**.

In the case of preconditions and postconditions, Ada 2012 introduces aspects Pre and Post. So to give the precondition for Pop we augment the specification of Pop by writing

```
procedure Pop(S: in out Stack; X: out Item)
  with Pre => not Is_Empty(S);
```

In a similar way we might give a postcondition as well which might be that the stack is not full. So altogether the specification of a generic package for stacks might be

```
generic
  type Item is private;
package Stacks is
  type Stack is private;

  function Is_Empty(S: Stack) return Boolean;
  function Is_Full(S: Stack) return Boolean;
```

    procedure Push(S: **in out** Stack; X: **in** Item)
      with
        Pre => **not** Is_Full(S),
        Post => **not** Is_Empty(S);

    procedure Pop(S: **in out** Stack; X: **out** Item)
      with
        Pre => **not** Is_Empty(S),
        Post => **not** Is_Full(S);

private
    ...
end Stacks;

Note how the individual aspects Pre and Post take the form of

    aspect_mark => expression

and that if there are several then they are separated by commas. The final semicolon is of course the semicolon at the end of the subprogram declaration as a whole. Thus the overall syntax is now

    subprogram_declaration ::=
    [overriding_indicator]
    subprogram_specification
    [aspect_specification] ;

and in general

    aspect_specification ::=
    with aspect_mark [=> expression] { ,
       aspect_mark [=> expression] }

Pre- and postconditions are controlled by the same mechanism as assertions using the pragma Assert. It will be recalled that these can be switched on and off by the pragma Assertion_Policy. Thus if we write

    pragma Assertion_Policy(Check);

then assertions are enabled whereas if the parameter of the pragma is Ignore then all assertions are ignored.

In the case of a precondition, whenever a subprogram with a precondition is called, if the policy is Check then the precondition is evaluated and if it is False then Assertion_Error is raised and the subprogram is not entered. Similarly, on return from a subprogram with a postcondition, if the policy is Check then the postcondition is evaluated and if it is False then Assertion_Error is raised.

So if the policy is Check and Pop is called when the stack is empty then Assertion_Error is raised whereas if the policy is Ignore then the predefined exception Constraint_Error would probably be raised (depending upon how the stack had been implemented).

Note that, unlike the pragma Assert, it is not possible to associate a specific message with the raising of Assertion_Error by a pre- or postcondition. The main reason is that it might be confusing with multiple conditions (which can arise with inheritance) and in any event it is expected that the implementation will give adequate information about which condition has been violated.

Note that it is not permitted to give the aspects Pre or Post for a null procedure; this is because all null procedures are meant to be interchangeable.

There are also aspects **Pre'Class** and **Post'Class** for use with tagged types (and they can be given with null procedures). The subtle topic of multiple inheritance of pre- and postconditions is discussed in detail in Section 2.3.

Two new attributes are useful in postconditions. **X'Old** denotes the value of **X** on entry to the subprogram whereas **X** denotes the value on exit. And in the case of a function **F**, the value returned by the function can be denoted by **F'Result** in a postcondition for **F**.

As a general rule, the new aspect specifications can be used instead of aspect clauses and pragmas for giving information regarding entities such as types and subprograms.

For example rather than

> **type** Bit_Vector **is array** (0 .. 15) **of** Boolean;

followed later by

> **for** Bit_Vector'Component_Size **use** 1;

we can more conveniently write

> **type** Bit_Vector **is array** (0 .. 15) **of** Boolean
>   **with** Component_Size => 1;

However, certain aspects such as record representation and enumeration representations cannot be given in this way because of the special syntax involved.

In cases where aspect specifications can now be used, the existing pragmas are mostly considered obsolescent and condemned to Annex J.

It should be noted that pragmas are still preferred for stating properties of program units such as **Pure**, **Preelaborable** and so on. However, we now talk about the pure property as being an aspect of a package. It is a general rule that the new aspect specifications are preferred with types and subprograms but pragmas continue to be preferred for program units. Nevertheless, the enthusiast for the new notation could write

> **package** Ada_Twin
>   **with** Pure **is**
> **end** Ada_Twin;

which illustrates that in some cases no value is required for the aspect (by default it is **True**).

A notable curiosity is that **Preelaborable_Initialization** still has to be specified by a pragma (this is because of problems with different views of the type).

Note incidentally that to avoid confusion with some other uses of the reserved word **with**, in the case of aspect specifications **with** is at the beginning of the line.

There are two other new facilities of a contractual nature concerning types and subtypes. One is known as type invariants and these describe properties of a type that remain true and can be relied upon. The other is known as subtype predicates which extend the idea of constraints. The distinction can be confusing at first sight and the following extract from one of the Ada Issues might be helpful.

"Note that type invariants are not the same thing as constraints, as invariants apply to all values of a type, while constraints are generally used to identify a subset of the values of a type. Invariants are only meaningful on private types, where there is a clear boundary (the enclosing package) that separates where the invariant applies (outside) and where it need not be satisfied (inside). In some ways, an invariant is more like the range of values specified when declaring a new integer type, as opposed to the constraint specified when defining an integer subtype. The specified range of an integer type can be violated (to some degree) in the middle of an arithmetic computation, but must be satisfied by the time the value is stored back into an object of the type."

Type invariants are useful if we want to ensure that some relationship between the components of a private type always holds. Thus suppose we have a stack and wish to ensure that no value is placed on the stack equal to an existing value on the stack. We can modify the earlier example to

```
package Stacks is
  type Stack is private
    with
      Type_Invariant => Is_Unduplicated(Stack);

  function Is_Empty(S: Stack) return Boolean;
  function Is_Full(S: Stack) return Boolean;
  function Is_Unduplicated(S: Stack) return Boolean;

  procedure Push(S: in out Stack; X: in Item)
    with
      Pre => not Is_Full(S),
      Post => not Is_Empty(S);

  -- and so on
```

The function Is_Unduplicated then has to be written (in the package body as usual) to check that all values of the stack are different.

Note that we have mentioned Is_Unduplicated in the type invariant before its specification. This violates the usual "linear order of elaboration". However, there is a general rule that all aspect specifications are only elaborated when the entity they refer to is frozen. Recall that one of the reasons for the introduction of aspect specifications was to overcome this problem with the existing mechanisms which caused information to become separated from the entities to which it relates.

The invariant on a private type T is checked when the value can be changed from the point of view of the outside user. That is primarily

- after default initialization of an object of type T,

- after a conversion to type T,

- after a call that returns a result of a type T or has an **out** or **in out** or access parameter of type T.

The checks also apply to subprograms with parameters or results whose components are of the type T.

In the case of the stack, the invariant Is_Unduplicated will be checked when we declare a new object of type Stack and each time we call Push and Pop.

Note that any subprograms internal to the package and not visible to the user can do what they like. It is only when a value of the type Stack emerges into the outside world that the invariant is checked.

The type invariant could be given on the full type in the private part rather than on the visible declaration of the private type (but not on both). Thus the user need not know that an invariant applies to the type.

Type invariants, like pre- and postconditions, are controlled by the pragma Assertion_Policy and only checked if the policy is Check. If an invariant fails to be true then Assertion_Error is raised at the appropriate point.

There is also an aspect Type_Invariant'Class for use with tagged types.

The subtype feature of Ada is very valuable and enables the early detection of errors that linger in many programs in other languages and cause disaster later. However, although valuable, the subtype mechanism is somewhat limited. We can only specify a contiguous range of values in the case of integer and enumeration types.

Accordingly, Ada 2012 introduces subtype predicates as an aspect that can be applied to type and subtype declarations. The requirements proved awkward to satisfy with a single feature so in fact there are two aspects: Static_Predicate and Dynamic_Predicate. They both take a Boolean expression and the key difference is that the static predicate is restricted to certain types of expressions so that it can be used in more contexts.

Suppose we are concerned with seasons and that we have a type Month thus

> **type** Month **is** (Jan, Feb, Mar, Apr, May, ..., Nov, Dec);

Now suppose we wish to declare subtypes for the seasons. For most people winter is December, January, February. (From the point of view of solstices and equinoxes, winter is from December 21 until March 21 or thereabouts, but March seems to me generally more like spring rather than winter and December feels more like winter than autumn.) So we would like to declare a subtype embracing Dec, Jan and Feb. We cannot do this with a constraint but we can use a static predicate by writing

> **subtype** Winter **is** Month
>   **with** Static_Predicate => Winter **in** Dec | Jan | Feb;

and then we are assured that objects of subtype Winter can only be Dec, Jan or Feb (provided once more that the Assertion_Policy pragma has set the Policy to Check). Note the use of the subtype name (Winter) in the expression where it stands for the current instance of the subtype.

The aspect is checked whenever an object is default initialized, on assignments, on conversions, on parameter passing and so on. If a check fails then Assertion_Error is raised.

The observant reader will note also that the membership test takes a more flexible form in Ada 2012 as explained in the next section.

If we want the expression to be dynamic then we have to use Dynamic_Predicate thus

> **type** T **is** ... ;
> **function** Is_Good(X: T) **return** Boolean;
> **subtype** Good_T **is** T
>   **with** Dynamic_Predicate => Is_Good(Good_T);

Note that a subtype with predicates cannot be used in some contexts such as index constraints. This is to avoid having arrays with holes and similar nasty things. However, static predicates are allowed in a for loop meaning to try every value. So we could write

> **for** M **in** Winter **loop**...

Beware that the loop uses values for M in the order, Jan, Feb, Dec and not Dec, Jan, Feb as the user might have wanted.

As another example, suppose we wish to specify that an integer is even. We might expect to be able to write

> **subtype** Even **is** Integer
>   **with** Static_Predicate => Even **mod** 2 = 0;   -- *illegal*

Sadly, this is illegal because the expression in a static predicate is restricted and cannot use some operations such as **mod**. We have to use a dynamic predicate thus

    subtype Even **is** Integer
      with Dynamic_Predicate => Even **mod** 2 = 0;   *--OK*

and then we cannot write

    for X **in** Even **loop** ...

but have to spell it out in detail such as

    for X **in** Integer **loop**
      if X **mod** 2 = 0 **then**   *-- or if X in Even then*
        ... *-- body of loop*
      end if;
    end loop;

The assurance given by type invariants and subtype predicates can depend upon the object having a sensible initial value. There is a school of thought that giving default initial values (such as zero) is bad since it can obscure flow errors. However, it is strange that Ada does allow default initial values to be given for components of records but not for scalar types or array types. This is rectified in Ada 2012 by aspects Default_Value and Default_Component_Value. We can write

    type Signal **is** (Red, Amber, Green)
      with Default_Value => Red;

    type Text **is new** String
      with Default_Component_Value => Ada.Characters.Latin_1.Space;

    type Day **is range** 1 .. 31
      with Default_Value => 1;

Note that, unlike default initial values for record components, these have to be static.

Finally, two new attributes are introduced to aid in the writing of preconditions. Sometimes it is necessary to check that two objects do not occupy the same storage in whole or in part. This can be done with two attributes thus

    X'Has_Same_Storage(Y)
    X'Overlaps_Storage(Y)

As an example we might have a procedure Exchange and wish to ensure that the parameters do not overlap in any way. We can write

    procedure Exchange(X, Y: **in out** T)
      with Pre => **not** X'Overlaps_Storage(Y);

Attributes are used rather than predefined functions since this enables the semantics to be written in a manner that permits X and Y to be of any type and moreover does not imply that X or Y are read.

1.3.2   Expressions

Those whose first language was Algol 60 or Algol 68 or who have had the misfortune to dabble in horrid languages such as C will have been surprised that a language of the richness of Ada does not have conditional expressions. Well, the good news is that Ada 2012 has at last introduced conditional expressions which take two forms, if expressions and case expressions.

The reason that Ada did not originally have conditional expressions is probably that there was a strong desire to avoid any confusion between statements and expressions. We know that many errors in C arise because assignments can be used as expressions. But the real problem with C is that it also treats Booleans as integers, and confuses equality and assignment. It is this combination of fluid styles that causes problems. But just introducing conditional expressions does not of itself introduce difficulties if the syntax is clear and unambiguous.

If expressions in Ada 2012 take the form as shown by the following statements:

S := (**if** N > 0 **then** +1 **else** 0);

Put(**if** N = 0 **then** "none" **elsif** N = 1 **then** "one" **else** "lots");

Note that there is no need for **end if** and indeed it is not permitted. Remember that **end if** is vital for good structuring of if statements because there can be more than one statement in each branch. This does not arise with if expressions so **end if** is unnecessary and moreover would be heavy as a closing bracket. However, there is a rule that an if expression must always be enclosed in parentheses. Thus we cannot write

X := **if** L > 0 **then** M **else** N + 1;   -- *illegal*

because there would be confusion between

X := (**if** L > 0 **then** M **else** N) + 1;   -- *and*

X := (**if** L > 0 **then** M **else** (N + 1));

The parentheses around N+1 are not necessary in the last line above but added to clarify the point.

However, if the context already provides parentheses then additional ones are unnecessary. Thus an if expression as a single parameter does not need double parentheses.

It is clear that if expressions will have many uses. However, the impetus for providing them in Ada 2012 was stimulated by the introduction of aspects of the form

Pre => expression

There will be many occasions when preconditions have a conditional form and without if expressions these would have to be wrapped in a function which would be both heavy and obscure. For example suppose a procedure P has two parameters P1 and P2 and that the precondition is that if P1 is positive then P2 must also be positive but if P1 is not positive then there is no restriction on P2. We could express this by writing a function such as

```
function Checkparas(P1, P2: Integer) return Boolean is
begin
  if P1 > 0 then
    return P2 > 0;
  else                   -- P1 is not positive
    return True;         -- so don't care about P2
  end if;
end Checkparas;
```

and then we can write

```
procedure P(P1, P2: Integer)
  with Pre => Checkparas(P1, P2);
```

This is truly gruesome. Apart from the effort of having to declare the wretched function Checkparas, the consequence is that the meaning of the precondition can only be determined by looking at the body of Checkparas and that could be miles away, typically in the body of the package containing the declaration of P. This would be a terrible violation of information hiding in reverse; we would be forced to hide something that should be visible.

However, using if expressions we can simply write

Pre => (**if** P1 > 0 **then** P2 > 0 **else** True);

and this can be abbreviated to

Pre => (**if** P1 > 0 **then** P2 > 0);

because there is a convenient rule that a trailing **else** True can be omitted when the type is a Boolean type. Many will find it much easier to read without **else** True anyway since it is similar to saying P1 > 0 implies P2 > 0. Adding an operation such as implies was considered but rejected as unnecessary.

The precondition could be extended to say that if P1 equals zero then P2 also has to be zero but if P1 is negative then we continue not to care about P2. This would be written thus

Pre => (**if** P1 > 0 **then** P2 > 0 **elsif** P1 = 0 **then** P2 = 0);

There are various sensible rules about the types of the various branches in an if expression as expected. Basically, they must all be of the same type or convertible to the same expected type. Thus consider a procedure Do_It taking a parameter of type Float and the call

Do_It (**if** B **then** X **else** 3.14);

where X is a variable of type Float. Clearly we wish to permit this but the two branches of the if statement are of different types, X is of type Float whereas 3.14 is of type *universal_real*. But a value of type *universal_real* can be implicitly converted to Float which is the type expected by Do_It and so all is well.

There are also rules about accessibility in the case where the various branches are of access types; the details need not concern us in this overview!

The other new form of conditional expression is the case expression and this follows similar rules to the if expression just discussed. Here is an amusing example based on one in the AI which introduces case expressions.

Suppose we are making a fruit salad and add various fruits to a bowl. We need to check that the fruit is in an appropriate state before being added to the bowl. Suppose we have just three fruits given by

type Fruit_Kind **is** (Apple, Banana, Pineapple);

then we might have a procedure Add_To_Salad thus

procedure Add_To_Salad(Fruit: **in** Fruit_Type);

where Fruit_Type is perhaps a discriminated type thus

type Fruit_Type (Kind: Fruit_Kind) **is private;**

In addition there might be functions such as Is_Peeled that interrogate the state of a fruit.

We could then have a precondition that checks that the fruit is in an edible state thus

Pre => (**if** Fruit.Kind = Apple **then** Is_Crisp(Fruit)
          elsif Fruit.Kind = Banana **then** Is_Peeled(Fruit)
          elsif Fruit.Kind = Pineapple **then** Is_Cored(Fruit));

(This example is all very well but it has allowed the apple to go in uncored and the pineapple still has its prickly skin.)

Now suppose we decide to add Orange to type Fruit_Kind. The precondition will still work in the sense that the implicit **else** True will allow the orange to pass the precondition unchecked and will go into the fruit salad possibly unpeeled, unripe or mouldy. The trouble is that we have lost the full coverage check which is such a valuable feature of case statements and aggregates in Ada.

We overcome this by using a case expression and writing

```
Pre => (case Fruit.Kind is
            when Apple => Is_Crisp(Fruit),
            when Banana => Is_Peeled(Fruit),
            when Pineapple => Is_Cored(Fruit),
            when Orange => Is_Peeled(Fruit));
```

and of course without the addition of the choice for Orange it would fail to compile.

Note that there is no **end case** just as there is no **end if** in an if expression. Moreover, like the if expression, the case expression must be in parentheses. Similar rules apply regarding the types of the various branches and so on.

Of course, the usual rules of case statements apply and so we might decide not to bother about checking the crispness of the apple but to check alongside the pineapple (another kind of apple!) that it has been cored by writing

```
Pre => (case Fruit.Kind is
            when Apple | Pineapple => Is_Cored(Fruit),
            when Banana | Orange => Is_Peeled(Fruit));
```

We can use **others** as the last choice as expected but this would lose the value of coverage checking. There is no default **when others** => True corresponding to **else** True for if expressions because that would defeat coverage checking completely.

A further new form of expression is the so-called quantified expression. Quantified expressions allow the checking of a Boolean expression for a given range of values and will again be found useful in pre- and postconditions. There are two forms using **for all** and **for some**. Note carefully that **some** is a new reserved word.

Suppose we have an integer array type

```
type Atype is array (Integer range <>) of Integer;
```

then we might have a procedure that sets each element of an array of integers equal to its index. Its specification might include a postcondition thus

```
procedure Set_Array(A: out Atype)
    with Post => (for all M in A'Range => A(M) = M);
```

This is saying that for all values of M in A'Range we want the expression A(M) = M to be true. Note how the two parts are separated by =>.

We could devise a function to check that some component of the array has a given value by

```
function Value_Present(A: Atype; X: Integer) return Boolean
    with Post => Value_Present'Result = (for some M in A'Range => A(M) = X);
```

Note the use of Value_Present'Result to denote the result returned by the function Value_Present.

As with conditional expressions, quantified expressions are always enclosed in parentheses.

The evaluation of quantified expressions is as expected. Each value of M is taken in turn (as in a for statement and indeed we could insert **reverse**) and the expression to the right of => then evaluated. In the case of universal quantification (a posh term meaning **for all**) as soon as one value is found to be False then the whole quantified expression is False and no further values are checked; if all values turn out to be True then the quantified expression is True. A similar process applies to existential quantification (that is **for some**) where the roles of True and False are reversed.

Those with a mathematical background will be familiar with the symbols ∀ and ∃ which correspond to **for all** and **for some** respectively. Readers are invited to discuss whether the A is upside down and the E backwards or whether they are both simply rotated.

As a somewhat more elaborate example suppose we have a function that finds the index of the first value of M such that A(M) equals a given value X. This needs a precondition to assert that such a value exists.

```
function Find(A: Atype; X: Integer) return Integer
   with
   Pre => (for some M in A'Range => A(M) = X),
   Post => A(Find'Result) = X and
      (for all M in A'First .. Find'Result–1 => A(M) /= X);
```

Note again the use of Find'Result to denote the result returned by the function Find.

Quantified expressions can be used in any context requiring an expression and are not just for pre- and postconditions. Thus we might test whether an integer N is prime by

```
RN := Integer(Sqrt(Float(N)));
if (for some K in 2 .. RN => N mod K = 0) then
   ...          -- N not prime
```

or we might reverse the test by

```
if (for all K in 2 .. RN => N mod K / = 0) then
   ...          -- N is prime
```

Beware that this is not a recommended technique if N is at all large!

We noted above that a major reason for introducing if expressions and case expressions was to avoid the need to introduce lots of auxiliary functions for contexts such as preconditions. Nevertheless the need still arises from time to time. A feature of existing functions is that the code is in the body and this is not visible in the region of the precondition – information hiding is usually a good thing but here it is a problem. What we need is a localized and visible shorthand for a little function. After much debate, Ada 2012 introduces expression functions which are essentially functions whose visible body comprises a single expression. Thus suppose we have a record type such as

```
type Point is tagged
   record
      X, Y: Float := 0.0;
   end record;
```

and the precondition we want for several subprograms is that a point is not at the origin. Then we could write

```
function Is_At_Origin(P: Point) return Boolean is
   (P.X = 0.0 and P.Y = 0.0);
```

and then

```
procedure Whatever(P: Point; ... )
   with Pre => not P.Is_At_Origin;
```

and so on.

Such a function is known as an expression function; naturally it does not have a distinct body. The expression could be any expression and could include calls of other functions (and not just expression functions). The parameters could be of any mode (see next section).

Expression functions can also be used as a completion. This arises typically if the type is private. In that case we cannot access the components P.X and P.Y in the visible part. However, we don't want to have to put the code in the package body. So we declare a function specification in the visible part in the normal way thus

```
function Is_At_Origin(P: Point) return Boolean;
```

and then an expression function in the private part thus

```
private
  type Point is ...

  function Is_At_Origin(P: Point) return Boolean is
    (P.X = 0.0 and P.Y = 0.0);
```

and the expression function then completes the declaration of Is_At_Origin and no function body is required in the package body.

Observe that we could also use an expression function for a completion in a package body so that rather than writing the body as

```
function Is_At_Origin(P: Point) return Boolean is
begin
  return P.X = 0.0 and P.Y = 0.0;
end Is_At_Origin;
```

we could write an expression function as a sort of shorthand.

Incidentally, in Ada 2012, we can abbreviate a null procedure body in a similar way by writing

```
procedure Nothing(...) is null;
```

as a shorthand for

```
procedure Nothing(...) is
begin
  null;
end Nothing;
```

and this will complete the procedure specification

```
procedure Nothing(...);
```

Another change in this area is that membership tests are now generalized. In previous versions of Ada, membership tests allowed one to see whether a value was in a range or in a subtype, thus we could write either of

```
if D in 1 .. 30 then
```

```
if D in Days_In_Month then
```

but we could not write something like

```
if D in 1 | 3 | 5 | 6 ..10 then
```

This is now rectified and following **in** we can now have one or more of a value, a range, or a subtype or any combination separated by vertical bars. Moreover, they do not have to be static.

A final minor change is that the form qualified expression is now treated as a name rather than as a primary. Remember that a function call is treated as a name and this allows a function call to be used as a prefix.

For example suppose F returns an array (or more likely an access to an array) then we can write

F(...)(N)

and this returns the value of the component with index N. However, suppose the function is overloaded so that this is ambiguous. The normal technique to overcome ambiguity is to use a qualified expression and write T'(F(...)). But in Ada 2005 this is not a name and so cannot be used as a prefix. This means that we typically have to copy the array (or access) and then do the indexing or (really ugly) introduce a dummy type conversion and write T(T'(F(...)))(N). Either way, this is a nuisance and hence the change in Ada 2012.

1.3.3   Structure and visibility

What will seem to many to be one of the most dramatic changes in Ada 2012 concerns functions. In previous versions of Ada, functions could only have parameters of mode **in**. Ada 2012 permits functions to have parameters of all modes.

There are various purposes of functions. The purest is simply as a means of looking at some state. Examples are the function Is_Empty applying to an object of type Stack. It doesn't change the state of the stack but just reports on some aspect of it. Other pure functions are mathematical ones such as Sqrt. For a given parameter, Sqrt always returns the same value. These functions never have any side effects. At the opposite extreme we could have a function that has no restrictions at all; any mode of parameters permitted, any side effects permitted, just like a general procedure in fact but also with the ability to return some result that can be immediately used in an expression.

An early version of Ada had such features, there were pure functions on the one hand and so-called value-returning procedures on the other. However, there was a desire for simplification and so we ended up with Ada 83 functions.

In a sense this was the worst of all possible worlds. A function can perform any side effects at all, provided they are not made visible to the user by appearing as parameters of mode **in out**! As a consequence, various tricks have been resorted to such as using access types (either directly or indirectly). A good example is the function Random in the Numerics annex. It has a parameter Generator of mode **in** but this does in fact get updated indirectly whenever Random is called. So parameters can change even if they are of mode **in**. Moreover, the situation has encouraged programmers to use access parameters unnecessarily with increased runtime cost and mental obscurity.

Ada 2012 has bitten the bullet and now allows parameters of functions to be of any mode. But note that operators are still restricted to only **in** parameters for obvious reasons.

However, there are risks with functions with side effects whether they are visible or not. This is because Ada does not specify the order in which parameters are evaluated nor the order in which parts of an expression are evaluated. So if we write

X := Random(G) + Random(G);

we have no idea which call of Random occurs first – not that it matters in this case. Allowing parameters of all modes provides further opportunities for programmers to inadvertently introduce order dependence into their programs.

So, in order to mitigate the problems of order dependence, Ada 2012 has a number of rules to catch the more obvious cases. These rules are all static and are mostly about aliasing. For example, it is illegal to pass the same actual parameter to two formal **in out** parameters – the rules apply to both functions and procedures. Consider

```
procedure Do_It(Double, Triple: in out Integer) is
begin
   Double := Double * 2;
   Triple := Triple * 3;
end Do_It;
```

Now if we write

```
Var: Integer := 2;
...
Do_It(Var, Var);            -- illegal in Ada 2012
```

then Var might become 4 or 6 in Ada 2005 according to the order in which the parameters are copied back.

These rules also apply to any context in which the order is not specified and which involves function calls with **out** or **in out** parameters. Thus an aggregate such as

```
(Var, F(Var))
```

where F has an **in out** parameter is illegal since the order of evaluation of the expressions in an aggregate is undefined and so the value of the first component of the aggregate will depend upon whether it is evaluated before or after F is called.

Full details of the rules need not concern the normal programmer – the compiler will tell you off!

Another change concerning parameters is that it is possible in Ada 2012 to explicitly state that a parameter is to be aliased. Thus we can write

```
procedure P(X: aliased in out T; ...);
```

An aliased parameter is always passed by reference and the accessibility rules are modified accordingly. This facility is used in a revision to the containers which avoids the need for expensive and unnecessary copying of complete elements when they are updated. The details will be found in Sections 4.2 and 6.3.

A major advance in Ada 2005 was the introduction of limited with clauses giving more flexibility to incomplete types. However, experience has revealed a few minor shortcomings.

One problem is that an incomplete type in Ada 2005 cannot be completed by a private type. This prevents the following mutually recursive structure of two types having each other as an access discriminant

```
type T1;
type T2 (X: access T1) is private;
type T1 (X: access T2) is private;        -- OK in Ada 2012
```

The rules in Ada 2012 are changed so that an incomplete type can be completed by any type, including a private type (but not another incomplete type obviously).

Another change concerns the use of incomplete types as parameters. Generally, we do not know whether a parameter of a private type is passed by copy or by reference. The one exception is that if it is tagged then we know it will be passed by reference. As a consequence there is a rule in Ada 2005 that an incomplete type cannot be used as a parameter unless it is tagged incomplete. This has forced the unnecessary use of access parameters.

In Ada 2012, this problem is remedied by permitting incomplete types to be used as parameters (and as function results) provided that they are fully defined at the point of call and where the body is declared.

A final change to incomplete types is that a new category of formal generic parameter is added that allows a generic unit to be instantiated with an incomplete type. Thus rather than having to write a signature package as

```
generic
   type Element is private;
   type Set is private;
   with function Empty return Set;
   with function Unit(E: Element) return Set;
   with function Union(S, T: Set) return Set;
   ...
package Set_Signature is end;
```

which must be instantiated with complete types, we can now write

```
generic
   type Element;
   type Set;
   with function Empty return Set;
   ...
package Set_Signature is end;
```

where the formal parameters Element and Set are categorized as incomplete. Instantiation can now be performed using any type, including incomplete or private types as actual parameters. This permits the cascading of generic packages which was elusive in Ada 2005 as will be illustrated in Section 4.3. Note that we can also write **type** Set **is tagged**; which requires the actual parameter to be tagged but still permits it to be incomplete.

There is a change regarding discriminants. In Ada 2005, a discriminant can only have a default value if the type is not tagged. Remember that giving a default value makes a type mutable. But not permitting a default value has proved to be an irritating restriction in the case of limited tagged types. Being limited they cannot be changed anyway and so a default value is not a problem and is permitted in Ada 2012. This feature is used in the declaration of the protected types for synchronized queues in Section 1.3.6.

Another small but useful improvement is in the area of use clauses. In Ada 83, use clauses only apply to packages and everything in the package specification is made visible. Programming guidelines often prohibit use clauses on the grounds that programs are hard to understand since the origin of entities is obscured. This was a nuisance with operators because it prevented the use of infixed notation and forced the writing of things such as

```
P."+"(X, Y)
```

Accordingly, Ada 95 introduced the use type clause which just makes the operators for a specific type in a package directly visible. Thus we write

```
use type P.T;
```

However, although this makes the primitive operators of T visible it does not make everything relating to T visible. Thus it does not make enumeration literals visible or other primitive operations of the type such as subprograms. This is a big nuisance.

To overcome this, Ada 2012 introduces a further variation on the use type clause. If we write

```
use all type P.T;
```

then *all* primitive operations of T are made visible (and not just primitive operators) and this includes enumeration literals in the case of an enumeration type and class wide operations of tagged types.

Finally, there are a couple of small changes to extended return statements which are really corrections to amend oversights in Ada 2005.

The first is that a return object can be declared as **constant**. For example

```
function F(...) return LT is
   ...
   return Result: constant LT := ... do
      ....
   end return;
end F;
```

We allow everything else to be declared as **constant** so we should here as well especially if LT is a limited type. This was really an oversight in the syntax.

The other change concerns class wide types. If the returned type is class wide then the object declared in the extended return statement need not be the same in Ada 2012 provided it can be converted to the class wide type. Thus

```
function F(...) return T'Class is
   ...
   return X: TT do
      ...
   end return;
end F;
```

is legal in Ada 2012 provided that TT is descended from T and thus covered by T'Class. In Ada 2005 it is required that the result type be identical to the return type and this is a nuisance with a class wide type because it then has to be initialized with something and so on. Note the analogy with constraints. The return type might be unconstrained such as String whereas the result (sub)type can be constrained such as String(1 .. 5).

1.3.4   Tasking and real-time facilities

There are a number of improvements regarding scheduling and dispatching in the Real-Time Systems annex.

A small addition concerns non-preemptive dispatching. In Ada 2005, a task wishing to indicate that it is willing to be preempted has to execute

```
delay 0.0;
```

(or **delay until** Ada.Real_Time.Time_First in Ravenscar). This is ugly and so a procedure Yield is added to the package Ada.Dispatching.

A further addition is the ability to indicate that a task is willing to be preempted by a task of higher priority (but not the same priority). This is done by calling Yield_To_Higher which is declared in a new child package with specification

```
package Ada.Dispatching.Non_Preemptive is
   pragma Preelaborate(Non_Preemptive);
   procedure Yield_To_Higher;
   procedure Yield_To_Same_Or_Higher renames Yield;
end Ada.Dispatching.Non_Preemptive;
```

Another low-level scheduling capability concerns suspension objects; these were introduced in Ada 95. Recall that we can declare an object of type Suspension_Object and call procedures to set it True or False. By calling Suspend_Until_True a task can suspend itself until the state of the object is true.

Ada 2005 introduced Earliest Deadline First (EDF) scheduling. The key feature here is that tasks are scheduled according to deadlines and not by priorities. A new facility introduced in Ada 2012 is the ability to suspend until a suspension object is true and then set its deadline sometime in the future. This is done by calling the aptly named procedure Suspend_Until_True_And_Set_Deadline in a new child package Ada.Synchronous_Task_Control.EDF.

A new scheduling feature is the introduction of synchronous barriers in a new child package Ada.Synchronous_Barriers. The main features are a type Synchronous_Barrier with a discriminant giving the number of tasks to be waited for.

> **type** Synchronous_Barrier(Release_Threshold: Barrier_Limit) **is limited private**;

There is also a procedure

> **procedure** Wait_For_Release(The_Barrier: **in out** Synchronous_Barrier;
>   Notified: **out** Boolean);

When a task calls Wait_For_Release it gets suspended until the number waiting equals the discriminant. All the tasks are then released and just one of them is told about it by the parameter Notified being True. The general idea is that this one task then does something on behalf of all the others. The count of tasks waiting is then reset to zero so that the synchronous barrier can be used again.

A number of other changes in this area are about the use of multiprocessors and again concern the Real-Time Systems annex.

A new package System.Multiprocessors is introduced as follows

```
package System.Multiprocessors is
  type CPU_Range is range 0..implementation-defined;
  Not_A_Specific_CPU: constant CPU_Range := 0:
  subtype CPU is CPU_Range range 1 .. CPU_Range'Last;
  function Number_Of_CPUs return CPU;
end System.Multiprocessors;
```

A value of subtype CPU denotes a specific processor. Zero indicates don't know or perhaps don't care. The total number of CPUs is determined by calling the function Number_Of_CPUs. This is a function rather than a constant because there could be several partitions with a different number of CPUs on each partition.

Tasks can be allocated to processors by an aspect specification. If we write

```
task My_Task
  with CPU => 10;
```

then My_Task will be executed by processor number 10. In the case of a task type then all tasks of that type will be executed by the given processor. The expression giving the processor for a task can be dynamic. The aspect can also be set by a corresponding pragma CPU. (This is an example of a pragma born obsolescent.) The aspect CPU can also be given to the main subprogram in which case the expression must be static.

Further facilities are provided by the child package System.Multiprocessors.Dispatching_Domains. The idea is that processors are grouped together into dispatching domains. A task may then be allocated to a domain and it will be executed on one of the processors of that domain.

Domains are of a type Dispatching_Domain. They are created by a function Create

> **function** Create(First, Last: CPU) **return** Dispatching_Domain;

that takes the first and last numbered CPU of the domain and then returns the domain. All CPUs are initially in the System_Dispatching_Domain. If we attempt to do something silly such as create overlapping domains, then Dispatching_Domain_Error is raised.

Tasks can be assigned to a domain in two ways. One way is to use an aspect

> **task** My_Task
>   **with** Dispatching_Domain => My_Domain;

The other way is by calling the procedure Assign_Task whose specification is

> **procedure** Assign_Task(Domain: **in out** Dispatching_Domain;
>   CPU: **in** CPU_Range := Not_A_Specific_CPU;
>   T: **in** Task_Id := Current_Task);

There are a number of other subprograms for manipulating domains and CPUs. An interesting one is Delay_Until_And_Set_CPU which delays the calling task until a given real time and then sets the processor.

The Ravenscar profile is now defined to be permissible with multiprocessors. However, there is a restriction that tasks may not change CPU. Accordingly the definition of the profile now includes the following restriction

> No_Dependence => System.Multiprocessors.Dispatching_Domains

In order to clarify the use of multiprocessors with group budgets the package Ada.Execution_Time.Group_Budgets introduced in Ada 2005 is slightly modified. The type Group_Budget (which in Ada 2005 is just **tagged limited private**) has a discriminant in Ada 2012 giving the CPU thus

> **type** Group_Budget(CPU: System.Multiprocessors.CPU :=
>   System.Multiprocessors.CPU'First) **is tagged limited private**;

This means that a group budget only applies to a single processor. If a task in a group is executed on another processor then the budget is not consumed. Note that the default value for CPU is CPU'First which is always 1.

Another improvement relating to times and budgets concerns interrupts. Two Boolean constants are added to the package Ada.Execution_Time

> Interrupt_Clocks_Supported: **constant** Boolean := *implementation-defined*;
> Separate_Interrupt_Clocks_Supported: **constant** Boolean := *implementation-defined*;

The constant Interrupt_Clocks_Supported indicates whether the time spent in interrupts is accounted for separately from the tasks and then Separate_Interrupt_Clocks_Supported indicates whether it is accounted for each interrupt individually. There is also a function

> **function** Clocks_For_Interrupts **return** CPU_Time;

This function gives the time used over all interrupts. Calling it if Interrupt_Clocks_Supported is false raises Program_Error.

A new child package accounts for the interrupts separately if Separate_Interrupt_Clocks_Supported is true.

```
package Ada.Execution_Time.Interrupts is
   function Clock(Interrupt: Ada.Interrupts.Interrupt_Id) return CPU_Time;
   function Supported(Interrupt: Ada.Interrupts.Interrupt_Id) return Boolean;
end Ada.Execution_Time.Interrupts;
```

The function Supported indicates whether the time for a particular interrupt is being monitored. If it is then Clock returns the accumulated time spent in that interrupt handler (otherwise it returns zero). However, if the overall constant Separate_Interrupt_Clocks_Supported is false then calling Clock for a particular interrupt raises Program_Error.

Multiprocessors have an impact on shared variables. The existing pragma Volatile (now the aspect Volatile) requires access to be in memory but this is strictly unnecessary. All we need is to ensure that reads and writes occur in the right order. A new aspect Coherent was considered but was rejected in favour of simply changing the definition of Volatile.

The final improvement in this section is in the core language and concerns synchronized interfaces and requeue. The procedures of a synchronized interface may be implemented by a procedure or entry or by a protected procedure. However, in Ada 2005 it is not possible to requeue on a procedure of a synchronized interface even if it is implemented by an entry. This is a nuisance and prevents certain high level abstractions.

Accordingly, Ada 2012 has an aspect Synchronization that takes one of By_Entry, By_Protected_Procedure, and Optional. So we might write

```
type Server is synchronized interface;
procedure Q(S: in out Server; X: in Item);
   with Synchronization => By_Entry;
```

and then we are assured that we are permitted to perform a requeue on any implementation of Q.

As expected there are a number of consistency rules. The aspect can also be applied to a task interface or to a protected interface. But for a task interface it obviously cannot be By_Protected_Procedure.

In the case of inheritance, any Synchronization property is inherited. Naturally, multiple aspect specifications must be consistent. Thus Optional can be overridden by By_Entry or by By_Protected_Procedure but other combinations conflict and so are forbidden.

A related change is that if an entry is renamed as a procedure then we can do a requeue using the procedure name. This was not allowed in Ada 95 or Ada 2005.

1.3.5 General improvements

As well as the major features discussed above there are also a number of improvements in various other areas.

We start with some gentle stuff. Ada 95 introduced the package Ada thus

```
package Ada is
   pragma Pure(Ada);
end Ada;
```

However, a close reading of the RM revealed that poor Ada is illegal since the pragma Pure is not in one of the allowed places for a pragma. Pragmas are allowed in the places where certain categories are allowed but not *in place of them*. In the case of a package specification the constructs are basic declarative items, but "items" were not one of the allowed things. This has been changed to keep Ada legal.

A related change concerns a sequence of statements. In a construction such as

```
if B then
    This;
else
    That;
end if;
```

there must be at least one statement in each branch so if we don't want any statements then we have to put a null statement. If we want a branch that is just a pragma Assert then we have to put a null statement as well thus

```
if B then
    pragma Assert(...); null;
end if;
```

This is really irritating and so the rules have been changed to permit a pragma in place of a statement in a sequence of statements. This and the problem with the package Ada are treated as Binding Interpretations which means that they apply to Ada 2005 as well.

A similar change concerns the position of labels. It is said that gotos are bad for you. However, gotos are useful for quitting an execution of a loop and going to the end in order to try the next iteration. Thus

```
for I in ... loop

    ...
        if this-one-no-good then goto End_Of_Loop; end if;

    ...
    <<End_Of_Loop>> null;                          -- try another iteration
end loop;
```

Ada provides no convenient way of doing this other than by using a goto statement. Remember that **exit** transfers control out of the loop. The possibility of a continue statement as in some other languages was discussed but it was concluded that this would obscure the transfer of control. The great thing about **goto** is that the label sticks out like a sore thumb. Indeed, a survey of the code in a well known compiler revealed an orgy of uses of this handy construction.

However, it was decided that having to put **null** was an ugly nuisance and so the syntax of Ada 2012 has been changed to permit the label to come right at the end.

There is a significant extension to the syntax of loops used for iteration. This arose out of a requirement to make iteration over containers easier (as outlined in the next section) but the general ideas can be illustrated with an array. Consider

```
for K in Table'Range loop
    Table(K) := Table(K) + 1;
end loop;
```

This can now be written as

```
for T of Table loop
    T := T + 1;
end loop;
```

The entity T is a sort of generalized reference and hides the indexing. This mechanism can also be used with multidimensional arrays in which case just one loop replaces a nested set of loops.

A minor problem has arisen with the use of tags and Generic_Dispatching_Constructor. There is no way of discovering whether a tag represents an abstract type other than by attempting to create an object of the type which then raises Tag_Error; this is disgusting. Accordingly, a new function

function Is_Abstract(T: Tag) **return** Boolean;

is added to the package Ada.Tags.

There were many changes to access types in Ada 2005 including the wide introduction of anonymous access types. Inevitably some problems have arisen.

The first problem is with the accessibility of stand-alone objects of anonymous access types such as

A: **access** T;

Without going into details, it turns out that such objects are not very useful unless they carry the accessibility level of their value in much the same way that access parameters carry the accessibility level of the actual parameter. They are therefore modified to do this.

Programmers have always moaned about the need for many explicit conversions in Ada. Accordingly, implicit conversions from anonymous access types to named access types are now permitted provided the explicit conversion is legal. The idea is that the need for an explicit conversion with access types should only arise if the conversion could fail. A curious consequence of this change is that a preference rule is needed for the equality of anonymous access types.

An issue regarding allocators concerns their alignment. It will be recalled that when implementing a storage pool, the attribute Max_Size_In_Storage_Units is useful since it indicates the maximum size that could be requested by a call of Allocate. Similarly, the new attribute Max_Alignment_ For_Allocation indicates the maximum alignment that could be requested.

Another problem is that allocators for anonymous access types cause difficulties in some areas. Rather than forbidding them completely a new restriction identifier is added so that we can write

pragma Restrictions(No_Anonymous_Allocators);

Another new restriction is

pragma Restrictions(No_Standard_Allocators_After_Elaboration);

This can be used to ensure that once the main subprogram has started no further allocation from standard storage pools is permitted. This prevents a long lived program suffering from rampant heap growth.

However, this does not prevent allocation from user-defined storage pools. To enable users to monitor such allocation, additional functions are provided in Ada.Task_Identification, namely Environment_Task (returns the Task_Id of the environment task) and Activation_Is_Complete (returns a Boolean result indicating whether a particular task has finished activation).

A new facility is the ability to define subpools using a new package System.Storage_ Pools.Subpools. A subpool is a separately reclaimable part of a storage pool and is identified by a subpool handle name. On allocation, a handle name can be given.

Further control over the use of storage pools is provided by the ability to define our own default storage pool. Thus we can write

pragma Default_Storage_Pool(My_Pool);

and then all allocation within the scope of the pragma will be from My_Pool unless a different specific pool is given for a type. This could be done using the aspect Storage_Pool as expected

type Cell_Ptr **is access** Cell
   with Storage_Pool => Cell_Ptr_Pool;

A pragma Default_Storage_Pool can be overridden by another one so that for example all allocation in a package (and its children) is from another pool. The default pool can be specified as **null** thus

pragma Default_Storage_Pool(**null**);

and this prevents any allocation from standard pools.

Note that coextensions and allocators as access parameters may nevertheless be allocated on the stack. This can be prevented (somewhat brutally) by the following restrictions

pragma Restrictions(No_Coextensions);

pragma Restrictions(No_Access_Parameter_Allocators);

A number of other restrictions have also been added. The introduction of aspects logically requires some new restrictions to control their use. Thus by analogy with No_Implementation_Pragmas, we can write

pragma Restrictions(No_Implementation_Aspect_Specifications);

and this prevents the use of any implementation-defined aspect specifications. The use of individual aspects such as Default_Value can be prevented by

pragma Restrictions(No_Specification_of_Aspect => Default_Value);

Implementations and indeed users are permitted to add descendant units of Ada, System and Interfaces such as another child of Ada.Containers. This can be confusing for maintainers since they may be not aware that they are using non-standard packages. The new restriction

pragma Restrictions(No_Implementation_Units);

prevents the use of such units.

In a similar vein, there is also

pragma Restrictions(No_Implementation_Identifiers);

and this prevents the use of additional identifiers declared in packages such as System.

A blanket restriction can be imposed by writing

pragma Profile(No_Implementation_Extensions);

and this is equivalent to the following five restrictions

No_Implementation_Aspect_Specifications,
No_Implementation_Attributes,
No_Implementation_Identifiers,
No_Implementation_Pragmas,
No_Implementation_Units.

Finally, the issue of composability of equality has been revisited. In Ada 2005, tagged record types compose but untagged record types do not. If we define a new type (a record type, array type or a derived type) then equality is defined in terms of equality for its various components. However, the behaviour of components which are records is different in Ada 2005 according to whether they are tagged or not. If a component is tagged then the primitive operation is used (which might have been redefined), whereas for an untagged type, predefined equality is used even though it might have been overridden. This is a bit surprising and so has been changed in Ada 2012 so that all record types behave the same way and use the primitive operation. This is often called composability of equality so that we can say that in Ada 2012, record types always compose for equality. Remember that this only applies to records; components which are of array types and elementary types always use predefined equality.

1.3.6 Standard library

The main improvements in the standard library concern containers. But there are a number of other changes which will be described first.

In Ada 2005, additional versions of Index and Index_Non_Blank were added to the package Ada.Strings.Fixed with an additional parameter From indicating the start of the search. The same should have been done for Find_Token. So Ada 2012 adds

```
procedure Find_Token(Source: in String;
                     Set: in Maps.Character_Set;
                     From: in Positive;
                     Test: in Membership;
                     First: out Positive;
                     Last: out Natural);
```

Similar versions are added for bounded and unbounded strings to the corresponding packages.

New child packages of Ada.Strings are added to provide conversions between strings, wide strings, or wide wide strings and UTF-8 or UTF-16 encodings. They are

Ada.Strings.UTF_Encoding – declares a function Encoding to convert a String into types UTF_8, UTF_16BE, or UTF_16LE where BE and LE denote Big Endian and Little Endian respectively.

Ada.Strings.UTF_Encoding.Conversions – declares five functions Convert between the UTF schemes.

Ada.Strings.UTF_Encoding.Strings – declares functions Encode and Decode between the type String and the UTF schemes.

Ada.Strings.UTF_Encoding.Wide_Strings – declares six similar functions for the type Wide_String.

Ada.Strings.UTF_Encoding.Wide_Wide_Strings – declares six similar functions for the type Wide_Wide_String.

Further new packages are Ada.Wide_Characters.Handling and Ada.Wide_Wide_Characters. Handling. These provide classification functions such as Is_Letter and Is_Lower and conversion functions such as To_Lower for the types Wide_Character and Wide_Wide_Character in a similar way to the existing package Ada.Characters.Handling for the type Character.

Experience with the package Ada.Directories added in Ada 2005 has revealed a few shortcomings.

One problem concerns case sensitivity. Unfortunately, common operating systems differ in their approach. To remedy this the following are added to Ada.Directories

```
type Name_Case_Kind is (Unknown, Case_Sensitive, Case_Insensitive, Case_Preserving);

function Name_Case_Equivalence(Name: in String) return Name_Case_Kind;
```

Calling Name_Case_Equivalence enables one to discover the situation for the operating system concerned.

Another problem is that the basic approach in Ada.Directories is a bit simplistic and assumes that file names can always be subdivided into a directory name and a simple name. Thus the existing function Compose is

```
function Compose(Containing_Directory: String := "";
                 Name: String; Extension: String := "") return String;
```

and this requires that the Name is a simple name such as "My_File" with possibly an extension if one is not provided.

Accordingly, an optional child package is introduced, Ada.Directories.Hierarchical_File_Names, and this adds the concept of relative names and a new version of Compose whose second parameter is a relative name and various functions such as Is_Simple_Name and Is_Relative_Name.

Programs often need information about where they are being used. This is commonly called the Locale. As an example, in some regions of the world, a sum such as a million dollars is written as $1,000,000.00 whereas in others it appears as $1.000.000,00 with point and comma interchanged. An early attempt at providing facilities for doing the right thing was fraught with complexity. So Ada 2012 has adopted the simple solution of enabling a program to determine the country code (two characters) and the language code (three characters) and then do its own thing. The codes are given by ISO standards. Canada is interesting in that it has one country code ("CA") but uses two language codes ("eng" and "fra").

The information is provided by a new package Ada.Locales which declares the codes and the two functions Language and Country to return the current active locale (that is, the locale associated with the current task).

And finally, we consider the container library. Containers were a major and very valuable addition to Ada 2005 but again, experience with use has indicated that some enhancements are necessary.

We start with a brief summary of what is in Ada 2005. The parent package Ada.Containers has six main children namely Vectors, Doubly_Linked_Lists, Hashed_Maps, Ordered_Maps, Hashed_Sets, and Ordered_Sets. These manipulate definite types.

In addition there are another six for manipulating indefinite types with names such as Indefinite_Vectors and so on.

There are also two packages for sorting generic arrays, one for unconstrained types and one for constrained types.

There are four new kinds of containers in Ada 2012

- bounded forms of the existing containers,

- a container for a single indefinite object,

- various containers for multiway trees, and

- various containers for queues.

In addition there are a number of auxiliary new facilities whose purpose is to simplify the use of containers.

We will start by briefly looking at each of the new kinds of containers in turn.

The existing containers are unbounded in the sense that there is no limit to the number of items that can be added to a list for example. The implementation is expected to use storage pools as necessary. However, many applications in high integrity and real-time areas forbid the use of access types and require a much more conservative approach. Accordingly, a range of containers is introduced with bounded capacity so that there is no need to acquire extra storage dynamically.

Thus there are additional packages with names such as Containers.Bounded_Doubly_Linked_Lists. A key thing is that the types List, Vector and so on all have a discriminant giving their capacity thus

    type List(Capacity: Count_Type) **is tagged private**;

so that when a container is declared its capacity is fixed. A number of consequential changes are made as well. For example, the bounded form has to have a procedure Assign

    procedure Assign(Target: **in out** List; Source: **in** List);

because using built-in assignment would raise Constraint_Error if the capacities were different. Using a procedure Assign means that the assignment will work provided the length of the source is not greater than the capacity of the target. If it is, the new exception Capacity_Error is raised. Moreover, a similar procedure Assign is added to all existing unbounded containers so that converting from a bounded to an unbounded container or vice versa is (reasonably) straightforward.

A new function Copy is also needed for the bounded containers and for uniformity is similarly added to the unbounded versions.

Conversion between bounded and unbounded containers is also guaranteed with respect to streaming.

There are no bounded indefinite containers; this is because if the components are indefinite then dynamic space allocation is required for the components anyway and making the overall container bounded would be pointless.

In Ada, it is not possible to declare an object of an indefinite type that can hold any value of the type. Thus if we declare an object of type String then it becomes constrained by the mandatory initial value.

> S: String := "Crocodile";

We can assign other strings to S but they must also have nine characters. We could assign "Alligator" but not "Elephant". (An elephant is clearly too small!)

This rigidity is rather a nuisance and so a new form of container is defined which enables the cunning declaration of an object of a definite type that can hold a single value of an indefinite type. In other words it is a wrapper. The new package is Ada.Containers.Indefinite_Holders and it takes a generic parameter of the indefinite type and declares a definite type Holder which is tagged private thus

```
generic
   type Element_Type (<>) is private;
   with function "="(Left, Right: Element_Type) return Boolean is <>;
package Ada.Containers.Indefinite_Holders is
   type Holder is tagged private;
   ...              -- various operations
end Ada.Containers. Indefinite_Holders;
```

The various operations include a procedure Replace_Element which puts a value into the holder and a function Element which returns the current value in the holder.

Three new containers are added for multiway trees (unbounded, bounded, and indefinite). It might have been thought that it would be easy to use the existing containers (such as the list container) to create a tree structure. But it is difficult for various reasons concerning memory management. And so it was concluded that new containers for multiway trees should be added to Ada 2012.

The package Ada.Containers.Multiway_Trees is the unbounded form similar to the existing containers for other structures. It has all the operations required to operate on a tree structure where each node can have multiple child nodes to any depth. Thus there are operations on subtrees, the ability to find siblings, to insert and remove children and so on. The other new containers are Ada.Containers.Bounded_Multiway_Trees and Ada.Containers.Indefinite_Multiway_Trees which provide bounded and indefinite forms respectively.

Finally, there is a group of containers for queues. This topic is particularly interesting because it has its origins in the desire to provide container operations that are task safe. However, it turned out that it was not easy to make the existing containers task safe in a general way which would satisfy all users because there are so many possibilities.

However, there was no existing container for queues and in the case of queues it is easy to see how to make them task safe.

There are in fact four queue containers and all apply to queues where the element type is definite; these come in both bounded and unbounded forms and for synchronized and priority queues. We get (writing AC as an abbreviation for Ada.Containers)

- AC.Unbounded_Synchronized_Queues,

- AC.Bounded_Synchronized_Queues,

- AC.Unbounded_Priority_Queues,

- AC.Bounded_Priority_Queues.

These in turn are all derived from a single synchronized interface. This is a good illustration of the use of synchronized interfaces and especially the aspect Synchronization discussed earlier (see Section 1.3.4). First there is the following generic package which declares the type Queue as a synchronized interface (writing AC as an abbreviation for Ada.Containers and ET for Element_Type)

```
generic
  type ET is private;  -- element type for definite queues
package AC.Synchronized_Queue_Interfaces is
  pragma Pure(...);
  type Queue is synchronized interface;

  procedure Enqueue(Container: in out Queue; New_Item: in ET) is abstract
    with Synchronization => By_Entry;

  procedure Dequeue(Container: in out Queue; Element: out ET) is abstract
    with Synchronization => By_Entry;

  function Current_Use(Container: Queue) return Count_Type is abstract;
  function Peak_Use(Container: Queue) return Count_Type is abstract;
end AC.Synchronized_Queue_Interfaces;
```

Then there are generic packages which enable us to declare actual queues. Thus the essence of the unbounded synchronized version is as follows (still with abbreviations AC for Ada.Containers, ET for Element_Type)

```
with System; use System;
with AC.Synchronized_Queue_Interfaces;
generic
  with package Queue_Interfaces is new AC.Synchronized_Queue_Interfaces(<>);
  Default_Ceiling: Any_Priority := Priority'Last;
package AC.Unbounded_Synchronized_Queues is
  pragma Preelaborate(...);

  package Implementation is
    -- not specified by the language
  end Implementation;

  protected type Queue(Ceiling: Any_Priority := Default_Ceiling)
            with Priority => Ceiling
            is new Queue_Interfaces.Queue with
```

```
    overriding
    entry Enqueue(New_Item: in Queue_Interfaces.ET);
    overriding
    entry Dequeue(Element: out Queue_Interfaces.ET);

    overriding
    function Current_Use return Count_Type;
    overriding
    function Peak_Use return Count_Type;

  private
      ...
  end Queue;

private
    ...
  end AC.Unbounded_Synchronized_Queues;
```

The discriminant gives the ceiling priority and for convenience has a default value. Remember that a protected type is limited and when used to implement an interface (as here) is considered to be tagged. In Ada 2012, defaults are allowed for discriminants of tagged types provided they are limited as mentioned in Section 1.3.3.

Note that the Priority is given by an aspect specification. Programmers who are allergic to the multiple uses of **with** could of course use the old pragma Priority in their own code.

(The need for the package Implementation will be briefly explained in Section 8.6 and can be completely ignored by the user.)

Now to declare our own queue of integers say we first write

```
  package My_Interface is new AC.Synchronized_Queue_Interfaces(ET => Integer);
```

This creates an interface for dealing with integers. Then to obtain an unbounded queue package for integers we write

```
  package My_Q_Package is new AC.Unbounded_Synchronized_Queues(My_Interface);
```

This creates a package which declares a protected type Queue. Now at last we can declare an object of this type and perform operations on it.

```
  The_Queue: My_Q_Package.Queue;
      ...
  The_Queue.Enqueue(37);
```

The various calls of Enqueue and Dequeue are likely to be in different tasks and the protected object ensures that all is well.

The other generic queue packages follow a similar style. Note that unlike the other containers, there are no queue packages for indefinite types. Indefinite types can be catered for by using the holder container as a wrapper or by using an access type.

In Ada 2005 there are two generic procedures for sorting arrays; one is for constrained arrays and one is for unconstrained arrays. In Ada 2012, a third generic procedure is added which can be used to sort any indexable structure. Its specification is

```
generic
   type Index_Type is (<>);
   with function Before(Left, Right: Index_Type) return Boolean;
   with procedure Swap(Left, Right: Index_Type);
procedure Ada.Containers.Generic_Sort(First, Last: Index_Type'Base);
pragma Pure(Ada.Containers.Generic_Sort);
```

Note that there is no parameter indicating the structure to be sorted; this is all done indirectly by the subprograms Before and Swap working over the range of values given by First and Last. It's almost magic!

A frequent requirement when dealing with containers is the need to visit every node and perform some action, in other words to iterate over the container. And there are probably many different iterations to be performed. In Ada 2005, this has to be done by the user defining a subprogram for each iteration or writing out detailed loops involving calling Next and checking for the last element of the container and so on. And we have to write out this mechanism for each such iteration.

In Ada 2012, after some preparatory work involving the new package Ada.Iterator.Interfaces it is possible to simplify such iterations hugely. For example, suppose we have a list container each of whose elements is a record containing two components of type Integer (P and Q say) and we want to add some global X to Q for all elements where P is a prime. In Ada 2005 we have to write the laborious

```
C := The_List.First;        -- C declared as of type Cursor
loop
   exit when C = No_Element;
   E := Element(C);
   if Is_Prime(E.P) then
      Replace_Element(The_List, C, (E.P, E.Q + X));
   end if;
   C := Next(C);
end loop;
```

Not only is this tedious but there is lots of scope for errors. However, in Ada 2012 we can simply write

```
for E of The_List loop
   if Is_Prime(E.P) then E.Q := E.Q + X; end if;
end loop;
```

The mechanism is thus similar to that introduced in the previous section for arrays.

There are also a number of minor new facilities designed to simplify the use of containers. These include the introduction of case insensitive operations for comparing strings and for writing hash functions.

1.4 Conclusions

This overview of Ada 2012 should have given the reader an appreciation of the important new features in Ada 2012. Some quite promising features failed to be included partly because the need for them was not clear and also because a conclusive design proved elusive.

The remaining chapters will expand on the six major topics of this overview in more detail.

It is worth briefly reviewing the guidelines (see Section 1.2 above) to see whether Ada 2012 meets them.

The group A items were about extending the advantages of Ada and specifically mentioned containers, contracts and real-time. There are many new features for containers, pre- and postconditions have been added and so have facilities for multiprocessors.

The group B items were about eliminating shortcomings, increasing safety and particularly mentioned improvements to access types and storage management. This has been achieved with corrections to accessibility checks, the introduction of subpools and so on.

It seems clear from this brief check that indeed Ada 2012 does meet the objectives set for it.

2 Contracts and Aspects

This chapter describes the mechanisms for including contracts in Ada 2012.

The main feature is that preconditions and postconditions can be given for subprograms. In addition, invariants can be given for types and predicates can be given for subtypes.

In attempting to find a satisfactory way of adding these features it was found expedient to introduce the concept of an aspect specification for describing properties of entities in general. It is thus convenient to describe aspect specifications in this chapter.

2.1 Overview of changes

The WG9 guidance document [1] identifies very large complex systems as a major application area for Ada. It further identifies four areas for improvements, one of which is

> Improving the ability to write and enforce contracts for Ada entities (for instance, via preconditions).

The idea of contracts has been a cornerstone of programming for many years. The very idea of specifying parameters for subroutines is a simple form of contract going back to languages such as Fortran over half a century ago. More recently the idea of contracts has been brought to the fore by languages such as SPARK and Eiffel.

SPARK is, as many readers will be aware, a subset of Ada with annotations providing assertions regarding state embedded as Ada comments. The subset excludes features such as access types and dynamic dispatching but it does include Ravenscar tasking and generics. The subset was chosen to enable the contracts to be proved prior to execution. Thus SPARK is a very appropriate vehicle for real programs that just have to be correct because of concerns of safety and security.

Eiffel, on the other hand, is a language with a range of dynamic facilities much as in Ada and has found favour as a vehicle for education. Eiffel includes mechanisms describing contracts which are monitored on a dynamic basis at program execution.

The goal of this amendment to Ada is to incorporate matters such as pre- and postconditions but with the recognition that they are, like those in Eiffel, essentially for checking at runtime.

Adding pre- and postconditions and similar features has had quite a wide ranging impact on Ada and has required much more flexibility in many areas such as the form of expressions which will be addressed in later chapter s.

The following Ada issues cover the key changes and are described in detail in this chapter:

145 Pre- and postconditions

146 Type invariants

153 Subtype predicates

183 Aspect specifications

191 Aliasing predicates

228 Default initial values for types

229 Specifiable aspects

230 Inheritance of null procedures with precondition

243 Clarification of categorization

247 Preconditions, postconditions, multiple inheritance and dispatching calls

250 Thoughts on type invariants

254 Do we really have contracts right?

267 Improvements for aspect specifications

287 Some questions on subtype predicates

289 Invariants and in mode parameters

297 First_Valid and Last_Valid attributes

These changes can be grouped as follows.

First we lay the syntactic foundations necessary to introduce features such as preconditions by discussing aspect specifications which essentially replace or provide an alternative to pragmas for specifying many features (183, 229, 243, 267).

Then we discuss the introduction of pre- and postconditions on subprograms including the problems introduced by multiple inheritance (145, 230, 247, 254).

Two other related topics are type invariants and subtype predicates which provide additional means of imposing restrictions on types (146, 153, 250, 287, 289, 297).

Finally, two auxiliary features are the ability to provide default values for scalar types and array types (228) and means of checking that aliasing does not occur between two objects (191).

2.2 Aspect specifications

Although in a sense the introduction of aspect specifications is incidental to the main themes of Ada 2012 which are contracts, real-time, and containers, the clarity (and some might say upheaval) brought by aspect specifications merits their description first.

An early proposal to introduce preconditions was by the use of pragmas. Thus to give a precondition **not** Is_Full to the usual Push procedure acting on a stack S and a corresponding postcondition **not** Is_Empty, it was proposed that this should be written as

```
pragma Precondition(Push, not Is_Full(S));
pragma Postcondition(Push, not Is_Empty(S));
```

But this looks ugly and is verbose since it mentions Push in both pragmas. Moreover, potential problems with overloading means that it has to be clarified to which procedure Push they apply if there happen to be several. As a consequence it was decreed that the pragmas had to apply to the immediately preceding subprogram. Which of course is not the case with pragma Inline which with overloading applies to all subprograms with the given name. Other curiosities include the need to refer to the formal parameters of Push (such as S) so that the expression has to be resolved taking heed of these even though it is detached from the actual specification of Push.

Other pragmas proposed were Inherited_Precondition and Inherited_Postcondition for use with dispatching subprograms.

So it was a mess and an alternative was sought. The solution which evolved was to get away from wretched pragmas in such circumstances. Indeed, the Ada 83 Rationale [6] says "In addition, a program text can include elements that have no influence on the meaning of the program but are included as information and guidance for the human reader or for the compiler. These are: Comments; Pragmas..."

So pragmas were meant to have no effect on the meaning of the program. Typical pragmas in Ada 83 were List, Inline, Optimize and Suppress. But in later versions of Ada, pragmas are used for all sorts of things. The days when pragmas had no effect are long gone!

The basic need was to tie the pre- and postconditions syntactically to the specification of Push so that there could be no doubt as to which subprogram they applied; this would also remove the need to mention the name of the subprogram again. And so, as described in the Introduction, we now have

```
procedure Push(S: in out Stack; X: in Item)
    with
      Pre => not Is_Full(S),
      Post => not Is_Empty(S);
```

The syntax for aspect specification is

```
aspect_specification ::=
    with aspect_mark [ => expression] { ,
        aspect_mark [ => expression] }
```

and this can be used with a variety of structures, subprogram declaration being the example here.

Note especially the use of the reserved word **with**. Serious attempts were made to think of another word so as to avoid using **with** again but nothing better was suggested. It might be thought that it would be confusing to use **with** which is firmly associated with context clauses. However, recall that **with** has also been used to introduce generic formal subprogram parameters without causing confusion since 1983. Thus

```
generic
    with function This ...
procedure That ...
```

Moreover, Ada 95 introduced the use of **with** for type extension as in

```
type Circle is new Object with
    record
        Radius: Float;
    end record;
```

So in Ada 95 there were already many distinct uses of **with** and another one will surely do no harm. It's a versatile little word.

Any risk of confusion is easily avoided by using a sensible layout. Thus a **with** clause should start on a new line at the left and aligned with the following unit to which it applies. A formal generic parameter starting with **with** should be aligned with other formal parameters and indented after the word generic. In the case of type extension, **with** should be at the end of the line. Finally, in the case of aspect specifications, **with** should be at the beginning of a line and indented after the entity to which it applies.

Having introduced aspect specifications which are generally so much nicer than pragmas, it was decided to allow aspect specifications for all those situations where pragmas are used and an aspect specification makes sense (typically where it applies to an entity rather than a region of text). And then to make most of the pragmas obsolete.

Before looking at the old pragmas concerned in detail, two general points are worth noting.

The usual linear elaboration rules do not apply to the expression in an aspect specification. It is essentially sorted out at the freezing point of the entity to which the aspect applies. The reason for this was illustrated by an example in the Introduction which was

```
type Stack is private
  with
    Type_Invariant => Is_Unduplicated(Stack);
```

The problem here is that the function Is_Unduplicated cannot be declared before that of the type Stack and yet it is needed in the aspect specification of the declaration of Stack. So there is a circularity which is broken by saying that the elaboration of aspect specifications is deferred.

The other general point is that some aspects essentially take a Boolean value. For example the pragma Inline is replaced by the aspect Inline so that rather than writing

```
procedure Do_It( ... );
pragma Inline(Do_It);
```

we now write

```
procedure Do_It( ... )
  with Inline;
```

The aspect Inline has type Boolean and so we could write

```
procedure Do_It( ... )
  with Inline => True;
```

To have insisted on this would have been both pedantic and tedious and so in the case of a Boolean aspect there is a rule that says that => True can be omitted and True is then taken by default. But this does not apply to Default_Value and Default_Component_Value as explained later in Section 2.6 on Default initial values.

Note however that omitting the whole aspect by just writing

```
procedure Do_It( ... );
```

results of course in the Inline aspect of Do_It being False.

A mad programmer could even use defaults for preconditions and postconditions. Thus writing

```
procedure Curious( ... )
  with Pre;
```

in which by default the precondition is taken to be True, results in the Curious procedure always being callable.

We will now consider the fate of the various pragmas in Ada 2005. Some are replaced by aspect specifications and the pragmas made obsolete (of course, they can still be used, but should be discouraged in new programs). Some are paralleled by aspect specifications and the user left with the choice. Some are unchanged since for various reasons aspect specifications were inappropriate. Some pragmas are new to Ada 2012 and born obsolete.

The following are the obsolete pragmas with some examples of corresponding aspect specifications.

The pragmas Inline, No_Return, and Pack are examples having Boolean aspects. We can now write

```
procedure Do_It( ... )
  with Inline;

procedure Fail( ... )
  with No_Return;

type T is ...
  with Pack;
```

Some thought was given as to whether the name of the Pack aspect should be Packing rather than Pack because this gave better resonance in English. But the possible confusion in having a different name to that of the pragma overrode the thought of niceties of (human) language.

Curiously enough the old pragmas Inline and No_Return could take several subprograms as arguments but naturally the aspect specification is explicitly given to each one.

If several aspects are given to a procedure then we simply put them together thus

> **procedure** Kill
>   **with** Inline, No_Return;

rather than having to supply several pragmas (which careless program maintenance might have scattered around).

In the case of a procedure without a distinct specification, the aspect specification goes in the procedure body before **is** thus

> **procedure** Do_It(...)
>   **with** Inline **is**
>
>   ...
>
> **begin**
>
>   ...
>
> **end** Do_It;

This arrangement is because the aspect specification is very much part of the specification of the subprogram. This will be familiar to users of SPARK where we might have

> **procedure** Do_It(...)
> --# **global in out** Stuff;
> **is** ...

If a subprogram has a distinct specification then we cannot give a language-defined aspect specification on the body; this avoids problems of conformance. If there is a stub but no specification then any aspect specification goes on the stub but not the body. Thus aspect specifications go on the first of specification, stub, and body but are never repeated. Note also that we can give aspect specifications on other forms of stubs and bodies such as package bodies, task bodies and entry bodies but none are defined by the language.

In the case of a stub, abstract subprogram, and null subprogram which never have bodies, the aspect specification goes after **is separate**, **is abstract** or **is null** thus

> **procedure** Action(D: **in** Data) **is separate**
>   **with** Convention => C;

> **procedure** Enqueue(...) **is abstract**
>   **with** Synchronization => By_Entry;

> **procedure** Nothing **is null**
>   **with** Something;

The above example of the use of Synchronization is from the package Synchronized_Queue_ Interfaces, a new child of Ada.Containers as mentioned in the Introduction.

The same style is followed by the newly introduced expression functions thus

> **function** Inc (A: Integer) **return** Integer **is** (A + 1)
>   **with** Inline;

Other examples of Boolean aspects are Atomic, Volatile, and Independent. We now write for example

> Converged: Boolean := False
>   **with** Atomic;

The aspects Atomic_Components, Volatile_Components and Independent_Components are similar.

The three pragmas Convention, Import and Export are replaced by five aspects, namely Import, Export, Convention, External_Name and Link_Name.

For example, rather than, (see [8] page 702)

> **type** Response **is access procedure** (D: **in** Data);
> **pragma** Convention(C, Response);
>
> **procedure** Set_Click(P: **in** Response);
> **pragma** Import(C, Set_Click);
>
> **procedure** Action(D: **in** Data) **is separate**;
> **pragma** Convention(C, Action);

we now more neatly write

> **type** Response **is access procedure** (D: **in** Data)
>   **with** Convention => C;
>
> **procedure** Set_Click(P: **in** Response)
>   **with** Import, Convention => C;
>
> **procedure** Action(D: **in** Data) **is separate**
>   **with** Convention => C;

Note that the aspects can be given in any order whereas in the case of pragmas, the parameters had to be in a particular order. We could have written **with** Import => True but that would have been pedantic. As another example (see the RM 7.4), instead of

> CPU_Identifier: **constant** String(1 .. 8);
> **pragma** Import(Assembler, CPU_Identifier, Link_Name => "CPU_ID");

we now have

> CPU_Identifier: **constant** String(1 .. 8)
>   **with** Import, Convention => Assembler, Link_Name => "CPU_ID";

Observe that we always have to give the aspect name such as Convention whereas with pragmas Import and Export, the parameter name Convention was optional. Clearly it is better to have to give the name.

The pragma Controlled which it may be recalled told the system to keep its filthy garbage collector off my nice access type is plain obsolete and essentially abandoned. It is doubted whether it was ever used. The subclause of the RM (13.11.3) relating to this pragma is now used by a new pragma Default_Storage_Pools which will be discussed in Section 6.4 on Access types and storage pools.

The pragma Unchecked_Union is another example of a pragma replaced by a Boolean aspect. So we now write

> **type** Number(Kind: Precision) **is**
>   **record**
>
>   ...

      end record
      with Unchecked_Union;

Many obsolete pragmas apply to tasks. The aspect Storage_Size takes an expression of any integer type. Thus in the case of a task type without a task definition part (and thus without **is** and matching **end**) we write

      task type T
      with Storage_Size => 1000;

In the case of a task type with entries we write

      task type T
      with Storage_Size => 1000 **is**
      entry E ...

         ...

      end T;

The interrupt pragmas Attach_Handler and Interrupt_Handler now become

      procedure P(...)
      with Interrupt_Handler;

which specifies that the protected procedure P can be a handler and

      procedure P(...)
      with Attach_Handler => Some_Id;

which actually attaches P to the interrupt Some_Id.

The pragmas Priority and Interrupt_Priority are replaced by corresponding aspect specifications for example

      task T
      with Interrupt_Priority => 31;

      protected Object
      with Priority => 20 **is**   -- *ceiling priority*

Note that a protected type or singleton protected object always has **is** and the aspect specification goes before it.

Similarly, instead of using the pragma Relative_Deadline we can write

      task T
      with Relative_Deadline => RD;

The final existing pragma that is now obsolete is the pragma Asynchronous used in the Distributed Systems Annex and which can be applied to a remote procedure or remote access type. It is replaced by the Boolean aspect Asynchronous.

That covers all the existing Ada 2005 pragmas that are now obsolete.

Two new pragmas in Ada 2012 are CPU and Dispatching_Domain but these are born obsolete. Thus we can write either of

      task My Task **is**
      pragma CPU(10);

or

      task My_Task
      with CPU => 10 **is**

and similarly

```
task Your_Task is
  pragma Dispatching_Domain(Your_Domain);
```

or

```
task Your_Task
  with Dispatching_Domain => Your_Domain is
```

The reason for introducing these pragmas is so that existing tasking programs with copious use of pragmas such as Priority can use the new facilities in a similar style. It was considered inelegant to write

```
task My_Task
  with CPU => 10 is
  pragma Priority(5);
```

and a burden to have to change programs to

```
task My_Task
  with CPU => 10, Priority => 5 is
```

So existing programs, can be updated to

```
task My_Task is
  pragma CPU(10);
  pragma Priority(5);
```

(One other pragma that was never born at all was Implemented which turned into the aspect Synchronization often used to ensure that an abstract procedure is actually implemented by an entry as illustrated earlier.)

A number of existing pragmas are paralleled by aspect specifications but the pragmas are not made obsolete. Examples are the pragmas relating to packages such as Pure, Preelaborate, Elaborate_Body and so on.

Thus we can write either of

```
package P is
  pragma Pure(P);
end P;
```

or

```
package P
  with Pure is
end P;
```

The author prefers the former but some avant garde programmers might like to use the latter.

Note that Preelaborable_Initialization is unusual in that it cannot be written as an aspect specification for reasons that need not bother us. The inquisitive reader can refer to AI-229 for the details.

Finally, there are many pragmas that do not relate to any particular entity and so for which an aspect specification would be impossible. These include Assert and Assertion_Policy, Suppress and Unsuppress, Page and List, Optimize and Restrictions.

As well as replacing pragmas, aspect specifications can be used instead of attribute definition clauses. For example rather than

```
type Byte is range 0 .. 255;
```

followed (perhaps much later) by

```
for Byte'Size use 8;
```

we can now write

```
type Byte is range 0 .. 255
   with Size => 8;
```

Similarly

```
type My_Float is digits 20
   with Alignment => 16;

Loose_Bits: array (1 .. 10) of Boolean
   with Component_Size => 4;

type Cell_Ptr is access Cell
   with Storage_Size => 500 * Cell'Size / Storage_Unit, Storage_Pool => Cell_Ptr_Pool;

S: Status
   with Address => 8#100#;

type T is delta 0.1 range −1.0 .. +1.0
   with Small => 0.1;
```

But we cannot use this technique to replace an enumeration representation clause or record representation clause. Thus although we can write

```
type RR is
   record
      Code: Opcode;
      R1: Register;
      R2: Register;
   end record                    .
      with Alignment => 2, Bit_Order => High_Order_First;
```

the layout information has to be done by writing

```
for RR use
   record
      Code at 0 range 0 .. 7;
      R1 at 1 range 0 .. 3;
      R2 at 1 range 4 .. 7;
   end record;
```

It is interesting to note that attribute definition clauses were not made redundant in the way that many pragmas were made redundant. This is because there are things that one can do with attribute definition clauses that cannot be done with aspect specifications. For example a visible type can be declared in a visible part and then details of its representation can be given in a private part. Thus we might have

```
package P is
   type T is ...
private
   Secret_Size: constant := 16;
   for T'Size use Secret_Size;
end P;
```

It's not that convincing because the user can use the attribute T'Size to find the Secret_Size anyway. But some existing programs are structured like that and hence the facility could hardly be made redundant.

The examples above have shown aspect specifications with the following constructions: subprogram declaration, subprogram body, stub, abstract subprogram declaration, null procedure declaration, full type declaration, private type declaration, object declaration, package declaration, task type declaration, single task declaration, and single protected declaration. In addition they can be used with subtype declaration, component declaration, private extension declaration, renaming declaration, protected type declaration, entry declaration, exception declaration, generic declaration, generic instantiation, and generic formal parameter declaration.

The appropriate layout should be obvious. In the case of a large structure such as a package specification and any body, the aspect specification goes before **is**. But when something is small and all in one piece such as a procedure specification, stub, null procedure, object declaration or generic instantiation any aspect specification goes at the end of the declaration; it is then more visible and less likely to interfere with the layout of the rest of the structure.

In some cases such as exception declarations there are no language defined aspects that apply but implementations might define their own aspects.

2.3 Preconditions and postconditions

We will look first at the simple case when inheritance is not involved and then look at more general cases. Specific preconditions and postconditions are applied using the aspects Pre and Post respectively whereas class wide conditions are applied using the aspects Pre'Class and Post'Class.

To apply a specific precondition Before and/or a specific postcondition After to a procedure P we write

> **procedure** P(P1: **in** T1; P2: **in out** T2; P3: **out** T3)
>   **with** Pre => Before,
>   Post => After;

where Before and After are expressions of a Boolean type (that is of type Boolean or a type derived from it).

The precondition Before and the postcondition After can involve the parameters P1 and P2 and P3 and any visible entities such as other variables, constants and functions. Note that Before can involve the **out** parameter P3 inasmuch as one can always read any constraints on an **out** parameter such as the bounds if it were an array.

The attribute X'Old will be found useful in postconditions; it denotes the value of X on entry to P. Old is typically applied to parameters of mode **in out** such as P2 but it can be applied to any visible entity such as a global variable. This can be useful for monitoring global variables which are updated by the call of P. But note that 'Old can only be used in postconditions and not in arbitrary text and it cannot be applied to objects of a limited type.

Perhaps surprisingly 'Old can also be applied to parameters of mode **out**. For example, in the case of a parameter of a record type that is updated as a whole, nevertheless we might want to check that a particular component has not changed. Thus in updating some personal details, such as address and occupation, we might want to ensure that the person's date of birth and sex are not tampered with by writing

> Post => P.Sex = P.Sex'Old **and** P.Dob = P.Dob'Old

In the case of an array, we can write A(I)'Old which means the original value of A(I). But A(I'Old) is different since it is the component of the final value of A but indexed by the old value of I.

Remember that the result of a function is an object and so 'Old can be applied to it. Note carefully the difference between F(X)'Old and F(X'Old). The former applies F to X on entry to the subprogram and saves it. The latter saves X and applies F to it when the postcondition is evaluated. These could be different because the function F might also involve global variables which have changed.

Generally 'Old can be applied to anything but there are restrictions on its use in certain conditional structures in which it can only be applied to statically determined objects. This is illustrated by the following (based on an example in the AARM)

```
Table: array (1 .. 10) of Integer := ... ;
procedure P(I: in out Natural)
   with Post => I > 0 and then Table(I)'Old = 1;   -- illegal
```

The programmer's intent is that the postcondition uses a short circuit form to avoid evaluating Table(I) if I is not positive on exit from the procedure. But, 'Old is evaluated and stored on entry and this could raise Constraint_Error because I might for example be zero. This is a conundrum since the compiler cannot know whether the value of Table(I) will be needed and also I can change so it cannot know which I anyway. So such structures are forbidden.

(The collector of Ada curiosities might be amused to note that we can write

```
subtype dlo is Character;
```

and then in a postcondition we could have

```
dlo'('I')'old
```

which is palindromic. If the subtype were blo rather than dlo then the expression would be mirror reflective!

I am grateful to Jean-Pierre Rosen for this example.)

In the case of a postcondition applying to a function F, the result of the function is denoted by the attribute F'Result. Again this attribute can only be used in postconditions.

Some trivial examples of declarations of a procedure Pinc and function Finc to perform an increment are

```
procedure Pinc(X: in out Integer)
   with Post => X = X'Old+1;

function Finc(X: Integer) return Integer
   with Post => Finc'Result = X'Old+1;
```

Preconditions and postconditions are controlled by the pragma Assertion_Policy. They are enabled by

```
pragma Assertion_Policy(Check);
```

and disabled by using parameter Ignore. It is the value in effect at the point of the subprogram declaration that matters. So we cannot have a situation where the policy changes during the call so that preconditions are switched on but postconditions are off or vice versa.

And so the overall effect of calling P with checks enabled is roughly that, after evaluating any parameters at the point of call, it as if the body were

```
if not Before then                    -- check precondition
   raise Assertion_Error;
end if;

evaluate and store any 'Old stuff;
```

call actual body of P;

if not After **then**   -- *check postcondition*
   raise Assertion_Error;
end if;

copy back any by-copy parameters;

return to point of call;

Occurrences of Assertion_Error are propagated and so raised at the point of call; they cannot be handled inside P. Of course, if the evaluation of Before or After themselves raise some exception then that will similarly be propagated to the point of call.

Note that conditions Pre and Post can also be applied to entries.

Before progressing to the problems of inheritance it is worth reconsidering the purpose of pre- and postconditions.

A precondition Before is an obligation on the caller to ensure that it is true before the subprogram is called and it is a guarantee to the implementer of the body that it can be relied upon on entry to the body.

A postcondition After is an obligation on the implementer of the body to ensure that it is true on return from the subprogram and it is a guarantee to the caller that it can be relied upon on return.

The symmetry is neatly illustrated by the diagram below

	Pre	Post
Call writer	obligation	guarantee
Body writer	guarantee	obligation

The simplest form of inheritance occurs with derived types that are not tagged. Suppose we declare the procedure Pinc as above with the postcondition shown and supply a body

```
procedure Pinc(X: in out Integer) is
begin
   X := X+1;
end Pinc;
```

and then declare a type

type Apples **is new** Integer;

then the procedure Pinc is inherited by the type Apples. So if we then write

No_Of_Apples: Apples;

...

Pinc(No_Of_Apples);

what actually happens is that the code of the procedure Pinc originally written for Integer is called and so the postcondition is inherited automatically.

If the user now wants to add a precondition to Pinc that the number of apples is not negative then a completely new subprogram has to be declared which overrides the old one thus

```
procedure Pinc(X: in out Apples)
   with Pre => X >= 0,
        Post => X = X'Old+1;
```

and a new body has to be supplied (which will of course in this curious case be essentially the same as the old one). So we cannot inherit an operation and change its conditions at the same time.

We now turn to tagged types and first continue to consider the specific conditions Pre and Post. As a perhaps familiar example, consider the hierarchy consisting of a type Object and then direct descendants Circle, Square and Triangle.

Suppose the type Object is

```
type Object is tagged
   record
      X_Coord, Y_Coord: Float;
   end record;
```

and we declare a function Area thus

```
function Area(O: Object) return Float
   with Pre => O.X_Coord > 0.0,
        Post => Area'Result = 0.0;
```

This imposes a requirement on the caller that the function is called only with objects with positive x-coordinate (for some obscure reason), and a requirement on the implementer of the body that the area is zero (raw objects are just points and have no area).

If we now declare a type Circle as

```
type Circle is new Object with
   record
      Radius: Float;
   end record;
```

and override the inherited function Area then the Pre and Post conditions on Area for Object are not inherited and we have to supply new ones, perhaps

```
function Area(C: Circle)
   with Pre => C.X_Coord – C.Radius > 0.0,
        Post => Area'Result > 3.1 * C.Radius**2 and
                Area'Result < 3.2 * C.Radius**2;
```

The conditions ensure that all of the circle is in the right half-plane and that the area is about right!

So the rules so far are exactly as for the untagged case. If an operation is not overridden then it inherits the conditions from its ancestor but if it is overridden then those conditions are lost and new ones have to be supplied. And if no new ones are supplied then they are by default taken to be True.

In conclusion, the conditions Pre and Post are very much part of the actual body. One consequence of this is that an abstract subprogram cannot have Pre and Post conditions because an abstract subprogram has no body.

We now turn to the class wide conditions Pre'Class and Post'Class which are subtly different. The first point is that the class wide ones apply to all descendants as well even if the operations are overridden. In the case of Post'Class if an overridden operation has no condition given then it is taken to be True (as in the case of Post). But in the case of Pre'Class, if an overridden operation has no condition given then it is only taken to be True if no other Pre'Class applies (no other is inherited). We will now look at the consequences of these rules.

It might be that we want certain conditions to hold throughout the hierarchy, perhaps that all objects concerned have a positive *x*-coordinate and nonnegative area. In that case we can use class wide conditions.

> **function** Area(O: Object) **return** Float
>   **with** Pre'Class => O.X_Coord > 0.0,
>   Post'Class => Area'Result >= 0.0;

Now when we declare Area for Circle, Pre'Class and Post'Class from Object will be inherited by the function Area for Circle. Note that within a class wide condition a formal parameter of type T is interpreted as of T'Class. Thus O is of type Object'Class and thus applies to Circle. The inherited postcondition is simply that the area is not negative and uses the attribute 'Result.

If we do not supply conditions for the overriding Area for Circle and simply write

> **overriding**
> **function** Area(C: Circle) **return** Float;

then the precondition inherited from Object still applies. In the case of the postcondition not only is the postcondition from Object inherited but there is also an implicit postcondition of True. So the applicable conditions for Area for Circle are

> Pre'Class for Object
>
> Post'Class for Object
> True

Suppose on the other hand that we give explicit Pre'Class and Post'Class for Area for Circle thus

> **overriding**
> **function** Area(C: Circle) **return** Float
>   **with** Pre'Class => ... ,
>   Post'Class => ... ;

We then find that the applicable conditions for Area for Circle are

> Pre'Class for Object
> Pre'Class for Circle
>
> Post'Class for Object
> Post'Class for Circle

Incidentally, it makes a lot of sense to declare the type Object as abstract so that we cannot declare pointless objects. In that case Area might as well be abstract as well. Although we cannot give conditions Pre and Post for an abstract operation we can still give the class wide conditions Pre'Class and Post'Class.

If the hierarchy extends further, perhaps Equilateral_Triangle is derived from Triangle which itself is derived from Object, then we could add class wide conditions to Area for Triangle and these would also apply to Area for Equilateral_Triangle. And we might add specific conditions for Equilateral_ Triangle as well. So we would then find that the following apply to Area for Equilateral_Triangle

> Pre'Class for Object
> Pre'Class for Triangle
> Pre for Equilateral Triangle
>
> Post'Class for Object
> Post'Class for Triangle
> Post for Equilateral_Triangle

The postconditions are quite straightforward, all apply and all must be true on return from the function Area. The compiler can see all these postconditions when the code for Area is compiled and so they are all checked in the body. Note that any default True makes no difference because B **and** True is the same as B.

However, the rules regarding preconditions are perhaps surprising. The specific precondition Pre for Equilateral_Triangle must be true (checked in the body) but so long as just one of the class wide preconditions Pre'Class for Object and Triangle is true then all is well. Note that class wide preconditions are checked at the point of call. Do not get confused over the use of the word apply. They all apply but only the ones seen at the point of call are actually checked.

The reason for this state of affairs concerns dispatching and especially redispatching. Consider the case of Ada airlines which has Basic, Nice and Posh passengers. Basic passengers just get a seat. Nice passengers also get a meal and Posh passengers also get a limo. The types Reservation, Nice_Reservation and Posh_Reservation form a hierarchy with Nice_Reservation being extended from Reservation and so on. The facilities are assigned when a reservation is made by calling an appropriate procedure Make thus

```
procedure Make(R: in out Reservation) is
begin
  Select_Seat(R);
end Make;

procedure Make(NR: in out Nice_Reservation) is
begin
  Make(Reservation(NR));
  Order_Meal(NR);
end Make;

procedure Make(PR: in out Posh_Reservation) is
  Make(Nice_Reservation(PR));
  Arrange_Limo(PR);
end Make;
```

Each Make calls its ancestor in order to avoid duplication of code and to ease maintenance.

A variation involving redispatching introduces two different procedures Order_Meal, one for Nice passengers and one for Posh passengers. We then need to ensure that Posh passengers get a posh meal rather than a nice meal. We write

```
procedure Make(NR: in out Nice_Reservation) is
begin
  Make(Reservation(NR));
            -- now redispatch to appropriate Order_Meal
  Order_Meal(Nice_Reservation'Class(NR));
end Make;
```

Now suppose we have a precondition Pre'Class on Order_Meal for Nice passengers and one on Order_Meal for Posh passengers. The call of Order_Meal sees that it is for Nice_Reservation'Class and so the code includes a test of Pre'Class on Nice_Reservation. It does not necessarily know of the existence of the type Posh_Reservation and cannot check Pre'Class on that Order_Meal. At a later date we might add Supersonic passengers (RIP Concorde) and this can be done without recompiling the rest of the system so it certainly cannot do anything about checking Pre'Class on Order_Meal for Supersonic_Reservation which does not exist when the call is compiled. So when we eventually get to the body of one of the procedures Order_Meal all we know is that some Pre'Class on Order_Meal has been checked somewhere. And that is all that the writer of the code of

Order_Meal can rely upon. Note that nowhere does the compiled code actually "or" a lot of preconditions together.

In summary, class wide preconditions are checked at the point of call. Class wide postconditions and both specific pre- and postconditions are checked in the actual body.

A small point to remember is that a class wide operation such as

> **procedure** Do_It(X: **in out** T'Class);

is not a primitive operation of T and so although we can specify Pre and Post for Do_It we cannot specify Pre'Class and Post'Class for Do_It.

We noted above that the aspects Pre and Post cannot be specified for an abstract subprogram because it doesn't have a body. They cannot be given for a null procedure either, since we want all null procedures to be identical and do nothing and that includes no conditions.

We now turn to the question of multiple inheritance and progenitors.

In the case of multiple inheritance we have to consider the so-called Liskov Substitution Principle (LSP). The usual consequence of LSP is that in the case of preconditions they are combined with "or" (thus weakening) and the rule for postconditions is that they are combined with "and" (thus strengthening). But the important thing is that a relevant concrete operation can be substituted for the corresponding operations of all its relevant ancestors.

In Ada, a type T can have one parent and several progenitors. Thus we might have

> **type** T **is new** P **and** G1 **and** G2 **with** ...

where P is the parent and G1 and G2 are progenitors. Remember that a progenitor cannot have components and cannot have concrete operations (apart possibly for null procedures). So the operations of the progenitors have to be abstract or null and cannot have Pre and Post conditions. However, they can have Pre'Class and Post'Class conditions. It is possible that the same operation Op is primitive for more than one of these. Thus the progenitors G1 and G2 might both have an operation Op thus

> **procedure** Op(X: G1) **is abstract**;
> **procedure** Op(X: G2) **is abstract**;

If they are conforming (as they are in this case) then the one concrete operation Op of the type T derived from both G1 and G2 will implement both of these. (If they don't conform then they are simply overloadings and two operations of T are required). Hence the one Op for T can be substituted for the Op of both G1 and G2 and LSP is satisfied.

Now suppose both abstract operations have pre- and postconditions. Take postconditions first, we might have

> **procedure** Op(X: G1) **is abstract**
>   **with** Post'Class => After1;

> **procedure** Op(X: G2) **is abstract**
>   **with** Post'Class => After2;

Users of the Op of G1 will expect the postcondition After1 to be satisfied by any implementation of that Op. So if using the Op of T which implements the abstract Op of G1, it follows that Op of T must satisfy the postcondition After1. By a similar argument regarding G2, it must also satisfy the postcondition After2.

It thus follows that the effective postcondition on the concrete Op of T is as if we had written

procedure Op(X: T)
   with Post'Class => After1 **and** After2;

But of course we don't actually have to write that since we simply write

overriding
procedure OP(X: T);

and it automatically inherits both postconditions and the compiler inserts the appropriate code in the body. Remember that if we don't give a condition then it is True by default but anding in True makes no difference.

If we do provide another postcondition thus

overriding
procedure OP(X: T)
   with Post'Class => After_T;

then the overall class wide postcondition to be checked before returning will be After1 **and** After2 **and** After_T.

Now consider preconditions. Suppose the declarations of the two versions of Op are

procedure Op(X: G1) **is abstract**
   with Pre'Class => Before1;

procedure Op(X: G2) **is abstract**
   with Pre'Class => Before2;

Assuming that there is no corresponding Op for P, we must provide a concrete operation for T thus

overriding
procedure Op(X: T)
   with Pre'Class => Before_T;

This means that at a point of call of Op the precondition to be checked is Before_T **or** Before1 **or** Before2. As long as this is satisfied it does not matter that Before1 and Before2 might have been different.

If we do not provide an explicit Pre'Class then the condition to be checked at the point of call is Before1 **or** Before2.

An interesting case arises if a progenitor (say G1) and the parent have a conforming operation. Thus suppose P itself has the operation

   procedure Op(X: P);

and moreover that the operation is not abstract. Then (ignoring preconditions for the moment) this Op for P is inherited by T and thus provides a satisfactory implementation of Op for G1 and all is well.

Now suppose that Op for P has a precondition thus

procedure OP(X: P)
   with Pre'Class => Before_P;

and that Before_P and Before1 are not the same. If we do not provide an explicit overriding for Op, it would be possible to call the body of Op for P when the precondition it knows about, Before_P, is False (since Before1 being True would be sufficient to allow the call to proceed). This would effectively mean that no class wide preconditions could be trusted within the subprogram body and that would be totally unacceptable. So in this case there is a rule that an explicit overriding is required for Op for T.

If Op for P is abstract then a concrete Op for T must be provided and the situation is just as in the case for the Op for G1 and G2.

If T itself is declared as abstract (and P is not abstract and Op for P is concrete) then the inherited Op for T is abstract.

(These rules are similar to those for functions returning a tagged type when the type is extended; it has to be overridden unless the type is abstract in which case the inherited operation is abstract.)

We finish this somewhat mechanical discussion of the rules by pointing out that if silly inappropriate preconditions are given then we will get a silly program.

At the end of the day, the real point is that programmers should not write preconditions that are not sensible and sensibly related to each other. Because of the generality, the compiler cannot tell so stupid things are hard to prohibit. There is no defence against stupid programmers.

A concrete example using simple numbers might help. Suppose we have a tagged type T1 and an operation Solve which takes a parameter of type T1 and perhaps finds the solution to an equation defined by the components of T1. Solve delivers the answer in a parameter A with a parameter D giving the number of significant digits required in the answer. Also we impose a precondition on the number of digits D thus

```
type T1 is tagged record ...

procedure Solve(X: in T1; A: out Float; D: in Integer)
    with Pre'Class => D < 5;
```

The intent here is that the version of Solve for the type T1 always works if the number of significant digits asked for is less than 5.

Now suppose we declare a type T2 derived from T1 and that we override the inherited Solve with a new version that works if the number of significant digits asked for is less than 10

```
type T2 is new T1 with ...

overriding
procedure Solve(X: in T2; A: out Float; D: in Integer)
    with Pre'Class => D < 10;
```

And so on with a type T3

```
type T3 is new T2 with ...

overriding
procedure Solve(X: in T3; A: out Float; D: in Integer)
    with Pre'Class => D < 15;
```

Thus we have a hierarchy of algorithms Solve with increasing capability.

Now suppose we have a dispatching call

```
An_X: T1'Class := ... ;
Solve(An_X, Answer, Digs);
```

this will dispatch to one of the Solve procedures but we do not know which one. The only precondition that applies is that on the Solve for T1 which is D < 5. That is fine because D < 5 implies D < 10 and D < 15 and so on. Thus the preconditions work because the hierarchy weakens them.

Similarly, if we have

>   An_X: T2'Class := ... ;
>   Solve(An_X, Answer, Digs);

then it will dispatch to a Solve for one of T2, T3, ..., but not to the Solve for T1. The applicable preconditions are D < 5 and D < 10 and these are notionally ored together which means D < 10 is actually required. To see this suppose we supply D = Digs = 7. Then D < 5 is False but D < 10 is True so by oring False and True we get True, so the call works.

On the other hand if we write

>   An_X: T2 := ... ;
>   Solve(An_X, Answer, Digs);

then no dispatching is involved and the Solve for T2 is called. But both class wide preconditions D < 5 and D < 10 apply and so again the resulting ored precondition that is required is D < 10.

Now it should be clear that if the preconditions do not form a weakening hierarchy then we will be in trouble. Thus if the preconditions were D < 15 for T1, D < 10 for T2, and D < 5 for T3, then dispatching from the root will only check D < 15. However, we could end up calling the Solve for T2 which expects the precondition D < 10 and this might not be satisfied.

Care is thus needed with preconditions that they are sensibly related.

Finally, note that pre- and postconditions are allowed on generic units but not on instances. See Section 9.5 of the Epilogue.

2.4 Type invariants

Type invariants are designed for use with private types where we want some relationship to always hold between components of the type. Like pre- and postconditions there are both specific invariants that can be applied to any type and class wide invariants that can only be applied to tagged types.

One example mentioned above and discussed in the Introduction was a type Stack with specific invariant Is_Unduplicated. Thus we write

>   **type** Stack **is private**
>   **with** Type_Invariant => Is_Unduplicated(Stack);

After calls of Push and Pop and any other operations that manipulate the stack, the function Is_Unduplicated is called to ensure that there are no duplicates on the stack.

The monitoring is controlled by the pragma Assertion_Policy in the same way as pre- and postconditions. If an invariant fails (that is, has value False) then Assertion_Error is raised.

The invariant Is_Unduplicated is a curious example because it cannot be violated by Pop anyway since if there were no duplicates then removing the top item cannot make one appear.

Moreover, Push needs to ensure that the item to be added is not a duplicate of one on the stack already and so essentially much of the checking is repeated. Indeed, when writing Push we should be able to assume that no items are already duplicated and hence all we need to do is check that the new item to be added is not equal to one of the existing items (so n comparisons). However, a general function Is_Unduplicated will need to compare all pairs and thus require a double loop (so $n(n+1)/2$ comparisons).

The reader is invited to meditate over this conundrum. One's first reaction might be that this is a bad example. However, one way to ensure reliability is to introduce redundancy. Thus if the encoding of Is_Unduplicated and Push are done independently then there is an increased probability that any error will be detected.

The aspect Type_Invariant requires an expression of a Boolean type. The mad programmer could therefore also write

```
type Stack is private
   with Type_Invariant;
```

which would thus be True by default and so useless! Actually it might not be entirely useless since it might act as a placeholder for an invariant to be defined later and meanwhile the program will compile and execute.

Type invariants are useful whenever a type is more than just the sum of its components. Note carefully that the invariant may not hold when an object is being manipulated by a subprogram having access to the full type. In the case of Push and Pop and the invariant Is_Unduplicated this will not happen but consider the following simple example.

Suppose we have a type Point which describes the position of an object in a plane. It might simply be

```
type Point is
   record
      X, Y: Float;
   end record;
```

Now suppose we want to ensure that all points are within a unit circle. We could ensure that a point lies within a square by means of range constraints by writing

```
type Point is
   record
      X, Y: Float range -1.0 .. +1.0;
   end record;
```

but we need to ensure that $X^{**}2 + Y^{**}2$ is not greater than 1.0, and that cannot be done by individual constraints. So we might declare a type Disc_Pt with an invariant as follows

```
package Places is

   type Disc_Pt is private
      with Type_Invariant => Check_In(Disc_Pt);

   function Check_In(D: Disc_Pt) return Boolean
      with Inline;
      ...                          -- various operations on disc points
private

   type Disc_Pt is
      record
         X, Y: Float range -1.0 .. +1.0;
      end record;

   function Check_In(D: Disc_Pt) return Boolean is
      (D.X**2 + D.Y**2 <= 1.0);

end Places;
```

Note that we have used an expression function for Check_In. Expression functions were outlined in the Introduction and will be discussed in detail in the next chapter. They are very useful for small functions in situations like this and typically will be given the aspect Inline on the specification as shown.

Now suppose that we wish to make available to the user a procedure Flip that reflects a Disc_Pt in the line $x = y$, or in other words interchanges its X and Y components. The body might be

```
procedure Flip(D: in out Disc_Pt) is
   T: Float;                      -- temporary
begin
   T := D.X;  D.X := D.Y;  D.Y := T;
end Flip;
```

This works just fine but note that just before the assignment to D.Y, it is quite likely that the invariant does not hold. If the original value of D was (0.1, 0.8) then at the intermediate stage it will be (0.8, 0.8) and so well outside the unit circle.

So there is a general principle that an intermediate value not visible externally need not satisfy the invariant. There is an analogy with numeric types. The intermediate value of an expression can fall outside the range of the type but will be within range when the final value is assigned to the object. For example, suppose type Integer is 16 bits (a small machine) but the registers perform arithmetic in 32 bits, then a statement such as

```
J := K * L / M;
```

could easily produce an intermediate result K * L outside the range of Integer but the final value could be in range.

In many cases it will not be necessary for the user to know that a type invariant applies to the type; it is after all merely a detail of the implementation. So perhaps the above should be rewritten as

```
package Places is

   type Disc_Pt is private;
      ...                         -- various operations on disc points
   private

   type Disc_Pt is
      record
         X, Y: Float range −1.0 .. +1.0;
      end record
      with Type_Invariant => Disc_Pt.X**2 + Disc_Pt.Y**2 <= 1.0;

end Places;
```

In this case we do not need to declare a function Check_In at all. Note the use of the type name Disc_Pt in the invariant expression. This is another example of the use of a type name to denote a current instance (this is familiar from way back in Ada 83 with task type names).

We now turn to consider the places where a type invariant on a private type T is checked. These are basically when it can be changed from the point of view of the outside user. They are

- after default initialization of an object of type T,

- after a conversion to type T,

- after assigning to a view conversion involving descendants and ancestors of type T,

- after a call of T'Read or T'Input,

- after a call of a subprogram declared in the immediate scope of T and visible outside that has a parameter (of any mode including an access parameter) with a part of type T or returns a result with a part of type T.

Note that by saying a part of type T, the checks not only apply to subprograms with parameters and results of type T but they also apply to parameters and results whose components are of the type T or are view conversions involving the type T. Observe that parameters of mode **in** are also checked because, as is well known, there are accepted techniques for changing such parameters.

But note that checks on **in** parameters only apply to procedures and not to functions. This was a retrospective change after ISO standardization as explained in Section 9.5 of the Epilogue.

Beware, however, that the checks do not extend to deeply nested situations, such as components with components that are access values to objects that themselves involve type T or worse. Thus there are holes in the protection offered by type invariants. However, if the types are straightforward and the writer does not do foolish things like surreptitiously exporting access types referring to T then all will be well. It is another example of there being no defence against foolish programmers.

The checks on type invariants regarding parameters and results can be conveniently implemented in the body of the subprogram in much the same way as for postconditions. This saves duplicating the code of the tests at each point of call.

If a subprogram such as Flip which is visible outside is called from inside then the checks still apply. This is not strictly necessary of course, but fits the simple model of the checks being in the body and so simplifies the implementation.

If an untagged type is derived then any existing specific invariant is inherited for inherited operations. However, a further invariant can be given as well and both will apply to the inherited operations. This fits in with the model of view conversions used to describe how an inherited subprogram works on derivation. The parameters of the derived type are view converted to the parent type before the body is called and back again afterwards. As mentioned above, view conversions are one of the places where invariants are checked.

However, if we add new operations then the old invariant does not apply to them. In truth, the specific invariant is not really inherited at all; it just comes along for free with the inherited operations that are not overridden. So if we do add new operations then we need to state the total invariant required.

Note that this is not quite the same model as specific postconditions. We cannot add postconditions to an inherited operation but have to override it and then any specific postconditions on the parent are lost. In any event, in both cases, if we want to use inheritance then we should really use tagged types and class wide aspects.

So there is also an aspect Type_Invariant'Class for use with private tagged types. The distinction between Type_Invariant and Type_Invariant 'Class has similarities to that between Post and Post'Class.

The specific aspect Type_Invariant can be applied to any type but Type_Invariant'Class can only be applied to tagged types. A tagged type can have both an aspect Type_Invariant and Type_Invariant'Class.

Type_Invariant cannot be applied to an abstract type.

Type_Invariant'Class is inherited by all derived types; it can also be applied to an abstract type.

Note the subtle difference between Type_Invariant and Type_Invariant'Class. Type_Invariant'Class is inherited for all operations of the type but as noted above Type_Invariant is only incidentally inherited by the operations that are inherited.

An interesting rule is that **Type_Invariant'Class** cannot be applied to a full type declaration which completes a private type such as **Disc_Pt** in the example above. This is because the writer of an extension will need to see the applicable invariants and this would not be possible if they were in the private part.

So if we have a type **T** with a class wide invariant thus

> **type T is tagged private**
>   **with** Type_Invariant'Class => F(T);
> **procedure** Op1(X: **in out** T);
> **procedure** Op2(X: **in out** T);

and then write

> **type NT is new** T **with private**
>   **with** Type_Invariant'Class => FN(NT);
> **overriding**
> **procedure** Op2(X: **in out** NT);
> **not overriding**
> **procedure** Op3(X: **in out** NT);

then both invariants **F** and **FN** will apply to **NT**.

Note that the procedure **Op1** is inherited unchanged by **NT**, procedure **Op2** is overridden for **NT** and procedure **Op3** is added.

Now consider various calls. The calls of **Op1** will involve view conversions as mentioned earlier and these will apply the checks for **FN** and the inherited body will apply the checks for **F**. The body of **Op2** will directly include checks for **F** and **FN** as will the body of **Op3**. So the invariant **F** is properly inherited and all is well.

Remember that if the invariants were specific and not class wide then although **Op1** will have checks for **F** and **FN**, **Op2** and **Op3** will only check **FN**.

In the case of the type **Disc_Pt** we might decide to derive a type which requires that all values are not only inside the unit circle but outside an inner circle – in other words in an annulus or ring. We use the class wide invariants so that the parent package is

> **package** Places **is**
>
> **type** Disc_Pt **is tagged private**
>   **with** Type_Invariant'Class => Check_In(Disc_Pt);
>
> **function** Check_In(D: Disc_Pt) **return** Boolean
>   **with** Inline;
>   ...   -- *various operations on disc points*
> **private**
>
> **type** Disc_Pt **is tagged**
>   **record**
>   X, Y: Float **range** –1.0 .. +1.0;
>   **end record**;
>
> **function** Check_In(D: Disc_Pt) **return** Boolean **is**
>   (D.X**2 + D.Y**2 <= 1.0);
>
> **end** Places;

And then we might write

```
package Places.Inner is

  type Ring_Pt is new Disc_Pt with null record
    with Type_Invariant'Class => Check_Out(Ring_Pt);

  function Check_Out(R: Ring_Pt) return Boolean
    with Inline;

private

  function Check_Out(R: Ring_Pt) return Boolean is
    (R.X**2 + R.Y**2 >= 0.25);

end Places.Inner;
```

And now the type Ring_Pt has both its own type invariant but also that inherited from Disc_Pt thereby ensuring that points are within the ring or annulus. It is unfortunate that we could not make the size of the inner circle a discriminant but a discriminant cannot be of a real type. Ah well, perhaps in Ada 2020??

Finally, it is worth emphasizing that it is good advice not to use inheritance with specific invariants but they are invaluable for checking internal and private properties of types.

2.5 Subtype predicates

The final major facility to be discussed here is subtype predicates. These are not really contractual in the sense that preconditions, postconditions and invariants are contractual but are more akin to constraints.

Subtype predicates are of two kinds, Static_Predicate and Dynamic_Predicate. They can be applied to subtype declarations and to type declarations using aspect specifications. For example, in the Introduction we met

```
subtype Even is Integer
  with Dynamic_Predicate => Even mod 2 = 0;

subtype Winter is Month
  with Static_Predicate => Winter in Dec | Jan | Feb;
```

The predicates take an expression of a Boolean type and again we note the use of the subtype name to denote the current instance. In the case of Dynamic_Predicate, the expression can be any Boolean expression.

However, in the case of Static_Predicate, the expression is restricted and can only be

- a static membership test where the choice is selected by the current instance,

- a case expression whose dependent expressions are static and selected by the current instance,

- a call of the predefined operations =, /=, <, <=, >, >= where one operand is the current instance,

- an ordinary static expression,

and, in addition, a call of a Boolean logical operator **and**, **or**, **xor**, **not** whose operands are such static predicate expressions, and, a static predicate expression in parentheses.

So we see that the predicate in the subtype Even cannot be a static predicate because the operator **mod** is not permitted with the current instance. But **mod** could be used in an inner static expression.

However, the predicate in the subtype Winter can be a static predicate because it takes the from of a membership test where the choice is selected by the current instance and whose individual items are static. Note that membership tests are considerably enhanced in Ada 2012; further details will be given in Section 3.6. Another useful example of this kind is

> **subtype** Letter **is** Character
>   **with** Static_Predicate => Letter **in** 'A' .. 'Z' | 'a' .. 'z';

Static case expressions are valuable because they provide the comfort of covering all values of the current instance. Suppose we have a type Animal

> **type** Animal **is** (Bear, Cat, Dog, Horse, Wolf);

We could then declare a subtype of friendly animals

> **subtype** Pet **is** Animal
>   **with** Static_Predicate => Pet **in** Cat | Dog | Horse;

and perhaps

> **subtype** Predator **is** Animal
>   **with** Static_Predicate => **not** (Predator **in** Pet);

or equivalently

> **subtype** Predator **is** Animal
>   **with** Static_Predicate => Predator **not in** Pet;

Now suppose we add Rabbit to the type Animal. Assuming that we consider that rabbits are pets and not food, we should change Pet to correspond but we might forget with awkward results. Maybe we have a procedure Hunt which aims to eliminate predators

> **procedure** Hunt(P: **in out** Predator);

and we will find that our poor rabbit is hunted rather than petted!

What we should have done is use a case expression controlled by the current instance thus

> **subtype** Pet **is** Animal
>   **with** Static_Predicate =>
>   (**case** Pet **is**
>   **when** Cat | Dog | Horse => True,
>   **when** Bear | Wolf => False);

and now if we add Rabbit to Animal and forget to update Pet to correspond then the program will fail to compile.

Note that a similar form of if expression where the current instance has to be of a Boolean type would not be useful and so is excluded.

Static subtypes with static predicates can also be used in case statements. Thus elsewhere in the program we might have

> **case** Animal **is**
>   **when** Pet =>   ...   *-- feed it*
>   **when** Predator =>   ...   *-- feed on it*
> **end case**;

Observe that we do not have to list all the individual animals and naturally there is no others clause. If other animals are added to Pet or Predator then this case statement will not need changing. Thus not only do we get the benefit of full coverage checking, but the code is also maintenance free. Of course if we add an animal that is neither a Pet nor Predator (Sloth perhaps?) then the case statement will need updating.

Subtype predicates, like pre- and postconditions and type invariants are similarly monitored by the pragma Assertion_Policy. If a predicate fails (that is, has value False) then Assertion_Error is raised.

Subtype predicates are checked in much the same sort of places as type invariants. Thus

- on a subtype conversion,

- on parameter passing (which covers expressions in general),

- on default initialization of an object.

Note an important difference from type invariants. If a type invariant is violated then the damage has been done. But subtype predicates are checked before any damage is done. This difference essentially arises because type invariants apply to private types and can become temporarily false inside the defining package as we saw with the procedure Flip applying to the type Disc_Pt.

If an object is declared without initialization and no default applies then any subtype predicate might be false in the same way that a subtype constraint might be violated.

Beware that subtype predicates like type invariants are not foolproof. Thus in the case of a record type they apply to the record as a whole but they are not checked if an individual component is modified.

Subtype predicates can be given for all types in principle. Thus we might have

```
type Date is
  record
    D: Integer range 1 .. 31;
    M: Month;
    Y: Integer;
  end record;
```

and then

```
subtype Winter_Date is Date
  with Dynamic_Predicate => Winter_Date.M in Winter;
```

Note how this uses the subtype Winter which was itself defined by a subtype predicate. However, Winter_Date has to have a Dynamic_Predicate because the selector is not simply the current instance but a component of it.

We can now declare and manipulate a Winter_Date

```
WD: Winter_Date := (25, Dec, 2011);

...

Do_Date(WD);
```

and the subtype predicate will be checked on the call of Do_Date. However, beware that if we write

```
WD.Month := Jun;                    -- dodgy
```

then the subtype predicate is not checked because we are modifying an individual component and not the record as a whole.

Subtype predicates can be given with type declarations as well as with subtype declarations. Consider for example declaring a type whose only allowed values are the possible scores for an individual throw when playing darts. These are 1 to 20 and doubles and trebles plus 50 and 25 for an inner and outer bull's eye.

We could write these all out explicitly

    type Score **is new** Integer
      with Static_Predicate **=>**
        Score **in** 1 | 2 | 3 | 4 | 5 | 6 | 7 | 8 | 9 | 10 | 11 | 12 | 13 | 14 | 15 | 16 | 17 | 18 | 19 | 20 | 21
          | 22 | 24 | 25 | 26 | 27 | 28 | 30 | 32 | 33 | 34 | 36 | 38 | 39 | 40 | 42 | 45 | 48 | 50
          | 51 | 54 | 57 | 60;

But that is rather boring and obscures the nature of the predicate. We can split it down by first defining individual subtypes for singles, doubles and trebles as follows

    subtype Single **is** Integer **range** 1 .. 20;

    subtype Double **is** Integer
      with Static_Predicate **=>**
        Double **in** 2 | 4 | 6 | 8 | 10 | 12 | 14 | 16 | 18 | 20;

    subtype Treble **is** Integer
      with Static_Predicate **=>**
        Treble **in** 3 | 6 | 9 | 12 | 15 | 18 | 21 | 24 | 27 | 30;

    subtype Score **is** Integer
      with Static_Predicate **=>**
        Score **in** Single **or** Score **in** Double **or** Score **in** Treble **or** Score **in** 25 | 50;

Note that it would be neater to write

    subtype Score **is** Integer
      with Static_Predicate **=>**
        Score **in** Single | Double | Treble | 25 | 50;

Observe that it does not matter that the individual predicates overlap. That is a score such as 12 is a Single, a Double and a Treble.

If we do not mind the predicates being dynamic then we can write

    subtype Double **is** Integer
      with Dynamic_Predicate **=>**
        Double **mod** 2 = 0 **and** Double / 2 **in** Single;

and so on. Or we could even use a quantified expression

    subtype Double **is** Integer
      with Dynamic_Predicate **=>**
        (**for some** K **in** Single **=>** Double = 2*K);

or go all the way in one lump

    type Dyn_Score **is new** Integer
      with Dynamic_Predicate **=>**
        (**for some** K **in** 1 .. 20 **=>** Score = K **or** Score = 2*K **or** Score = 3*K) **or** Score **in** 25 | 50;

There are some restrictions on the use of subtypes with predicates.

If a subtype has a static or dynamic predicate then it cannot be used as an array index subtype. This is to avoid arrays with holes. So we cannot write

    type Winter_Hours **is array** (Winter) **of** Hours;   *-- illegal*

    type Hits **is array** (Score **range** <>) **of** Integer;   *-- illegal*

Similarly, we cannot use a subtype with a predicate to declare the range of an array object or to select a slice. So if we have

```
type Month_Days is array (Month range <>) of Integer;
The_Days: Month_Days := (31, 28, 31, 30, ... );
```

then we cannot write

```
Winter_Days: Month_Days(Winter);                    -- illegal array

The_Days(Winter) := (Jan | Dec => 31, Feb => 29);   -- really nasty illegal slice
```

However, a subtype with a static predicate can be used in a for loop thus

```
for W in Winter loop ...
```

and in a named aggregate such as

```
(Winter => 10.0, others => 14.0);                   -- OK
```

but a subtype with a dynamic predicate cannot be used in these ways. Actually the restriction is slightly more complicated. If the original subtype is not static such as

```
subtype To_N is Integer range 1 .. N;
```

then even if To_N has a static predicate it still cannot be used in a for loop or named aggregate.

These rules can also be illustrated by considering the dartboard. We might like to accumulate a count of the number of times each particular score has been achieved. So we might like to declare

```
type Hit_Count is array (Score) of Integer;         -- illegal
```

but sadly this would result in an array with holes and so is forbidden. However, we could declare an array from 1 to 60 and then initialize it with 0 for those components used for hits and −1 for the unused components. Of course, we ought not to repeat literals such as 1 and 60 because of potential maintenance problems. But, we can use new attributes First_Valid and Last_Valid thus

```
type Hit_Count is array (Score'First_Valid .. Score'Last_Valid) of Integer :=
                                (Score => 0, others => −1);
```

which uses Score to indicate the used components. The attributes First_Valid and Last_Valid can be applied to any static subtype but are particularly useful with static predicates.

In detail, First_Valid returns the smallest valid value of the subtype. It takes any range and/or predicate into account whereas First only takes the range into account. Similarly Last_Valid returns the largest value. Incidentally, they are illegal on null subtypes (because null subtypes have no valid values at all).

The Hit_Count array can then be updated by the value of each hit as expected

```
A_Hit: Score := ... ;                               -- next dart

Hit_Count(A_Hit) := Hit_Count(A_Hit) + 1;
```

If we attempt to assign a value of type Integer which is not in the subtype Score to A_Hit then Assertion_Error is raised.

After the game, we can now loop through the subtype Score and print out the number of times each hit has been achieved and perhaps accumulate the total at the same time thus

```
for K in Score loop
   New_Line;  Put(Hit);  Put(Hit_Count(K));
   Total := Total + K * Hit_Count(K);
end loop;
```

The reason for the distinction between static and dynamic predicates is that the static form can be implemented as small sets with static operations on the small sets. Hence the loop

for K **in** Score **loop** ...

can be implemented simply as a sequence of 43 iterations. However, a loop such as

for X **in** Even **loop** ...

which might look innocuous requires iterating over the whole set of integers. Thus we insist on having to write

for X **in** Integer **loop**
if X **in** Even **then** ...

which makes the situation quite clear.

Another restriction on the use of subtypes with predicates is that the attributes First, Last and Range cannot be applied. But Pred and Succ are permitted because they apply to the underlying type. As a consequence, if a generic body uses First, Last or Range on a formal type and the actual type has a subtype predicate then Program_Error is raised.

Subtype predicates can be applied to abstract types but not to incomplete types.

Subtype predicates are inherited as expected on derivation. Thus if we have

type T **is** ...
with Static_Predicate => SP(T);

and then

type NT **is new** T
with Dynamic_Predicate => DP(NT);

the result is that both predicates apply to NT rather as if we had written the predicate as SP(NT) **and** DP(NT). So if several apply they are anded together. If any one is dynamic then restrictions on the use of subtypes with a dynamic predicate apply.

There is no need for special predicates for class wide types in the way that we have both Type_Invariant and Type_Invariant'Class. So in the general case where a tagged type is derived from a parent and several progenitors

type T **is new** P **and** G1 **and** G2 **with** ...

where P is the parent and G1 and G2 are progenitors, the subtype predicate applicable to T is simply those for P, G1 and G2 all anded together.

A number of improvements were made in this area after ISO standardization as described in Section 9.5 of the Epilogue. These concern a new aspect Predicate_Failure which enables specific messages to be associated with a failure and rules regarding the order of evaluation of predicates if several apply.

2.6 Default initial values

It is often important that we can rely upon an object having a value within its subtype even before it is assigned to and this especially applies in the face of type invariants and subtype predicates. Consider a type Location whose type invariant In_Place requires the point to be within some place.

package Places **is**
type Location **is private**
with Type_Invariant => In_Place(Location);

function In_Place(L: Location) **return** Boolean;
procedure Do_It(X: **in out** Location; ...);

```
private

   type Location is
     record
       X, Y: Float range –1.0 .. +1.0;
     end record;

     ...

   end Places;
```

If we just declare an object of type Location thus

```
   Somewhere: Location;
```

then there is no guarantee that Somewhere is anywhere in particular. If the type invariant In_Place applies and a subprogram with an **in out** parameter such as Do_It is called

```
   Do_It(Somewhere);
```

then it might be that some paths through Do_It do not assign a new value to X. Nevertheless, on return from Do_It, the type invariant In_Place will be checked on the parameter. If Somewhere by chance had an accidental initial value outside the space implied by In_Place then the call will fail. Now it might be that other parameters of the procedure indicate to the caller that Somewhere has not been updated in this case but unfortunately this information is unlikely to be available to the invariant.

One solution to this is to ensure that objects always have an initial value satisfying the requisite constraints, predicates or invariants. One might do this by assigning a safe initial value thus

```
   Somewhere: Location := (0.0, 0.0);                    -- illegal
```

but this is illegal because the type is private. We could of course export from the package Places a safe initial value so that we could write

```
   Somewhere: Location := Places.Haven;
```

But this is often frowned upon because giving an explicit initial value can hide flow errors. It is thus best to ensure that the object automatically has a safe default value by writing perhaps

```
   type Location is
     record
       X, Y: Float range –1.0 .. +1.0 := 0.0;
     end record;
```

It is curious that Ada allows default initial values for components of records and provides them automatically for access types (**null**) but not for scalar types or for array types. This is remedied in Ada 2012 by the introduction of aspects Default_Value and Default_Component_Value for scalar types and arrays of scalar types respectively. The format is as expected

```
   type My_Float is digits 20
     with Default_Value => 0.5;

   type OK is new Boolean
     with Default_Value => True;
```

The usual rule regarding the omission of => True does not apply in the case of Default_Value for Boolean types for obvious reasons.

If possible, a special value indicating the status of the default should be supplied. This particularly applies to enumeration types. For example

```
type Switch is (On, Off, Unknown)
   with Default_Value => Unknown;
```

In the case of an array type this can be constrained or unconstrained and the default value will apply to all components.

```
type Vector is array (Integer range <>) of Integer
   with Default_Component_Value => 0;
```

Default initial values cannot be given to the predefined types but they can be given to types derived from them such as the Boolean type OK above.

In the case of a private type, any default has to be given on the full type declaration.

It is important to note that default initial values can only be given for types and not for subtypes. If a default initial value lies outside the range of a subtype then declaring an object of a subtype without its own specific initial value will raise Constraint_Error. So writing

```
subtype Known_Switch is Switch range On .. Off;
A_Switch: Known_Switch;
```

raises Constraint_Error because the default initial value Unknown is outside the range of the subtype Known_Switch.

If a record type is declared and some components are given initial values but others are not then explicitly given initial values take precedence over default values given by these aspects. Thus if we have

```
type Location is
   record
      X: My_Float range −1.0 .. +1.0 := 0.0;
      Y: My_Float range  −1.0 .. +1.0;
   end record;
```

then the component X has default value 0.0 but component Y has default value 0.5, (since My_Float declared above has default value 0.5).

A final important point is that default initial values supplied by these aspects have to be static unlike default initial values for record components.

2.7   Storage occupancy checks

Finally, two new attributes are introduced to aid in the writing of preconditions. Sometimes it is necessary to check that two objects do not occupy the same storage in whole or in part. This can be done with two functional attributes X'Has_Same_Storage and X'Overlaps_Storage which apply to an object X of any type.

Their specifications are

```
function X'Has_Same_Storage(Arg: any_type) return Boolean;

function X'Overlaps_Storage(Arg: any_type) return Boolean;
```

As an example we might have a procedure Exchange and wish to ensure that the parameters do not overlap in any way. We can write

```
procedure Exchange(X, Y: in out T)
   with Pre => not X'Overlaps_Storage(Y);
```

Attributes are used rather than predefined functions since this enables the semantics to be written in a manner that permits X and Y to be of any type and moreover does not imply that X or Y are read.

The object X and the parameter Y could be components such as A(5) or indeed A(J) or even a slice A(1 .. N). Thus the actual addresses to be checked may not be statically determined but have to be determined at the point of call.

AI-191 shows the following curious example

```
procedure Count(A: in out Arrtype; B: in Arrtype)
  with Pre => not A'Overlaps_Storage(B)
is
  -- intended to count in A the number of value
  -- occurrences in B as part of a distribution sort
begin
  for I in B'Range loop
    A(B(I)) := A(B(I)) + 1;
  end loop;
end Count;
```

The author seems to have assumed that the array A has appropriate components and that they are initialized to zero. This also illustrates the use of an aspect specification in a subprogram body.

At the machine level Overlaps_Storage means that at least one bit is in common and Has_Same_Storage means that all bits are in common. Hence X'Has_Same_Storage(Y) implies X'Overlaps_Storage(Y).

In some applications involving the possibility of aliasing (messing with tree structures comes to mind) we do really want to check that two entities are not in the same place rather than just overlapping in which case it is more logical to use Has_Same_Storage.

3 Expressions

This chapter describes the introduction of more flexible forms of expressions in Ada 2012.

There are four new forms of expressions. If expressions and case expressions define a value and closely resemble if statements and case statements. Quantified expressions take two forms using for all and for some to return a Boolean value. Finally, expression functions provide a simple means of parameterizing an expression without the formality of providing a function body.

These more flexible forms of expressions will be found invaluable in formulating contracts such as preconditions. It is interesting to note that Ada now has conditional expressions over 50 years after their introduction in Algol 60.

3.1 Overview of changes

One of the key areas identified by the WG9 guidance document [1] as needing attention was improving the ability to write and enforce contracts. These were discussed in detail in the previous chapter.

When defining the new aspects for preconditions, postconditions, type invariants and subtype predicates it became clear that without more flexible forms of expressions, many functions would need to be introduced because in all cases the aspect was given by an expression.

However, declaring a function and thus giving the detail of the condition, invariant or predicate in the function body makes the detail of the contract rather remote for the human reader. Information hiding is usually a good thing but in this case, it just introduces obscurity.

Four forms are introduced, namely, if expressions, case expressions, quantified expressions and expression functions. Together they give Ada some of the flexible feel of a functional language.

In addition, membership tests are generalized to allow greater flexibility which is particularly useful for subtype predicates.

The following Ada issues cover the key changes and are described in detail in this chapter:

   3 Qualified expressions and names

147 Conditional expressions

158 Generalizing membership tests

176 Quantified expressions

177 Expression functions

188 Case expressions

These changes can be grouped as follows.

First there are conditional expressions which come in two forms, if expressions and case expressions, which have a number of features in common (147, 188).

Then there is the introduction of quantified expressions which use **for all** to describe a universal quantifier and **for some** to describe an existential quantifier. Note that **some** is a new reserved word (176).

Next comes the fourth new form of expression which is the expression function (177).

Finally, membership tests are generalized (158) and there is a minor change regarding qualified expressions (3).

3.2 If expressions

It is perhaps very surprising that Ada does not have if expressions as well as if statements. In order to provide some background context we briefly look at two historic languages that are perhaps the main precursors to modern languages; these are Algol 60 [8] and CPL [9].

Algol 60 had conditional expressions of the form

    Z := if X = Y then P else Q

which can be contrasted with the conditional statement

    if X = Y then
      Z := P
    else
      Z := Q

Conditional statements in Algol 60 allowed only a single statement in each branch, so if several were required then they had to be grouped into a compound statement thus

    if X = Y then
      begin
        Z := P; A := B
      end
    else
      begin
        Z := Q; A := C
      end

It may be recalled that statements were not terminated by semicolons in Algol 60 but separated by them. However, a null statement was simply nothing so the effect of adding an extra semicolon in some cases was harmless. However, accidentally writing

    if X = Y then ;
      begin
        Z := P; A := B
      end;

results in a disaster because the test then just covers a null statement and the assignments to Z and A always take place. The complexity of compound statements did not arise with conditional expressions.

The designers of Algol 68 [10] sensibly recognized the problem and introduced closing brackets thus

    if X = Y then
      Z := P; A := B;
    fi;

where **fi** matches the **if**. Conditional expressions in Algol 68 were similar

    Z := if X = Y then P else Q fi;

An alternative shorthand notation was

    Z := (X = Y | P | Q);

which was perhaps a bit too short.

The next major language in this series was Pascal [11]. The designers of Pascal rejected everything that had been learnt from Algol 68 and foolishly continued the Algol 60 style for compound statements and also dropped conditional expressions. Only with Modula did they realise the need for bracketing rather than compounding.

The other foundation language was CPL [9]. Conditional statements in CPL took the following form

> **if** X = Y **then do** Z := P
>
> **if** X = Y **then do** § Z := P; A := B §

where compound statements were delimited by section symbols (note that the closing symbol has a vertical line through it).

From CPL came BCPL, B and C. Along the way, the expressive := for assignment got lost in favour of = which then meant that = had to be replaced by == for equality. And the section brackets became { and } so in C the above conditional statements become

> if (X == Y) Z = P;
>
> if (X == Y) {Z = P; A = B;}

This suffers from the same stray semicolon problem mentioned above with reference to Algol 60.

Steelman [12] did not require Ada to have conditional expressions and since they were not required they were not provided (the requirements were treated with considerable reverence). A further influence might have been that the new language had to be based on one of Pascal, Algol 68 and PL/I and Ada is based on Pascal which did not have conditional expressions as mentioned above.

Moreover, the Ada designers felt that the Algol 68 style with reversed keywords such as **fi** (or worse **esac**) for conditional statements would not be acceptable to the USDoD or the public at large and so we have **end if** as the closing bracket thus

> **if** X = Y **then**
>   Z := P;
>   A := B;
> **end if**;

Remember that semicolons terminate statements in Ada and so those above are all required. Moreover, since null statements in Ada have to be given explicitly, placing a stray semicolon after **then** gives a compiler error.

The absence of conditional expressions is a pain. It leads to unnecessary duplication such as having to write

> **if** X > 0 **then**
>   P(A, B, D, E);
> **else**
>   P(A, C, D, E);
> **end if**;

where all parameters but one are the same. This can even lead to disgusting coding using the fact that Boolean'Pos(True) is 1 whereas Boolean'Pos(False) is 0. Thus (assuming that B and C are of type Integer) the above could be written as a single procedure call thus

> P(A, Boolean'Pos(X>0)*B+Boolean'Pos(X<=0)*C, D, E);

So it is a great relief in Ada 2012 to be able to write

P(A, (**if** X>0 **then** B **else** C), D, E);

A worse problem was when a static expression was required such as the initial value for a named number as in the following gruesome code

Febdays: **constant** := Boolean'Pos(Leap)*29 + Boolean'Pos(**not** Leap)*28;

which we can now thankfully write as

Febdays: **constant** := (**if** Leap **then** 29 **else** 28);

Note carefully that there is no **end if**. One reason is simply that it is logically unnecessary since there can be only a single expression after **else** and also **end if** would have been obtrusively heavy (compared say with **fi** of Algol 68). However, it was felt that some demarcation was required to aid clarity and so a conditional expression is always enclosed in parentheses. If the context already has parentheses then additional ones are not required. Thus in the case of a positional call with a single parameter we just write

P(**if** X > 0 **then** B **else** C);

but if we use named notation then extra parentheses are required

P(Para => (**if** X > 0 **then** B **else** C));

Note carefully that the term conditional expression in Ada 2012 embraces both if expressions and case expressions (which are discussed in the next section).

As expected, a series of tests can be done using **elsif** thus

P(**if** X > 0 **then** B **elsif** X < 0 **then** C **else** D);

and expressions can be nested

P(**if** X > 0 **then** (**if** Y > 0 **then** B **else** C) **else** D);

Without the rule requiring enclosing parentheses this could be written as

P(**if** X > 0 **then if** Y > 0 **then** B **else** C **else** D);   -- *illegal*

which seems more than a little confusing.

There is a special rule if the type of the expression is Boolean (that is of the predefined type Boolean or derived from it). In that case a final else part can be omitted and is taken to be true by default. Thus the following are equivalent

P(**if** C1 **then** C2 **else** True);

P(**if** C1 **then** C2);

Such abbreviations appear frequently in preconditions as was illustrated in the Introduction where we had

Pre => (**if** P1 > 0 **then** P2 > 0);

which has the obvious meaning that the precondition requires that if P1 is positive then P2 must be positive as well but if P1 is not positive then all is well and we don't care about P2.

This abbreviated form has the same effect as an implies operation.

R := C1 **implies** C2;   -- *not Ada!*

with the following truth table

	C1 = False	C1 = True
C2 = False	R = True	R = False
C2 = True	R = True	R = True

Some consideration was given to including such an operation in Ada 2012 (it existed in Algol 60). However, this is exactly the same as

R := **not** C1 **or** C2;

and so somewhat unnecessary. Moreover, although **implies** might appeal to some programmers it could lead to maintenance problems since it might be considered incomprehensible by many others.

There are important rules regarding the types of the various dependent expressions in the branches of an if expression. Basically they have to all be of the same type or convertible to the same expected type. But there are some interesting situations.

If the conditional expression is the argument of a type conversion then effectively the conversion is considered pushed down to the dependent expressions. Thus

X := Float(**if** P **then** A **else** B);

is equivalent to

X := (**if** P **then** Float(A) **else** Float(B));

As a consequence we can write

X := Float(**if** P **then** 27 **else** 0.3);

and it doesn't matter that 27 and 0.3 are not of the same type.

If the expected type is class wide, perhaps giving the initial value for a class wide variable V, then the individual dependent expressions have that same expected class wide type but they need not all be of the same specific type within the class. Thus we might write

V: Object'Class := (**if** B **then** A_Circle **else** A_Triangle);

where A_Circle and A_Triangle are objects of specific types Circle and Triangle which are themselves descended from the type Object.

If the expected type is a specific tagged type then various situations can arise regarding the various branches which are similar to the rules for calling a subprogram with several controlling operands. Either they all have to be dynamically tagged (that is class wide) or all have to be statically tagged. They might all be tag indeterminate in which case the conditional expression as a whole is also tag indeterminate.

Some obscure curiosities arise. Remember that the controlling condition for an if statement can be any Boolean type. Consider

type My_Boolean **is new** Boolean;

My_Cond: My_Boolean := ... ;

if (**if** K > 10 **then** X = Y **else** My_Cond) **then**   -- *illegal*

   ...

end if;

The problem here is that X = Y is of type **Boolean** but **My_Cond** is of type **My_Boolean**. Moreover, the expected type for the condition in the if statement is any Boolean type so it cannot make up its mind. We could overcome this foolishness by putting a type conversion around the if expression.

There are also rules regarding staticness. If all branches are static then a conditional expression as a whole is static as in the example of **Febdays** above. Thus the definition of a static expression has been extended to permit the inclusion of static conditional expressions.

The avid reader of the Reference Manual will find that the term *statically unevaluated* has been introduced. This relates to situations where expressions are not evaluated because a prior expression is static. Consider

> X := (**if** B **then** P **else** Q);

If B, P and Q are all static then the conditional expression as a whole is static. If B is true then the answer is P and there is not any need to even look at Q. We say that Q is statically unevaluated and indeed it does not matter that if Q had been evaluated it would have raised an exception. Thus we might write

> Average := (**if** Count = 0 **then** 0.0 **else** Total/Count);

and there is no risk of dividing by zero.

Similar rules regarding being statically unevaluated apply to short circuit conditions, case expressions, and membership tests.

As might be expected there are rules regarding access types and accessibility. The accessibility level of a conditional expression is simply that of the chosen dependent expression and thus (generally) determined dynamically.

Readers might feel that Ada has embarked on a slippery slope by introducing more flexibility thereby possibly damaging Ada's reputation for reliability. Certainly a number of additional rules have been required but from the users' point of view these are almost intuitive. It should be remembered that the difficulties in C stem from a combination of things

- that assignment is permitted as an expression,
- that integer values are used as Booleans,
- that null statements are invisible.

None of these applies to Ada so all is well.

3.3 Case expressions

Case expressions have much in common with if expressions and the two are collectively known as conditional expressions.

Thus given a variable D of the familiar type **Day**, we can assign the number of hours in a working day by

> Hours := (**case** D **is**
>   **when** Mon .. Thurs => 8,
>   **when** Fri => 6,
>   **when** Sat | Sun => 0);

A slightly more adventurous example involving nested if expressions is

> Days := (**case** M **is**
>   **when** September | April | June | November => 30,
>   **when** February =>

> (**if** Year **mod** 100 = 0 **then**
> (**if** Year **mod** 400 =0 **then** 29 **else** 28)
> **else**
> (**if** Year **mod** 4 = 0 **then** 29 **else** 28)),
> **when others** => 31);

The reader is invited to improve this!

Note the similarity to the rules for if expressions. There is no closing **end case**. Case expressions are always enclosed in parentheses but they can be omitted if the context already provides parentheses.

If M and Year are static then the case expression as a whole is also static. If M is static and equal to September, April, June or November then the value is statically known to be 30 so that the expression for February is statically unevaluated even if Year is not static. Note that the various choices are evaluated in order.

The rules regarding the types of the dependent expressions are exactly as for if expressions. Thus if the case expression is the argument of a type conversion then the conversion is effectively pushed down to the dependent expressions.

It is always worth emphasizing that an important advantage of case constructions is that they give a coverage check. Thus in the previous chapter we had

> **subtype** Pet **is** Animal
> **with** Static_Predicate =>
> (**case** Pet **is**
> **when** Cat | Dog | Horse => True,
> **when** Bear | Wolf => False);

which is much more reliable than

> **subtype** Pet **is** Animal
> **with** Static_Predicate => Pet **in** Cat | Dog | Horse;

because when we add Rabbit to the type Animal, we are forced to include it in one branch of the case expression whereas it is all too easy to forget it using an if expression.

3.4 Quantified expressions

Another new form of expression in Ada 2012 is the quantified expression. The syntax is

> quantified_expression ::=
> **for** quantifier loop_parameter_specification => predicate
> | **for** quantifier iterator_specification => predicate

> quantifier ::= **all** | **some**

> predicate ::= *boolean*_expression

The form involving iterator_specification concerns generalized iterators and will be found particularly useful with containers; it will be discussed in detail in Section 6.3 on Iteration. Here we will concentrate on the use of the familiar loop parameter specification.

The type of a quantified expression is Boolean. So we might write

> B := (**for all** K **in** A'Range => A(K) = 0);

which assigns true to B if every component of the array A has value 0. We might also write

> B := (**for some** K **in** A'Range => A(K) = 0);

which assigns true to B if some component of the array A has value 0.

Note that the loop parameter is almost inevitably used in the predicate. A quantified expression is very much like a for statement except that we evaluate the expression after => on each iteration rather than executing one or more statements. The iteration is somewhat implicit and the words **loop** and **end loop** do not appear.

The expression is evaluated for each iteration in the appropriate order (**reverse** can be inserted of course) and the iteration stops as soon as the value of the expression is determined. Thus in the case of **for all**, as soon as one value is found to be False, the overall expression is False whereas in the case of **for some** as soon as one value is found to be True, the overall expression is True. An iteration could raise an exception which would then be propagated in the usual way.

Like conditional expressions, a quantified expression is always enclosed in parentheses which can be omitted if the context already provides them, such as in a procedure call with a single positional parameter.

Incidentally, predicate is a fancy word meaning Boolean expression. Older folk might recall that it also means the part of a sentence after the subject. Thus in the sentence "I love Ada", the subject is "I" and the predicate is "love Ada".

The forms **for all** and **for some** are technically known as the universal quantifier and existential quantifier respectively.

Note that **some** is a new reserved word (the only one in Ada 2012). There were six new ones in Ada 95 (**abstract, aliased, protected, requeue, tagged** and **until**) and three new ones in Ada 2005 (**interface, overriding** and **synchronized**). Hopefully we are converging.

The type of a quantified expression can be any Boolean type (that is the predefined type **Boolean** or perhaps **My_Boolean** derived from Boolean). The predicate must be of the same type as the expression as a whole. Thus if the predicate is of type **My_Boolean** then the quantified expression is also of type **My_Boolean**.

The syntax for quantified expressions uses => to introduce the predicate. This is similar to the established notation in SPARK [13]. Consideration was given to using a vertical bar which is common in mathematics but that would have been confusing because of its use in membership tests and other situations with multiple choices.

As illustrated in the Introduction, quantified expressions will find their major uses in pre- and postconditions. Thus a procedure Sort on an array A of type Atype such as

    type Atype **is array** (Index) **of** Float;

might have specification

    procedure Sort(A: **in out** Atype)
      with Post => A'Length < 2 **or else**
        (**for all** K **in** A'First .. Index'Pred(A'Last) => A(K) <= A(Index'Succ(K)));

where we are assuming that the index type need not be an integer type and so we have to use Succ and Pred. Note how the trivial cases of a null array or an array with a single component are dismissed first.

Quantified expressions can be nested. So we might check that all components of a two-dimensional array are zero by writing

    B := (**for all** I **in** AA'Range(1) => (**for all** J **in** AA'Range(2) => AA(I, J) = 0));

This can be done rather more neatly using the syntactic form

> **for** quantifier iterator_specification => predicate

as will be discussed in detail in Section 6.3 on Iteration. We just write

> B := (**for all** E **of** AA => E = 0);

which iterates over all elements of the array AA however many dimensions it has.

3.5 Expression functions

The final new form to be discussed is the expression function. As outlined in the Introduction, an expression function provides the effect of a small function without the formality of introducing a body. It is important to appreciate that strictly speaking an expression function is basically another form of function and not another form of expression. But it is convenient to discuss expression functions in this chapter because like conditional expressions and quantified expressions they arose for use with aspect clauses such as pre- and postconditions.

The syntax is

> expression_function_declaration ::=
>   [overriding_indicator]
>   function_specification **is**
>   (expression)
>   [aspect_specification] ;

As an example we can reconsider the type Point and the function Is_At_Origin thus

```
package P is
  type Point is tagged
    record
      X, Y: Float := 0.0;
    end record;

  function Is_At_Origin(P: Point) return Boolean is
    (P.X = 0.0 and P.Y = 0.0)
      with Inline;

    ...
  end P;
```

The expression function Is_At_Origin is a primitive operation of Point just as if it were a normal function with a body. If a type My_Point is derived from Point then Is_At_Origin would be inherited or could be overridden with a normal function or another expression function. Thus an expression function can be prefixed by an overriding indicator as indicated by the syntax.

Expression functions can have an aspect clause and since by their very nature they will be short, this will frequently be **with** Inline as in this example.

The result of an expression function is given by an expression in parentheses. The parentheses are included to immediately distinguish the structure from a normal body which could start with an arbitrary local declaration. The expression can be any expression having the required type. It could for example be a quantified expression as in the following

```
function Is_Zero(A: Atype) return Boolean is
  (for all J in A'Range => A(J) = 0);
```

This is another example of a situation where the quantified expression does not need to be enclosed in its own parentheses because the context supplied by the expression function provides parentheses.

Expression functions can be completions as well as standing alone and this introduces a number of possibilities. Remember that many declarations require completing. For example an incomplete type such as

>   **type** Cell;   *-- an incomplete type*

is typically completed by a full type declaration later on

>   **type** Cell **is**
>   **record** ... **end record**;   *-- its completion*

Completion also applies to subprograms. Typically the declaration (that is the specification plus semicolon) of a subprogram appears in a package specification thus

>   **package** P **is**
>   **function** F(X: T);   *-- declaration*
>
>   ...
>   **end** P;

and then the body of F which completes it appears in the body of P thus

>   **package body** P **is**
>   **function** F(X: T) **is**   *-- completion*
>   **begin**
>
>   ...
>   **end** F;
>
>   ...
>   **end** P;

A function body cannot appear in a package specification. The only combinations are

function declaration F	function body F
in spec of P	in body of P
in body of P	in body of P
none	in body of P

Remember that mutual recursion may require that a body be given later so it is possible for a distinct declaration of F to appear in the body of P before the full body of F. In addition to the above the function body could be replaced by a stub and the proper body compiled separately but that is another story.

The rules regarding expression functions are rather different. An expression function can be declared alone as in the example of Is_At_Origin above; or it can be a completion of a function declaration and that completion can be in either the package specification or body. A frequently useful combination occurs with a private type where we need to make a function visible so that it can be used in a precondition and the expression function then occurs in the private part as a completion thus

>   **package** P **is**
>   **type** Point **is tagged private**;
>   **function** Is_At_Origin(P: Point) **return** Boolean
>   **with** Inline;

```
procedure Do_It(P: in Point; ... )
   with Pre => not Is_At_Origin;

private

   type Point is tagged
      record
         X, Y: Float := 0.0;
      end record;

   function Is_At_Origin(P: Point) return Boolean is
      (P.X = 0.0 and P.Y = 0.0);

      ...

end P;
```

Note that we cannot give an aspect specification on an expression function used as a completion so it is given on the function specification; this makes it visible to the user. (This rule applies to all completions such as subprogram bodies and is not special to expression functions.)

An expression function can also be used in a package body as an abbreviation for

```
function Is_At_Origin(P: Point) return Boolean is
begin
   return P.X = 0.0 and P.Y = 0.0;
end Is_At_Origin;
```

The possible combinations regarding a function in a package are

function declaration F	expression function F
in spec of P	in spec or body of P
in body of P	in body of P
none	in spec or body of P

We perhaps naturally think of an expression function used as a completion to be in the private part of a package. But we could declare a function in the visible part of a package and then an expression function to complete it in the visible part as well. This is illustrated by the following interesting example of two mutually recursive functions.

```
package Hof is

   function M(K: Natural) return Natural;
   function F(K: Natural) return Natural;

   function M(K: Natural) return Natural is
      (if K = 0 then 0 else K − F(M(K−1)));

   function F(K: Natural) return Natural is
      (if K =0 then 1 else K − M(F(K−1)));

end Hof;
```

These are the Male and Female functions described by Hofstadter [14]. They are inextricably intertwined and both are given with completions for symmetry.

Almost inevitably, at least one of the expression functions in a mutually recursive pair will include an if expression (or else **or else**) otherwise the recursion will not stop.

Expression functions can also be declared in subprograms and blocks (they are basic declarative items). Moreover, an expression function that completes a function can also be declared in the subprogram or block.

This is illustrated by the following Gauss-Legendre algorithm which computes π to an amazing accuracy determined by the value of the constant K.

```
with Ada.Text_IO; use Ada.Text_IO;
with Ada.Long_Long_Float_Text_IO;
use Ada.Long_Long_Float_Text_IO;
with Ada.Numerics.Long_Long_Elementary_Functions;
use Ada.Numerics.Long_Long_Elementary_Functions;
procedure Compute_Pi is

    function B(N: Natural) return Long_Long_Float;

    function A(N: Natural) return Long_Long_Float is
        (if N = 0 then 1.0 else (A(N–1)+B(N–1))/2.0);

    function B(N: Natural) return Long_Long_Float is
        (if N = 0 then Sqrt(0.5) else Sqrt(A(N–1)*B(N–1)));

    function T(N: Natural) return Long_Long_Float is
        (if N = 0 then 0.25 else
            T(N–1)–2.0**(N–1)*(A(N–1)–A(N))**2);

    K: constant := 5;                  -- for example
    Pi: constant Long_Long_Float := ((A(K) + B(K))**2 / (4.0*T(K));
begin
    Put(Pi, Exp => 0);
    New_Line;
end Compute_Pi;
```

With luck this will output 3.14159265358979324 (depending on the accuracy of Long_Long_Float).

The functions A and B give successive arithmetic and geometric means. They call each other and so B is given as a function specification which is then completed by the expression function.

I am grateful to Brad Moore and to Ed Schonberg for these instructive examples.

The rules regarding null procedures (introduced in Ada 2005 primarily for use with interfaces) are modified in Ada 2012 to be uniform with those for expression functions regarding completion. Thus

```
    procedure Nothing(X: in T) is null;
```

can be used alone as a declaration of a null operation for a type or as a shorthand for a traditional null procedure thus possibly completing the declaration

```
    procedure Nothing(X: in T);
```

Expression functions and null procedures do not count as subprogram declarations and so cannot be declared at library level. Nor can they be used as proper bodies to complete stubs. Library subprograms are mainly intended for use as main subprograms and to use an expression function in that way would be somewhat undignified!

Thus if we wanted to declare a useful function to compute sin 2*x* from time to time, we cannot write

```
with Ada.Numerics.Elementary_Functions;
use Ada.Numerics.Elementary_Functions;
function Sin2(X: Float) is                    -- illegal
    (2.0 * Sin(X) * Cos(X));
```

but either have to write it out the long way or wrap the expression function in a package.

3.6 Membership tests

Membership tests in Ada 83 to Ada 2005 are somewhat restrictive. They take two forms

- to test whether a value is in a given range, or

- to test whether a value is in a given subtype.

Examples of these are

```
if M in June .. August then
```

```
if I in Index then
```

However, the restrictions are annoying. If we want to test whether it is safe to eat an oyster (there has to be an R in the month) then we would really like to write

```
if M in Jan .. April | Sep .. Dec then        -- illegal in Ada 2005
```

whereas we are forced to write something like

```
if M in Jan .. April or M in Sep .. Dec then
```

which means repeating M and then perhaps worrying about whether to use **or** or **or else**. Or in this case we could do the test the other way

```
if M not in May .. Aug then
```

What we would really like to do is use the vertical bar as in case statements and aggregates to select a combination of ranges, subtypes, and values.

Ada 2012 is much more flexible in this area. To see the differences it is probably easiest to look at the old and new syntax. The relevant old syntax for Ada 2005 is

```
relation ::=
        simple_expression [relational_operator simple_expression]
      | simple_expression [not] in range
      | simple_expression [not] in subtype_mark
```

where the last two productions define membership tests. The syntax regarding choices in aggregates and case statements in Ada 2005 is

```
discrete_choice_list ::= discrete_choice { | discrete_choice}
```

```
discrete_choice ::= expression | discrete_range | others
```

```
discrete_range ::= discrete_subtype_indication | range
```

The syntax in Ada 2012 is rather different and changes relation to use new productions for membership_choice_list and membership_choice (this enables the vertical bar to be used in membership tests). And then a membership choice in turn uses choice_expression and choice_relation as follows

```
relation ::=
        simple_expression [relational_operator simple_expression]
      | simple_expression [not] in membership_choice_list
```

membership_choice_list ::= membership_choice { | membership_choice}

membership_choice ::= choice_expression | range | subtype_mark

choice_expression ::=
        choice_relation {**and** choice_relation}
       | choice_relation {**or** choice_relation}
       | choice_relation {**xor** choice_relation}
       | choice_relation {**and then** choice_relation}
       | choice_relation {**or else** choice_relation}

choice_relation ::= simple_expression [relational_operator simple_expression]

The difference between a choice_relation and a relation is that the choice_relation does not include membership tests. Moreover, discrete_choice is changed to

discrete_choice ::= choice_expression | *discrete*_subtype_indication | range | **others**

the difference being that a discrete_choice now uses a choice_expression rather than an expression as one of its possibilities.

The overall effect of the changes is to permit the vertical bar in membership tests without getting too confused by nesting membership tests.

Here are some examples that are now permitted in Ada 2012 but were not permitted in Ada 2005

if N **in** 6 | 28 | 496 **then**   *-- N is small and perfect!*

if M **in** Spring | June | October .. December **then**
                                        -- combination of subtype, single value and range

if X **in** 0.5 .. Z | 2.0*Z .. 10.0 **then**   *-- not discrete or static*

if Obj **in** Triangle | Circle **then**   *-- with tagged types*

if Letter **in** 'A' | 'E' | 'I' | 'O' | 'U' **then**   *-- characters*

Membership tests are permitted for any type and values do not have to be static. There is no change here but it should be remembered that existing uses of the vertical bar in case statements and aggregates do require the type to be discrete and the values to be static.

Another important point about membership tests is that the membership choices are evaluated in order and as soon as one is found to be true (or false if **not** is present) then the relation as a whole is determined and the other membership choices are not evaluated. This is therefore the same as using short circuit forms such as **or else** and so gives another example of expressions which are statically unevaluated.

There is one very minor incompatibility. In Ada 2005 we can write

```
X: Boolean := ...
case X is
  when Y in 1 .. 10  => F(10);
  when others => F(5);
end case;
```

This is rather peculiar. The discrete choice Y **in** 1 .. 10 must be static. Suppose Y is 5, so that Y **in** 1 .. 10 is true; then if X is True, we call F(10) whereas if X is false we call F(5). And vice versa for values of Y not in the range 1 to 10.

This is syntactically illegal in Ada 2012 because a discrete choice can no longer be an expression and so be a membership test. This was imposed because otherwise we might have been tempted to write

```
X: Boolean := ...
case X is
   when Y in 1 .. 10 | 20 => F(10);
   when others => F(5);
end case;
```

and this is syntactically ambiguous because it might be parsed as (Y in 1 .. 10) | 20 rather than as if we were allowed to write Y in (1 .. 10) | 20. Although it would be rejected anyway because of the type mismatch.

A nastier example might make this clearer. Consider

```
case X is
   when Y in False | True => Do_This;
   when others => Do_That;
end case;
```

Now suppose that Y itself is of type Boolean. Is it (Y in False) | True rather than Y in (False | True)? If Y happens to have the value True then the first interpretation gives False | True so whatever the value of X we always Do_This but in the second interpretation we get just True so if X happens to be False we Do_That. So it really is seriously ambiguous without any type mismatch in sight and has to be forbidden.

However, this is clearly very unlikely to be a problem. Case statements over Boolean types are pretty rare anyway.

There is one other change to membership tests which concerns access types and so will be considered again in Section 6.4 when we discuss Access types and storage pools. The change is that membership tests can be used to check accessibility.

It is often the case that one uses a membership test before a conversion to ensure that the conversion will succeed. This avoids raising an exception which then has to be handled. Thus we might have

```
subtype Score is Integer range 1 .. 60;
Total: Integer;
S: Score;
   ...                          -- compute Total somehow
if Total in Score then
   S := Score(Total)            -- reliable conversion
   ...                          -- now use S knowing that it is OK
else
   ...                          -- Total was excessive
end if;
```

If we are indexing some arrays whose range is Score then it is an advantage to use S as an index since we know it will work and no checks are needed.

However, in Ada 2005, we cannot use a membership test to check accessibility. But Ada 2012 permits this and we can write

```
type Ptr is access all T;
```

```
procedure P(X: access T) is
   Local: Ptr;
begin
   if X in Ptr then
      Local := Ptr(X);          -- reliable conversion
      ...                       -- now use Ptr knowing that it is OK
   else
      ...                       -- would have failed accessibility check
   end if;
end P;
```

We could also do the check in a precondition thus

```
procedure P(X: access T)
   with Pre => X in Ptr;
```

Here we have a precondition where the expression is simply a membership test **X in** Ptr. Of course this does not avoid the exception because it will raise Assertion_Error if the accessibility is wrong.

Finally, note that two changes have been made in the syntax for relation since ISO standardization. One concerns the addition of a new form of expression, the raise expression; the other concerns an ambiguity discovered in membership tests. These changes are described in Section 9.5 of the Epilogue.

3.7 Qualified expressions

We conclude this discussion of expressions by considering some points regarding names and primaries.

In Ada 2005 we have

> name ::= direct_name | explicit_dereference | indexed_component
> | slice | selected_component | attribute_reference
> | type_conversion | function_call | character_literal

> primary ::= numeric_literal | **null** | string_literal | aggregate | name
> | qualified_expression | allocator | (expression)

And in Ada 2012 we have

> name ::= direct_name | explicit_dereference | indexed_component
> | slice | selected_component | attribute_reference
> | type_conversion | function_call | character_literal
> | qualified_expression | generalized_reference | generalized_indexing

> primary ::= numeric_literal | **null** | string_literal | aggregate | name
> | allocator | (expression) | (conditional_expression) | (quantified_expression)

The important thing to observe here is that qualified_expression has moved from being a form of primary to being a name.

We also note the addition of conditional_expression and quantified_expression (both in parentheses) as forms of primary as discussed earlier in this chapter and the addition of generalized_reference and generalized_indexing as forms of name. These are used in the new forms of iterator briefly alluded to at the end of the discussion on quantified expressions and which will be discussed in detail in Section 6.3.

Returning to qualified expressions, the main reason for allowing them as names is to avoid unnecessary conversions as mentioned in the Introduction.

Consider

```
A: T;                                    -- object of type T
type Art is array (1 .. 10) of T;        -- array of type T
function F(X: Integer) return Art;
```

A function call can be used as a prefix and so a call returning an array can be indexed as in

```
A := F(3)(7);
```

which assigns to A the value of the 7th component of the array returned by the call of F.

Now suppose that F is overloaded so that F(3) is ambiguous. The normal solution to such ambiguities is to use qualification and write Art'(F(3)) as in

```
A := Art'(F(3))(7);                      -- illegal in Ada 2005
```

but this is illegal in Ada 2005 because a qualified expression is not a name and so cannot be used as a prefix. What one has to do in Ada 2005 is either copy the wretched array (really naughty) or add a type conversion (a type conversion *is* a name) thus

```
A := Art(Art'(F(3)))(7);
```

This is really gruesome; but in Ada 2012, qualification is permitted as a name so we can simply write

```
A := Art'(F(3))(7);                      -- OK in Ada 2012
```

Although a qualified expression is now classed as a name rather than a primary, a qualified variable is not considered to be a variable. As a consequence, a qualified variable cannot be used as the destination of an assignment or as an actual parameter corresponding to an **out** or **in out** parameter. This would have added complexity for no useful purpose. Ambiguity generally involves calls on overloaded functions, and the result of a function call is always a constant, so ambiguous names of variables are unlikely!

Other uses might involve strings which can also give rise to ambiguities. For example

```
("a string")'Length
```

is ambiguous (it could be a String or Wide_String). But now we can write

```
String'("a string")'Length
```

which was not permitted in Ada 2005.

4 Structure and Visibility

This chapter describes various improvements in the areas of structure and visibility for Ada 2012.

*Perhaps the most amazing change is that functions may now have parameters of all modes. In earlier versions of Ada, functions could only have parameters of mode **in** and so could not change variables explicitly passed as parameters; however, they could silently manipulate global variables in any way whatsoever. In order to ameliorate any risks of foolishness with this new freedom, there are new rules regarding order dependence.*

There are also important improvements to incomplete types which make them much more useful; these include completion by a private type, their use as parameters and a new form of generic parameter.

Other improvements include a new form of use clause and changes to extended return statements.

4.1 Overview of changes

The WG9 guidance document [1] does not specifically identify problems in this area other than through a general exhortation to remedy shortcomings.

The following Ada Issues cover the relevant changes and are described in detail in this chapter:

15 Constant return objects

19 Primitive subprograms are frozen with a tagged type

32 Extended return statements for class-wide functions

53 Aliased views of unaliased objects

142 Explicitly aliased parameters

143 In out parameters for functions

144 Detecting dangerous order dependencies

150 Use all type clause

151 Incomplete types as parameters and result

162 Incomplete types completed by partial views

213 Formal incomplete types

214 Default discriminants for limited tagged types

235 Accessibility of explicitly aliased parameters

277 Aliased views of extended return objects

296 Freezing of subprograms with incomplete parameters

These changes can be grouped as follows.

First there is the exciting business of allowing parameters of all modes for functions (143) and the associated rules to prevent certain order dependences (144). Another change concerning parameters is permitting explicitly aliased parameters (142, 235).

There are then a number of improvements in the area of incomplete types (151, 162) including the ability to permit them as formal generic parameters (213, 296). There are also related changes to the freezing rules (19).

There is also a minor change regarding discriminants (214).

The existing two forms of use clause (use package clause and use type clause) are augmented by a third form: the use all type clause (150).

Finally, there are a number of changes (corrections really) to extended return statements which were introduced in Ada 2005 (15, 32, 277). An associated change is the introduction of the idea of an immutably limited type (53).

4.2 Subprogram parameters

The main topic here is the fact that functions (but not operators) in Ada 2012 can have parameters of any mode.

This is a topic left over from Ada 2005. The epilogue to the Rationale for Ada 2005 [15] discusses a number of topics that were abandoned and in the case of function modes says:

"Clearly, Ada functions are indeed curious. But strangely this AI (that is AI95-323) was abandoned quite early in the revision process on the grounds that it was 'too late'. (Perhaps too late in this context meant 25 years too late.)" It was not possible to agree on a way forward and so effort was devoted to other topics.

But mists clear with time. The big concern was that allowing parameters of all modes might open the door to dangerous programming practices but a solution to that was found in the introduction of stricter rules preventing many order dependences.

It is instructive to quickly go through the various historical documents.

A probably little known document is one written in 1976 by David Fisher of the Institute for Defense Analyses [16] which provided the foundation for the requirements for the development of a new language. It doesn't seem to distinguish between procedures and functions; it does mention the need for parameters which are constant and those which effectively rename a variable. Moreover, it does say (item C1 on page 81): *Side effects which are dependent on the evaluation order among the arguments of an expression will be evaluated left-to-right.* This does not actually require left-to-right evaluation but the behaviour must be as if it were. I have always thought it tragic that this was not observed.

This document was followed by a series known as Strawman, Woodenman, Tinman, Ironman [17] and finishing with Steelman [12].

The requirement on left-to-right evaluation remained in Tinman and was even stronger in Ironman but was somewhat weakened in Steelman to allow instrumentation and ends with a warning about being erroneous.

Further requirements are introduced in Ironman which requires both functions and procedures as we know them. Moreover, Ironman has a requirement about assignment to variables non-local to a function; they must be encapsulated in a region that has no calls on the function; this same requirement notes that it implies that functions can only have input parameters. This requirement does not seem to have carried forward to Steelman.

However, Ironman also introduces a requirement on restrictions to prevent aliasing. One is that the same actual parameter of a procedure cannot correspond to more than one input-output parameter. This requirement does survive into Steelman. But, it only seems to apply to procedures and not to functions and Steelman appears not to have noticed that the implied requirement that functions can only have input parameters has vanished.

It interesting to then see what was proposed in the sequence of languages leading to Ada 83, namely, Preliminary Green [18], Green [19], Preliminary Ada [20], and Ada [21]. Note that Preliminary Green was based on Ironman whereas Green was based on Steelman.

In Preliminary Green we find procedures and functions. Procedures can have parameters of three modes, **in**, **out** and **access** (don't get excited, **access** meant **in out**). Functions can only have parameters of mode **in**. Moreover,

> side effects to variables accessible at the function call are not allowed. In particular, variables that are global to the function body may not be updated in the function body. The rationale for Preliminary Green makes it quite clear that functions can have no side effects whatsoever.

In Green we find the three modes **in**, **out**, and **in out**. But the big difference is that as well as procedures and functions as in preliminary Green, there are now value returning procedures such as

procedure Random **return** Real **range** −1.0 .. 1.0;

The intent is that functions are still free of all side effects whereas value returning procedures have more flexibility. However, value returning procedures can only have parameters of mode **in** and

> assignments to global variables are permitted within value returning procedures. Calls of such procedures are only valid at points of the program where the corresponding variables are not within the scope of their declaration. The order of evaluation of these calls is strictly that given in the text of the program. Calls to value returning procedures are only allowed in assignment statements, initializations and procedure calls.

The rationale for Green notes that if you want to instrument a function then use a pragma. It also notes that functions

> with arbitrary side effects would undermine the advantage of the functional approach to software. In addition it would complicate the semantics of all language structures where expressions involving such calls may occur. Hence this form of function is not provided.

And now we come to Ada herself. There are manuals dated July 1979 (preliminary Ada), July 1980 (draft mil-std), July 1982 (proposed ANSI standard), and January 1983 (the ANSI standard usually known as Ada 83).

In Preliminary Ada, we have procedures, functions and value returning procedures exactly as in Green. Indeed, it seems that the only difference between Green and Preliminary Ada is that the name Green has been converted to Ada.

But the 1980 Ada manual omits value returning procedures and any mention of any restrictions on what you can do in a function. And by 1982 we find that we are warned that parameters can be evaluated in any order and so on.

The Rationale for Ada 83 [6] didn't finally emerge until 1986 and discusses briefly the reason for the change which is basically that benevolent side effects are important. It concludes by quoting from a paper regarding Algol 60 [22]

> The plain fact of the matter is (1) that side-effects are sometimes necessary, and (2) programmers who are irresponsible enough to introduce side-effects unnecessarily will soon lose the confidence of their colleagues and rightly so.

However, an interesting remark in the Rationale for Ada 83 in the light of the change in Ada 2012 is

The only limitation imposed in Ada on functions is that the mode of all parameters must be **in**: it would not be logical to allow **in out** and **out** parameters for functions in a language that excludes nested assignments within an expression.

Hmm. That doesn't really seem to follow. Allowing assignments in expressions as in C is obnoxious and one of the sources of errors in C programs. It is not so much that permitting side-effects in expressions via functions is unwise but more that treating the result of an assignment as a value nested within an expression is confusing. Such nested constructions are naturally still excluded from Ada 2012 and so it is very unlikely that the change will be regretted.

Now we must turn to the question of order dependences. Primarily, to enable optimization, Ada does not define the order of evaluation of a number of constructions. These include

- the parameters in a subprogram or entry call,
- the operands of a binary operator,
- the destination and value in an assignment,
- the components in an aggregate,
- the index expressions in a multidimensional name,
- the expressions in a range,
- the barriers in a protected object,
- the guards in a select statement,
- the elaboration of library units.

The expressions involved in the above constructions can include function calls. Indeed, as AI-144 states "Arguably, Ada has selected the worst possible solution to evaluation order dependences (by not specifying an order of evaluation), it does not detect them in any way, and then says that if you depend upon one (even if by accident), your code will fail at some point in the future when your compiler changes. Something should be done about this."

It is far too late to do anything about specifying the order of evaluation so the approach taken is to prevent as much aliasing as possible since aliasing is an important cause of order of evaluation problems. Ada 2012 introduces rules for determining when two names are "known to denote the same object".

Thus they denote the same object if

- both names statically denote the same stand-alone object or parameter; or
- both names are selected components, their prefixes are known to denote the same object, and their selector names denote the same component.

and so on with similar rules for dereferences, indexed components and slices. There is also a rule about renaming so that if we have

    C: Character **renames** S(5);

then C and S(5) are known to denote the same object. The index naturally has to be static.

A further step is to define when two names "are known to refer to the same object". This covers some cases of overlapping. Thus given a record R of type T with a component C, we say that R and R.C are known to refer to the same object. Similarly with an array A we say that A and A(K) are known to refer to the same object (K does not need to be static in this example).

Given these definitions we can now state the two basic restrictions.

The first concerns parameters of elementary types:

- For each name N that is passed as a parameter of mode **in out** or **out** to a call of a subprogram S, there is no other name among the other parameters of mode **in out** or **out** to that call of S that is known to denote the same object.

Roughly speaking this comes down to saying two or more parameters of mode **out** or **in out** of an elementary type cannot denote the same object. This applies to both functions and procedures.

This excludes the example given in the Introduction which was

```
procedure Do_It(Double, Triple: in out Integer) is
begin
  Double := Double * 2;
  Triple := Triple * 3;
end Do_It;
```

with

```
Var: Integer := 2;
...
Do_It(Var, Var);                    -- illegal in Ada 2012
```

The key problem is that parameters of elementary types are always passed by copy and the order in which the parameters are copied back is not specified. Thus Var might end up with either the value of Double or the value of Triple.

The other restriction concerns constructions which have several constituents that can be evaluated in any order and can contain function calls. Basically it says:

- If a name N is passed as a parameter with mode **out** or **in out** to a function call that occurs in one of the constituents, then no other constituent can involve a name that is known to refer to the same object.

Constructions cover many situations such as aggregates, assignments, ranges and so on as listed earlier.

This rule excludes the other example in the Introduction, namely, the aggregate

```
(Var, F(Var))                       -- illegal in Ada 2012
```

where F has an **in out** parameter.

The rule also excludes the assignment

```
Var := F(Var);                      -- illegal
```

if the parameter of F has mode **in out**. Remember that the destination of an assignment can be evaluated before or after the expression. So if Var were an array element such as A(I) then the behaviour could vary according to the order. To encourage good practice, it is also forbidden even when Var is a stand-alone object.

Similarly, the procedure call

```
Proc(Var, F(Var));                  -- illegal
```

is illegal if the parameter of F has mode **in out**. Examples of overlapping are also forbidden such as

```
ProcA(A, F(A(K)));                  -- illegal
ProcR(R, F(R.C));                   -- illegal
```

assuming still that F has an **in out** parameter and that ProcA and ProcR have appropriate profiles because, as explained above, A and A(K) are known to refer to the same object as are R and R.C.

On the other hand

    Proc(A(J), F(A(K)));   -- OK

is permitted provided that J and K are different objects because this is only a problem if J and K happen to have the same value.

For more details the reader is referred to the AI. The intent is to detect situations that are clearly troublesome. Other situations that might be troublesome (such as if J and K happen to have the same value) are allowed, since to prevent them would make many programs illegal that are not actually dubious. This would cause incompatibilities and upset many users whose programs are perfectly correct.

The other change in Ada 2012 concerning parameters is that they may be explicitly marked **aliased** thus

    procedure P(X: **aliased in out** T; ...);

As a consequence within P we can write X'Access. Recall that tagged types were always considered implicitly aliased anyway and always passed by reference. If the type T is a by-copy type such as Integer, then adding **aliased** causes it to be passed by reference. (So by-copy types are not always passed by copy!)

The possibility of permitting explicitly aliased function results such as

    function F(...) **return aliased** T;   -- *illegal Ada 2012*

was considered but this led to difficulties and so was not pursued.

The syntax for parameter specification is modified thus

      parameter_specification ::=
        defining_identifier_list: **[aliased]** mode [null exclusion] subtype_mark
                                        [:= default_expression]
        | defining_identifier_list: access_definition [:= default_expression]

showing that **aliased** comes first as it does in all contexts where it is permitted.

The rules for mode conformance are modified as expected. Two profiles are only mode conformant if both or neither are explicitly marked as aliased. Although adding **aliased** for a tagged type parameter makes little difference since tagged types are implicitly aliased, if this is done for a subprogram declaration then it must be done for the corresponding body as well.

There are (of course) rules regarding accessibility; these are much as expected although a special case arises in function return statements. These allow a function to safely return an access to a part of an explicitly aliased parameter and be assured that the result will not outlive the parameter. As usual, if the foolish programmer does something silly, the compiler will draw attention to the error.

Explicitly aliased parameters are used in the functions Reference (and Constant_Reference) declared in the various container packages. See Section 6.3 on Iteration and Section 8.3 on Iterating and updating containers.

4.3 Incomplete types

Incomplete types in Ada 83 were very incomplete. They were mostly used for the traditional linked list such as

```
type Cell;                          -- incomplete
type Cell_Ptr is access Cell;

type Cell is                        -- the completion
   record
      Next: Cell_Ptr;
      Element: Pointer;
   end record;
```

The incomplete type could only be used in the declaration of an access type. Moreover, the incomplete declaration and its completion had to be in the same list of declarations. However, if the incomplete declaration is in a private part then the completion can be deferred to the body; this is the so-called Taft Amendment added to Ada 83 at the last minute.

Ada 95 introduced tagged types and generalized access types and so made the language much more flexible but made no changes to incomplete types as such. However, it soon became clear that the restrictive nature of incomplete types was a burden regarding mutually dependent types and was a key issue in the requirements for Ada 2005.

The big step forward in Ada 2005 was the introduction of the limited with clause. This enables a package to have an incomplete view of a type in another package and solves many problems of mutually recursive types.

However, the overall rule remained that an incomplete type could only be completed by a full type declaration and, moreover, a parameter could not (generally) be of an incomplete type. This latter restriction encouraged the use of access parameters.

As mentioned in the Introduction, the first rule prevented the following

```
type T1;
type T2 (X: access T1) is private;
type T1 (X: access T2) is private;      -- illegal in Ada 2005
```

since the completion of T1 could not be by a private type.

This is changed in Ada 2012 so that an incomplete type can be completed by any type (other than another incomplete type). Note especially that an incomplete type can be completed by a private extension as well as by a private type.

The other major problem in Ada 2005 was that with mutually dependent types in different packages we could not use incomplete types as parameters because it was not known whether they were by-copy or by-reference. Of course, if they were tagged then we did know they were by reference but that was a severe restriction.

The need to know whether parameters are by reference or by copy was really a red herring. The model used for parameter passing in versions of Ada up to and including Ada 2005 was basically that at the point of the declaration of a subprogram we need to have all the information required to call the subprogram. Thus we needed to know how to pass parameters and so whether they were by reference or by copy.

But this is quite unnecessary; we don't need to know the mechanisms involved until a point where the subprogram is actually called or the body itself is encountered since it is only at those points that the parameter mechanism is really required. It is only at those points that the compiler has to grind out the code for the call or for the body.

So the rules in Ada 2012 are changed to use this "when we need to know" model. This is discussed in AI-19 which is actually a binding interpretation and thus retrospectively applies to Ada 2005 as well. This is formally expressed by the difference between freezing a subprogram and freezing its profile. This was motivated by a problem with tagged types whose details need not concern us.

As a highly benevolent consequence, we are allowed to use incomplete types as both parameters and function results provided that they are fully defined at the point of call and at the point where the body is defined.

But another consequence of this approach is that we cannot defer the completion of an incomplete type declared in a private part to the corresponding body. In other words, parameters of an incomplete type are allowed provided the Taft Amendment is not used for completing the type.

The other exciting change regarding incomplete types is that in Ada 2012 they are allowed as generic parameters. In Ada 2005 the syntax is

> formal_type_declaration ::=
>   **type** defining_identifier [discriminant_part] **is** formal_type_definition ;

whereas in Ada 2012 we have

> formal_type_declaration ::=
>   formal_complete_type_declaration
> | formal_incomplete_type_declaration

> formal_complete_type_declaration ::=
>   **type** defining_identifier [discriminant_part] **is** formal_type_definition ;

> formal_incomplete_type_declaration ::=
>   **type** defining_identifier [discriminant_part] **[is tagged]** ;

So the new kind of formal generic parameter has exactly the same form as the declaration of an incomplete type. It can be simply **type** T; or can require that the actual be tagged by writing **type** T **is tagged**; – and in both cases a discriminant can be given.

A formal incomplete type can then be matched by any appropriate incomplete type. If the formal specifies **tagged**, then so must the actual. If the formal does not specify **tagged** then the actual might or might not be tagged. Of course, a formal incomplete type can also be matched by an appropriate complete type. And also, in all cases, any discriminants must match as well.

An example of the use of a formal incomplete type occurs in the package Ada.Iterator_Interfaces whose generic formal part is

```
generic
   type Cursor;
   with function Has_Element(Position: Cursor) return Boolean;
package Ada.Iterator_Interfaces is ...
```

The formal type Cursor is incomplete and can be matched by an actual incomplete type. The details of this package will be described in Section 6.3 on Iteration.

Another example is provided by a signature package as mentioned in the Introduction. We can write

```
generic
   type Element;
   type Set;
   with function Empty return Set is <>;
   with function Unit(E: Element) return Set is <>;
   with function Union(S, T: Set) return Set is <>;
   with function Intersection(S, T: Set) return Set is <>;
```

```
     ...
   package Set_Signature is end;
```

Such a signature generic can be instantiated with an actual set type and then the instance can be passed into other generics that have a formal package such as

```
generic
  type VN is private;
  type VN_Set is private;
  with package Sets is
    new Set_Signature(Element => VN, Set => VN_Set, others => <>);
     ...
   package Analyse is ...
```

This allows the construction of a generic that needs a Set abstraction such as a flow analysis package. Remember that the purpose of a signature is to group several entities together and to check that various relationships hold between the entities. In this case the relationships are that the types Set and Element do have the various operations Empty, Unit and so on.

The set generic could be included in a set container package thus

```
generic
  type Element is private;
package My_Sets is
  type Set is tagged private;

  function Empty return Set;
  function Unit(E: Element) return Set;
  function Union(S, T: Set) return Set;
  function Intersection(S, T: Set) return Set;
     ...
   package My_Set is new Set_Signature(Element, Set);
private
     ...
   end My_Sets;
```

The key point is that normally an instantiation freezes a type passed as a generic parameter. But in the case of a formal incomplete untagged type, this does not happen. Hence the actual in the instantiation of Set_Signature in the generic package My_Sets can be a private type such as Set.

This echoes back to the earlier discussion of changing the freezing rules. We cannot call a subprogram with untagged incomplete parameters (whether formal or not) because we do not know whether they are to be passed by copy or by reference. But we can call a subprogram with tagged incomplete parameters because we do know that they are passed by reference (and this has to remain true for compatibility with Ada 2005). So just in case the actual subprogram in the tagged case is called within the generic, the instantiation freezes the profile. But in the untagged case, we know that the subprogram cannot be called and so there is no need to freeze the profile.

This means that the type Set should not be given as tagged incomplete in the package Set_Signature since we could not then use the signature in the package My_Sets.

If a subprogram has both tagged and untagged formal incomplete parameters then the untagged incomplete parameters win and the subprogram cannot be called.

(If this is all too confusing, do not worry, the compiler will moan at you if you make a mistake.)

Another rule regarding incomplete formal types is that the controlling type of a formal abstract subprogram cannot be incomplete.

4.4 Discriminants

There is one minor change in this area which was mentioned in the Introduction.

In Ada 2005, a discriminant can only have a default if it is not tagged. But in Ada 2012, a default is also permitted in the case of a limited tagged type.

Ada typically uses defaults as a convenience so that in many cases standard information can be omitted. Thus it is convenient that the procedure New_Line has a default of 1 since it would be boring to have to write New_Line(1); all the time.

In the case of discriminants however, a default as in

```
type Polynomial(N: Index := 0) is
  record
    A: Integer_Vector(0 .. N);
  end record;
```

also indicates that the type is mutable. This means that the value of the discriminant of an object of the type can be changed by a whole record assignment. However, tagged types in Ada 2005 never have defaults because we do not want tagged types to be mutable. On the other hand, if a tagged type is limited then it is immutable anyway. And so it was concluded that there is no harm in permitting a limited tagged type to have a default discriminant.

This may seem rather academic but the problem arose in designing containers for queues. It was felt desirable that the protected type Queue should have a discriminant giving its ceiling priority and that this should have a default for convenience. As illustrated in the Introduction this resulted in a structure as follows

```
generic
  with package Queue_Interfaces is new ...
  Default_Ceiling: Any_Priority := Priority'Last;
package AC.Unbounded_Synchronized_Queues is

  ...

  protected type Queue(Ceiling: Any_Priority := Default_Ceiling)
    with Priority => Ceiling
      is new Queue_Interfaces.Queue with ...
```

Now the problem is that a protected type such as Queue which is derived from an interface is considered to be tagged because interfaces are tagged. On the other hand a protected type is always limited and its discriminant provides a convenient way of providing the ceiling priority. So there was a genuine need for a change to the rule.

Note incidentally that the default is itself provided with the default value of Priority'Last since it is a generic parameter with its own default.

4.5 Use clauses

Ada 2012 introduces a further form of use clause. In order to understand the benefit it is perhaps worth just recalling the background to this topic.

The original use clause in Ada 83 made everything in a package directly visible. Consider the following package

```
package P is
  I, J, K: Integer;

  type Colour is (Red, Orange, Yellow, Green, Blue, ... );
  function Mix(This, That: Colour) return Colour;

  type Complex is
    record
      Rl, Im: Float;
    end record;
  function "+"(Left, Right: Complex) return Complex;
    ...
end P;
```

Now suppose we have a package Q which manipulates entities declared in P. We need a with clause for P, thus

```
with P;
package Q is ...
```

With just a with clause for P we have to refer to entities in P using the prefix P. So we get statements and declarations in Q such as

```
P.I := P.J + P.K;
```

```
Mucky: P.Colour := P.Mix(P.Red, P.Green);
```

```
W: P.Complex := (1.0, 2.0);
Z: P.Complex := (4.0, 5.0);
D: P.Complex := P."+"(W, Z);
```

This is generally considered tedious especially if the package name is not P but A_Very_Long_Name. However, adding a package use clause to Q thus

```
with P; use P;
package Q ...
```

enables the P prefix to be omitted and in particular allows infix notation for operators so we can now simply write

```
D: Complex := W + Z;
```

But as is well known, the universal use of such use clauses introduces ambiguity (if the same identifier is in two different packages and we have a use clause for both), obscurity (you can't find the wretched declaration of Red) and possibly a maintenance headache (another package is added which duplicates some identifiers). So there is a school of thought that use clauses are bad for you.

However, although the prefix denoting the package is generally beneficial it is a pain to be forced to always use the prefix notation for operators. So in Ada 95, the use type clause was added enabling us to write

```
with P;  use type P.Complex;
package Q is ...
```

This has the effect that only the primitive *operators* of the type Complex are directly visible. So we can now write

```
D: P.Complex := W + Z;
```

Note that the type name Complex is not itself directly visible so we still have to write P.Complex in the declaration of D.

However, some users still grumbled. Why should only those primitive operations that happen to be denoted by operators be visible? Why indeed? Why cannot Mucky be declared similarly without using the prefix P for Mix, Red and Green?

It might be worth briefly recalling exactly which operations of a type T are primitive operations of T. They are basically

- predefined operations such as "=" and "+",

- subprograms declared in the same package as T and which operate on T,

- enumeration literals of T,

- for a derived type, inherited or overridden subprograms.

The irritation is solved in Ada 2012 by the **use all type** clause which makes all primitive operations visible. (Note another use for the reserved word **all**.)

So we can write

> **with** P; **use all type** P.Colour;
> **package** Q **is** ...

and now within Q we can write

> Mucky: P.Colour := Mix(Red, Green);

Thus the enumeration literals such as Red are made directly visible as well as obvious primitive subprograms such as Mix.

Another impact concerns tagged types and in particular operations on class wide types.

Remember that subprograms with a parameter (or result) of type T'Class are not primitive operations unless they also have a parameter (or result of type T) as well.

Actually it is usually very convenient that operations on a class wide type are not primitive operations because it means that they are not inherited and so cannot be overridden. Thus we are assured that they do apply to all types of the class.

So, suppose we have

```
package P is
  type T is tagged private;
  procedure Op1(X: in out T);
  procedure Op2(Y: in T; Z: out T);
  function Fop(W: T) return Integer;
  procedure List(TC: in T'Class);
private
  ...
end P;
```

Then although List is not a primitive operation of T it will certainly look to many users that it belongs to T in some broad sense. Accordingly, writing **use all type** P.T; makes not only the primitive operations such as Op1, Op2 and Fop, visible but it also makes List visible as well.

Note that this is the same as the rule regarding the prefixed form of subprogram calls which can also be used for both primitive operations and class wide operations. Thus given an object A of type T, as well as statements A.Op1; and A.Op2(B); and a function call A.Fop we can equally write

> A.List;   -- *prefixed call of class wide procedure*

Moreover, suppose we declare a type NT in a package NP thus

```
package NP is
   type NT is new T with ...

   ...
end NP;
```

If we have an object AN of type NT then not only can we use prefixed calls for inherited and overridden operations but we can also use prefixed calls for class wide operations in ancestor packages such as P. So we can write

> AN.List;   -- *prefixed call of List in ancestor package*

Similarly, writing **use all type** NP.NT; on Q makes the inherited (or overridden) operations Op1, Op2 and Fop visible and also makes the class wide operation List declared in P visible. We do not also have to write **use all type** P.T; on Q as well.

We conclude by remarking that the maintenance problem of name clashes really only applies to use package clauses. In the case of use type and use all type clauses, the entities made visible are overloadable and a clash only occurs if two have the same profile which is very unlikely and almost inevitably indicates a bug.

4.6   Extended return statements

The final topic in this chapter is the extended return statement. This was introduced in Ada 2005 largely to solve problems with limited types. However, some glitches have come to light and these are corrected in Ada 2012.

A description of the reasons for and general properties of the extended return statement will be found in [15].

The syntax for extended return statement in Ada 2005 as found in [5] is

> extended_return_statement ::=
>   **return** defining_identifier: [**aliased**] return_subtype_indication [:= expression] [**do**
>   handled_sequence_of_statements
>   **end return**] ;

Before going further, it should be mentioned that there was some confusion regarding limited types and so the term immutably limited was introduced in the course of the maintenance of Ada 2005. There were various problems. Basically, limitedness is a property of a view of a type. Thus even in Ada 83 a private type might be limited but the full view found in the private part would not be limited. Ada 95 introduced explicitly limited types. Ada 2005 introduced coextensions and these could even include such obviously limited things as task types thus adding a limited part to what was otherwise a seemingly nonlimited type. It became clear that it was necessary to introduce a term which meant that a type was really and truly limited and could not subsequently become nonlimited for example in a private part or in a child unit. So a type is immutably limited if

- it is an explicitly limited record type,

- it is a task type, protected type or synchronized interface,

- it is a non-formal limited private type that is tagged or has an access discriminant with a default expression,

- it is derived from an immutably limited type.

It was then realised that there were problems with extended return statements containing an explicit **aliased**. Consequently, it was decided that there was really no need for **aliased** if there was a rule that immutably limited return objects were implicitly aliased. So **aliased** was removed from the syntax. However, some users had already written **aliased** and this would have introduced an irritating incompatibility. So finally it was decided that **aliased** could be written but only if the type were immutably limited.

Another small problem concerned constants. Thus we might write

> **return** X: T **do**
>
>   ...   -- *compute X*
> **end return**;

However, especially in the case of a limited type LT, we might also give the return object an initial value, thus

> **return** X: LT := (A, B, C) **do**
>
>   ...   -- *other stuff*
> **end return**;

Now it might be that although the type as a whole is limited one or more of its components might not be and so could be manipulated in the sequence of statements. But if we want to ensure that this does not happen, it would be appropriate to indicate that X were constant. But, almost surely by an oversight, we cannot do that since it is not permitted by the syntax. So the syntax needed changing to permit the addition of constant.

To aid the description the syntax in Ada 2012 is actually written as two productions as follows

> extended_return_object_declaration ::=
>   defining_identifier: **[aliased] [constant]** return_subtype_indication [:= expression]

> extended_return_statement ::=
>   **return** extended_return_object_declaration [**do**
>   handled_sequence_of_statements
>   **end return**] ;

The other small change to the extended return statement concerns the subtype give in the profile of the function and that in the extended return statement itself. The result type of the function can be constrained or unconstrained but that given in the extended return statement must be constrained.

This can be illustrated by considering array types. (These examples are from [15].) Suppose we have

> **type** UA **is array** (Integer **range** <>) **of** Float;
> **subtype** CA **is** UA(1 .. 10);

then we can write

> **function** Make(...) **return** CA **is**
> **begin**
>
>   ...
>   **return** R: UA(1 .. 10) **do**   -- *statically matches*
>
>   ...
>   **end return**;
> **end** Make;

This is allowed because the subtypes statically match.

If the subtype in the function profile is unconstrained then the result must be constrained either by its subtype or by its initial value. For example

> **function** Make(...) **return** UA **is**
> **begin**
>
>   ...
>   **return** R: UA(1 .. N) **do**

```
       ...
     end return;
   end Make;
```

and here the result R is constrained by its subtype. A similar situation can arise with records with discriminants. Thus we can have

```
   type Person(Sex: Gender) is ... ;

   function F( ... ) return Person is
   begin
     if ... then
       return R: Person(Sex => Male) do
         ...
       end return;
     else
       return R: Person(Sex => Female) do
         ...
       end return;
     end if;
   end F;
```

which shows that we have the possibility of returning a person of either gender.

However, what is missing from Ada 2005 is that we can have analogous situations with tagged types in that a function might wish to return a value of some type in a class.

So we would like to write things such as

```
   function F( ... ) return Object'Class is
   begin
     if ... then
       return C: Circle do
         ...
       end return;
     elsif ... then
       return S: Square do
         ...
       end return;
     end if;
   end F;
```

This is not permitted in Ada 2005 which required the types to be the same. This can be overcome by writing

```
   return C: Object'Class := Circle_Func do
     ...
   end return;
```

where Circle_Func is some local function that returns the required object of type Circle.

This is all rather irksome so the wording is changed in Ada 2012 to say that in this situation the subtype in the extended return statement need not be the same as that in the profile but simply must be covered by it. There are also related slight changes to the accessibility rules.

5 Tasking and Real-Time

This chapter describes various improvements in the tasking and real-time areas for Ada 2012.

The most important is perhaps the recognition of the need to provide control over task allocation on multiprocessor architectures.

There are also various improvements to the scheduling mechanisms and control of budgets with regard to interrupts.

An interesting addition to the core language is the ability to specify restrictions on how a procedure of a synchronized interface is to be implemented.

5.1 Overview of changes

The WG9 guidance document [1] identifies real-time systems as an important application area for Ada. In particular it says that attention should be paid to

improving the capabilities of Ada on multicore and multiprocessor architectures.

Ada 2012 does indeed address the issues of multiprocessors as well as other real-time improvements.

The following Ada Issues cover the relevant changes and are described in detail in this chapter:

 30 Requeue on synchronized interfaces

117 Memory barriers and Volatile objects

166 Yield for non-preemptive dispatching

167 Affinities for programs on multiprocessor platforms

168 Extended suspension objects

169 Group budgets for multiprocessors

170 Monitoring time spent in interrupt handlers

171 Pragma CPU and Ravenscar profile

174 Implement task barriers in Ada

215 Pragma Implemented should be an aspect

278 Set_CPU called during a protected action

These changes can be grouped as follows.

First there are a number of improvements and additions to the scheduling mechanisms (166, 168, 174). These are in the Real-Time Systems annex (D).

A number of additions recognise the importance of the widespread introduction of multiprocessors and provide mechanisms for associating tasks with particular CPUs or groups of CPUs known as dispatching domains (167, 171, 278). There is an associated change to group budgets which were introduced in Ada 2005 (169). These changes also concern Annex D.

Other changes concerning budgets relate to the time spent in interrupt handlers (170). In some systems it may be possible to account for time spent in individual interrupts whereas in others it might only be possible to account for time spent in interrupts as a whole. Again these changes concern Annex D.

The definition of Volatile is updated to take account of multiprocessors (117).

Finally, there are changes to the core language regarding synchronized interfaces and requeue (30, 215).

5.2 Scheduling

Ada 83 was remarkably silent about the scheduling of tasks. It muttered about tasks being implemented on multiprocessors or using interleaved execution on a single processor. But it said nothing about how such interleaving might be achieved. It also indicated that a single Ada task might be implemented using several actual processors if the effect would be the same.

Ada 83 introduced the pragma Priority and stated

> if two task with different priorities are both eligible for execution ... then it cannot be the case that the task with the lower priority is executing while the task with the higher priority is not.

The Rationale for Ada 83 says that this rule requires preemptive scheduling. But it says nothing about what happens if several tasks have the same priority. It does however have a dire warning

> Priorities are provided as a tool for indicating relevant degrees of urgency and on no account should their manipulation be used as a technique for attempting to obtain mutual exclusion.

So, apart from the existence of priorities, implementations were free to use whatever scheduling algorithms they liked such as Round Robin time slicing or simply running until blocked.

There was also a bit of a mystery about the delay statement. On the one hand Ada 83 says

> suspends execution of the task for at least the duration specified.

The words "at least" caused much confusion. The intent was simply a reminder that a task might not get the processor back at the end of the interval because another task might have become eligible for execution meanwhile. It did not mean that the implementation could willy-nilly delay execution for a longer time.

Another mystery surrounded the meaning of

> **delay** 0.0;

Ada 83 did state that delay with a negative value is equivalent to a delay statement with a zero value. But it did not say what a delay with a zero value meant. The Rationale remained mute on the topic as well.

However, a general convention seemed to arise that **delay** 0.0; indicated that the task was willing to relinquish the processor and so force a scheduling point.

Ada 95 brought some clarity to the situation in the new Real-Time Systems annex by introducing the pragma Task_Dispatching_Policy and the standard argument of FIFO_Within_Priorities. But the core language did not clarify the effect of a delay of zero. It does say that a delay causes a task to be blocked but if the expiration time has already passed, the task is not blocked. So clearly a negative delay does not block. However, it still has the note that a negative delay is equivalent to delay zero so we could deduce that delay zero does not block and so cannot force scheduling.

But help is at hand in the Real-Time Systems annex where it clearly states that even if a delay does not result in blocking, nevertheless the task goes to the end of the ready queue for its active priority. But that is only for the standard policy of FIFO_Within_Priorities. If a malevolent vendor introduces a curious policy called perhaps Dodgy_Scheduling then it need not follow this rule.

Ada 2005 added further policies namely

Non_Preemptive_FIFO_Within_Priorities

Round_Robin_Within_Priorities

EDF_Across_Priorities

In the case of Non_Preemptive_FIFO_Within_Priorities a non-blocking delay also sends the task to the end of the ready queue for its active priority. However, a non-blocking delay has absolutely no effect in the case of Round_Robin_Within_Priorities and EDF_Across_Priorities.

The introduction of non-preemptive dispatching revealed a shortcoming that is cured in Ada 2012. The problem is that in such a system there is a need to be able to indicate that a task is willing to be preempted by a task of a higher priority but not by one of the same priority. So somehow we need to say Yield_To_Higher.

Moreover, some felt that it was time to get rid of this strange habit of writing **delay** 0.0; to indicate a scheduling point. Those restricted to the Ravenscar profile, had been forced to write something really gruesome such as

delay until Ada.Real_Time.Time_First;

Accordingly, the procedure Yield is added to the package Ada.Dispatching so that it becomes

```
package Ada.Dispatching is
  pragma Preelaborate(Dispatching);
  procedure Yield;
  Dispatching_Policy_Error: exception;
end Ada.Dispatching;
```

Calling Yield is exactly equivalent to **delay** 0.0; and similarly causes a bounded error if called from within a protected operation.

There is also a new child package thus

```
package Ada.Dispatching.Non_Preemptive is
  pragma Preelaborate(Non_Preemptive);
  procedure Yield_To_Higher;
  procedure Yield_To_Same_Or_Higher renames Yield;
end Ada.Dispatching.Non_Preemptive;
```

Calling Yield_To_Higher provides the additional facility required for non-preemptive scheduling. Note that, unlike Yield, it can be called from within a protected operation and does not cause a bounded error.

The pedantic programmer can call the precisely named Yield_To_Same_Or_Higher which simply renames Yield in the parent package.

Incidentally, note that since Yield has a side effect, Ada.Dispatching has been downgraded to preelaborable whereas it was pure in Ada 2005.

We now turn to consider an interaction between suspension objects introduced in Ada 95 and EDF scheduling introduced in Ada 2005.

Remember that suspension objects are manipulated by the following package

```
package Ada.Synchronous_Task_Control is
  type Suspension_Object is limited private;
  procedure Set_True(S: in out Suspension_Object);
  procedure Set_False(S: in out Suspension_Object);
  function Current_State(S: Suspension_Object) return Boolean;
  procedure Suspend_Until_True(S: in out Suspension_Object);
private
```

```
    ...
    end Ada.Synchronous_Task_Control;
```

The state of a suspension object can be set by calls of **Set_True** and **Set_False**. The key feature is that the procedure **Suspend_Until_True** enables a task to be suspended until the suspension object is set true by some other task. Thus this provides a neat mechanism for signalling between tasks.

Earliest Deadline First (EDF) scheduling is manipulated by the following child package of Ada.Dispatching introduced in Ada 2005 (with use clauses added to save space)

```
    with Ada.Real_Time; with Ada.Task_Identification;
    use Ada.Real_Time; use Ada.Task_Identification;
    package Ada.Dispatching.EDF is
      subtype Deadline is Ada.Real_Time.Time;
      Default_Deadline: constant Deadline := Time_Last;

      procedure Set_Deadline(D: in Deadline; TT: in Task_Id := Current_Task);
      procedure Delay_Until_And_Set_Deadline(Delay_Until_Time: in Time;
                                             Deadline_Offset: in Time_Span);
      function Get_Deadline(T: Task_Id := Current_Task) return Deadline;
    end Ada.Dispatching.EDF;
```

The procedure Delay_Until_And_Set_Deadline is the key feature. It enables a task to be blocked until the time given by the parameter Delay_Until_Time and sets the deadline so that it is Deadline_Offset after that.

But what is missing in Ada 2005 is the ability for a sporadic task triggered by a suspension object to have its deadline set in a similar manner. This is remedied in Ada 2012 by the addition of the following child package

```
    with Ada.Real_Time;
    package Ada.Synchronous_Task_Control.EDF is
      procedure Suspend_Until_True_And_Set_Deadline(S: in out Suspension_Object;
                                             TS: in Ada.Real_Time.Span);
    end Ada.Synchronous_Task_Control.EDF;
```

This enables a task to be blocked until the suspension object S is set true; it then becomes ready with a deadline of Ada.Real_Time.Clock + TS.

The other new feature concerning scheduling in Ada 2012 is the addition of a package Ada.Synchronous_Barriers. This enables many tasks to be blocked and to be released together.

The rationale for needing this facility is explained in the AI concerned. As general purpose computing is moving to parallel architectures and eventually to massively parallel machines, there is a need to efficiently schedule many tasks using barrier primitives. The POSIX OS interface provides a barrier primitive where N tasks wait on a barrier and are released simultaneously when all are ready to execute.

There are many situations where the release of N tasks is required to execute an algorithm in parallel. Often the calculation is relatively small for each task on each iteration but the number of tasks is relatively high. As an example consider the solution of partial differential equations where one task is allocated to each node of a grid; there might easily be several thousand nodes. Such an example is outlined in [7]. The cost of linearly scheduling and releasing them could remove almost all gains made through parallelization in the first place.

The new package is

```
package Ada.Synchronous_Barriers is
  pragma Preelaborate(Synchronous_Barriers);

  subtype Barrier_Limit is range 1 .. implementation-defined;
  type Synchronous_Barrier(Release_Threshold: Barrier_Limit) is limited private;
  procedure Wait_For_Release(The_Barrier: in out Synchronous_Barrier;
                             Notified: out Boolean);
private
  ...
end Ada.Synchronous_Barriers;
```

The type Synchronous_Barrier has a discriminant whose value indicates the number of tasks to be waited for. When an object of the type is declared its internal counter is set to zero. Thus we might write

```
SB: Synchronous_Barrier(Release_Threshold => 100);
```

When a task calls the procedure Wait_For_Release thus

```
Wait_For_Release(SB, My_Flag);
```

then the task is blocked and the internal counter in SB is incremented. If the counter is then equal to the release threshold for that object (100 in this example), then all the tasks are released. Just one task will have the parameter Notified set to true (the mechanism for selecting the chosen task is not defined). This specially chosen task is then expected to do some work on behalf of all the others. Typically all the tasks will be of the same task type so the code of that type might have

```
Wait_For_Release(SB, My_Flag);
if My_Flag then                         -- Gosh, I am the chosen one
  ...                                   -- do stuff
end if;
```

Once all the tasks are released, the counter in SB is reset to zero so that the synchronous barrier can be used again.

Care is needed regarding finalization, aborting tasks and other awkward activities. For example, if a synchronous barrier is finalized, then any tasks blocked on it are released and Program_Error is raised at the point of the call of Wait_For_Release.

Many embedded real-time programs, such as those conforming to the Ravenscar profile, run forever. However, there are soft multitasking programs which are hosted on systems such as Windows or Linux and these require closing down in an orderly manner. There are also programs that have mode changes in which the set of tasks involved can be changed dramatically. In such situations it is important that synchronous barriers are finalized neatly.

5.3 Multiprocessors

In recent years the cost of processors has fallen dramatically and for many applications it is now more sensible to use several individual processors rather than one high performance processor.

Moreover, society has got accustomed to the concept that computers keep on getting faster. This makes them applicable to more and more high volume but low quality applications. But this cannot go on. The finite value of the velocity of light means that increase in processor speed can only be achieved by using devices of ever smaller size. But here we run into problems concerning the nonzero size of Planck's constant. When devices get very small, quantum effects cause problems with reliability.

No doubt, in due course, genuine quantum processors will emerge based perhaps on attributes such as spin. But meanwhile, the current approach is to use multiprocessors to gain extra speed.

One special feature of Ada 2012 aimed at helping to use multiprocessors is the concept of synchronous barriers which were described above. We now turn to facilities for generally mapping tasks onto numbers of processors.

The key feature is a new child package of System thus

```
package System.Multiprocessors is
  pragma Preelaborate(Multiprocessors);

  type CPU_Range is range 0 .. implementation-defined;
  Not_A_Specific_CPU: constant CPU_Range := 0;
  subtype CPU is CPU_Range range 1 .. CPU_Range'Last;

  function Number_Of_CPUs return CPU;
end System.Multiprocessors;
```

Note that this is a child of System rather than a child of Ada. This is because System is generally used for hardware related features.

Processors are given a unique positive integer value from the subtype CPU. This is a subtype of CPU_Range which also includes zero; zero is reserved to mean not allocated or unknown and for clarity is the value of the constant Not_A_Specific_CPU.

The total number of CPUs is determined by calling the function Number_Of_CPUs. This is a function rather than a constant because there could be several partitions with a different number of CPUs on each partition. And moreover, the compiler might not know the number of CPUs anyway.

Since this is not a Remote Types package, it is not intended to be used across partitions. It follows that a CPU cannot be used by more than one partition. The allocation of CPU numbers to partitions is not defined; each partition could have a set starting at 1, but they might be numbered in some other way.

Tasks can be allocated to processors by an aspect specification. If we write

```
task My_Task
  with CPU => 10;
```

then My_Task will be executed by processor number 10. In the case of a task type then all tasks of that type will be executed by the given processor. The expression giving the processor for a task can be dynamic.

Moreover, in the case of a task type, the CPU can be given by a discriminant. So we can have

```
task type Slave(N: CPU_Range)
  with CPU => N;
```

and then we can declare

```
Tom: Slave(1);
Dick: Slave(2);
Harry: Slave(3);
```

and Tom, Dick and Harry are then assigned CPUs 1, 2 and 3 respectively. We could also have

```
Fred: Slave(0);
```

and Fred could then be executed by any CPU since 0 is Not_A_Specific_CPU.

The aspect can also be set by a corresponding pragma CPU. (This is an example of a pragma born obsolescent as explained in Section 2.2 on Aspect specifications.) The aspect CPU can also be given to the main subprogram in which case the expression must be static.

Further facilities are provided by the child package System.Multiprocessors.Dispatching_Domains as shown below. Again we have added use clauses to save space and also have often abbreviated Dispatching_Domain to D_D.

```
with Ada.Real_Time; with Ada.Task_Identification;
use Ada.Real_Time; use Ada.Task_Identification;
package System.Multiprocessors.Dispatching_Domains is
   pragma Preelaborate(Dispatching_Domains);

   Dispatching_Domain_Error: exception;

   type Dispatching_Domain(<>) is limited private;
   System_Dispatching_Domain: constant D_D;

   function Create(First, Last: CPU) return D_D;
   function Get_First_CPU(Domain: D_D) return CPU;
   function Get_Last_CPU(Domain: D_D) return CPU;

   function Get_Dispatching_Domain(T: Task_Id := Current_Task) return D_D;

   procedure Assign_Task(Domain: in out Dispatching_Domain;
                         CPU: in CPU_Range := Not_A_Specific_CPU;
                         T: in Task_Id := Current_Task);

   procedure Set_CPU(CPU: in CPU_Range; T: in Task_Id := Current_Task);

   function Get_CPU(T: in Task_Id := Current_Task) return CPU_Range;

   procedure Delay_Until_And_Set_CPU(Delay_Until_Time: in Time;
                                     CPU: in CPU_Range);
private
   ...
end System.Multiprocessors.Dispatching_Domains;
```

The idea is that processors are grouped together into dispatching domains. A task may then be allocated to a domain and it will be executed on one of the processors of that domain.

Domains are of the type Dispatching_Domain. This has unknown discriminants and consequently uninitialized objects of the type cannot be declared. But such an object can be initialized by the function Create. So to declare My_Domain covering processors from 10 to 20 inclusive we can write

```
My_Domain: Dispatching_Domain := Create(10, 20);
```

All CPUs are initially in the System_Dispatching_Domain. A CPU can only be in one domain. If we attempt to do something silly such as create overlapping domains by for example also writing

```
My_Domain_2: Dispatching_Domain := Create(20, 30);
```

then Dispatching_Domain_Error is raised because in this case, CPU number 20 has been assigned to both My_Domain and My_Domain_2.

The environment task is always executed on a CPU in the System_Dispatching_Domain. Clearly we cannot move all the CPUs from the System_Dispatching_Domain other wise the environment task would be left high and dry. Again an attempt to do so would raise Dispatching_Domain_Error.

A very important rule is that Create cannot be called once the main subprogram is called. Moreover, there is no operation to remove a CPU from a domain once the domain has been created. So the general approach is to create all domains during library package elaboration. This then sets a fixed arrangement for the program as a whole and we can then call the main subprogram.

Each partition has its own scheduler and so its own set of CPUs, dispatching domains and so on.

Tasks can be assigned to a domain in two ways. One way is to use an aspect

```
task My_Task
   with Dispatching_Domain => My_Domain;
```

If we give both the domain and an explicit CPU thus

```
task My_Task
   with CPU => 10, Dispatching_Domain => My_Domain;
```

then they must be consistent. That is the CPU given must be in the domain given. If it is not then task activation fails (hands up all those readers who thought it was going to raise Dispatching_Domain_Error). If for some reason we write

```
task My_Task
   with CPU => 0, Dispatching_Domain => My_Domain;
```

then no harm is done. Remember that there is not a CPU with number zero but zero simply indicates Not_A_Specific_CPU. In such a case it would be better to write

```
task My_Task
   with CPU => Not_A_Specific_CPU, Dispatching_Domain => My_Domain;
```

The other way to assign a task to a domain is by calling the procedure Assign_Task. Thus the above examples could be written as

```
Assign_Task(My_Domain, 10, My_Task'Identity);
```

giving both domain and CPU, and

```
Assign_Task(My_Domain, T => My_Task'Identity);
```

which uses the default value Not_A_Specific_CPU for the CPU.

Similarly, we can assign a CPU to a task by

```
Set_CPU(A_CPU, My_Task'Identity);
```

Various checks are necessary. If the task has been assigned to a domain there is a check to ensure that the new CPU value is in that domain. If this check fails then Dispatching_Domain_Error is raised. Of course, if the new CPU value is zero, that is Not_A_Specific_CPU then it simply means that the task can then be executed on any CPU in the domain.

To summarize the various possibilities, a task can be assigned a domain and possibly a specific CPU in that domain. If no specific CPU is given then the scheduling algorithm is free to use any CPU in the domain for that task.

If a task is not assigned to a specific domain then it will execute in the domain of its activating task. In the case of a library task the activating task is the environment task and since this executes in the System_Dispatching_Domain, this will be the domain of the library task.

The domain and any specific CPU assigned to a task can be set at any time by calls of Assign_Task and Set_CPU. But note carefully that once a task is assigned to a domain other than the system dispatching domain then it cannot be assigned to a different domain. But the CPU within a domain can be changed at any time; from one specific value to another specific value or maybe to zero indicating no specific CPU.

It is also possible to change CPU but for the change to be delayed. Thus we might write

Delay_Until_And_Set_CPU(Delay_Until_Time => Sometime, CPU => A_CPU);

Recall we also have Delay_Until_And_Set_Deadline in Ada.Dispatching.EDF mentioned earlier.

Note that calls of Set_CPU and Assign_Task are defined to be task dispatching points. However, if the task is within a protected operation then the change is deferred until the next task dispatching point for the task concerned. If the task is the current task then the effect is immediate unless it is within a protected operation in which case it is deferred as just mentioned. Finally, if we pointlessly assign a task to the system dispatching domain when it is already in that domain, then nothing happens (it is not a dispatching point).

There are various functions for interrogating the situation regarding domains. Given a domain we can find its range of CPU values by calling the functions Get_First_CPU and Get_Last_CPU. Given a task we can find its domain and CPU by calling Get_Dispatching_Domain and Get_CPU. If a task is not assigned a specific CPU then Get_CPU naturally returns Not_A_Specific_CPU.

In order to accommodate interrupt handling the package Ada.Interrupts is slightly modified and now includes the following function

function Get_CPU(Interrupt: Interrupt_Id) **return** System.Multiprocessors.CPU_Range;

This function returns the CPU on which the handler for the given interrupt is executed. Again the returned value might be Not_A_Specific_CPU.

The Ravenscar profile is now defined to be permissible with multiprocessors. However, there is a restriction that tasks may not change CPU. Accordingly the definition of the profile now includes the following restriction

No_Dependence => System.Multiprocessors.Dispatching_Domains

In order to clarify the use of multiprocessors with group budgets the package Ada.Execution_Time.Group_Budgets introduced in Ada 2005 is slightly modified. The Ada 2005 version is

with System;
package Ada.Execution_Time.Group_Budgets **is**

  type Group_Budget **is tagged limited private**;

  type Group_Budget_Handler **is access protected procedure** (GB: **in out** Group_Budget);

    ...   *-- and so on*
private
    ...
end Ada.Execution_Time.Group_Budgets;

However, in Ada 2012 the type Group_Budget has a discriminant giving the CPU thus

type Group_Budget(CPU: System.Multiprocessors.CPU :=
                          System.Multiprocessors.CPU'First)
                                is tagged limited private;

This means that a group budget only applies to a single processor. If a task in a group is executed on another processor then the budget is not consumed. Note that the default value for CPU is CPU'First which is always 1.

Note that the definition of dispatching domains above assumes that the set of CPU values is contiguous. After ISO standardization it was realised that this was unreasonable and accordingly the definition was changed to allow any set of values as described in Section 9.5 of the Epilogue.

5.4 Interrupt timers and budgets

It will be recalled that Ada 2005 introduced three packages for monitoring the CPU time used by tasks. They are a root package Ada.Execution_Time plus two child packages thus

Ada.Execution_Time – this is the root package and enables the monitoring of execution time of individual tasks.

Ada.Execution_Time.Timers – this provides facilities for defining and enabling timers and for establishing a handler which is called by the run time system when the execution time of the task reaches a given value.

Ada.Execution_Time.Group_Budgets – this enables several tasks to share a budget and provides means whereby action can be taken when the budget expires.

The execution time of a task, or CPU time, is the time spent by the system executing the task and services on its behalf. CPU times are represented by the private type CPU_Time declared in the root package Ada.Execution_Time.

However, it was left implementation defined in Ada 2005 as to how the time spent in interrupts was to be accounted. The Ada 2005 RM says

> It is implementation defined which task, if any, is charged the execution time that is consumed by interrupt handlers and run-time services on behalf of the system.

As noted in the AI, a common and simple implementation will charge the time consumed by the interrupt handlers to the task executing when the interrupt is generated. This is done under the assumption that the effect of interrupt handlers on the execution time clocks is negligible since the interrupt handlers are usually very short pieces of code. However, in real-time systems that undertake an intensive use of interrupts, this assumption may not be realistic. For example, Ada 2005 introduced timed events that can execute handlers in interrupt context. The facility is convenient and has low overheads, and therefore programmers are tempted to put more code into these handlers.

It is thus considered important to be able to measure time spent in interrupts and so facilities to do this are added in Ada 2012.

The root package is extended by the addition of two Boolean constants, Interrupt_Clocks_Supported and Separate_Interrupt_Clocks_Supported, and also a function Clocks_For_Interrupts so in outline it becomes

```
with Ada.Task_Identification; use Ada.Task_Identification;
with Ada.Real_Time;  use Ada.Real_Time;
package Ada.Execution_Time is

  type CPU_Time is private;

    ...

  function Clock(T: Task_Id := Current_Task) return CPU_Time;

    ...

  Interrupt_Clocks_Supported: constant Boolean := implementation-defined;
  Separate_Interrupt_Clocks_Supported: constant Boolean := implementation-defined;

  function Clocks_For_Interrupts return CPU_Time;
```

```
    private
       ...              -- not specified by the language
    end Ada.Execution_Time;
```

The constant Interrupt_Clocks_Supported indicates whether the time spent in interrupts is accounted for separately from the tasks and then Separate_Interrupt_Clocks_Supported indicates whether the time is accounted for each interrupt individually.

The new function Clocks_For_Interrupts returns the CPU_Time used over all interrupts. It is initialized to zero.

Time accounted for in interrupts is not also accounted for in individual tasks. In other words there is never any double accounting.

Calling the function Clocks_For_Interrupts if Interrupt_Clocks_Supported is false raises Program_Error. Note that the existing function Clock has a parameter giving the task concerned whereas Clocks_For_Interrupts does not since it covers all interrupts.

A new child package of Ada.Execution_Time is provided for monitoring the time spent in individual interrupts. Note that this package always exists even if the Boolean constant Separate_Interrupt_Clocks_Supported is false. Its specification is

```
    package Ada.Execution_Time.Interrupts is
       function Clock(Interrupt: Ada.Interrupts.Interrupt_Id) return CPU_Time;
       function Supported(Interrupt: Ada.Interrupts.Interrupt_Id) return Boolean;
    end Ada.Execution_Time.Interrupts;
```

The function Supported indicates whether the time for a particular interrupt is being monitored. If it is then Clock returns the accumulated CPU_Time spent in that interrupt handler (otherwise it returns zero). However, if the overall constant Separate_Interrupt_Clocks_Supported is false then calling this function Clock for any particular interrupt raises Program_Error.

The package Ada.Execution_Time.Timers is exactly the same in Ada 2012. However, as mentioned earlier, the package Ada.Execution_Time.Group_Budgets is now defined to work on a single processor and the type Group_Budget is modified to include a discriminant giving the CPU concerned.

5.5   Volatile

This is a curious topic and created much debate. For the collector of statistics the real part of the AI is less than two pages but the appendix has nearly twenty pages of chatter!

The problem is all about sharing variables and ensuring that things happen in the correct order. Moreover, we need to avoid the overhead of protected objects particularly on microprocessors where we might be using low level features such as memory barriers discussed in Section 2 above.

Suppose we have two tasks A and B which access some shared data perhaps in a nice package Common thus

```
    package Common is
       ...
       Data: Integer;
       pragma Volatile(Data);
       Flag: Boolean;
       pragma Volatile(Flag);
       ...
    end Common;
```

and in task A we write

```
with Common; use Common;
task A is
   ...
   Data := 42;
   Flag := True;
   ...
end A;
```

whereas in task B we have

```
with Common; use Common;
task B is
   Copy: Integer;
begin
   ...
   loop
      exit when Flag;            -- spin
   end loop;
   Copy := Data;
   ...
end B;
```

The idea is that task A assigns some value to Data and then indicates this to task B by setting Flag to true. Meanwhile, task B loops checking Flag and when it is found to be true, then reads the Data.

Does this work in Ada 2005? Hmm. Nearly. There are three things that need to be ensured. One is that Flag gets changed in one lump. Another is that the new value of Data assigned by task A truly is updated when task B reads it. And the third is that the actions happen sequentially. Well, we should have applied pragma Atomic to Flag to ensure the first but since it is of type Boolean we might get away with it. And note that Atomic implies Volatile anyway. Also Atomic ensures that the actions are sequential.

So, with the pragma Volatile changed to Atomic for Flag, it does indeed work in Ada 2005 because Volatile ensures that read and writes are to memory and so things do happen in the correct order. However, this is overkill. It is not necessary that all accesses are to memory; all that matters is that they happen in the correct order so they could be to some intermediate cache. Indeed, there might be nested caches and as hardware evolves it is becoming more difficult to make general statements about its structure; hence we can really only make statements about the effect.

The possibility of introducing a new pragma Coherent was debated for some time. However, it was ultimately concluded that the definition of Volatile should be weakened. In Ada 2005 it says

> For a volatile object all reads and updates of the object as a whole are performed directly to memory.

In Ada 2012 it says

> All tasks of the program (on all processors) that read or write volatile variables see the same order of updates to the variables.

Of course, in Ada 2012, we use aspects so the package Common becomes

```
package Common is
   ...
   Data: Integer
      with Volatile;
```

```
    Flag: Boolean
      with Atomic;              -- Atomic implies Volatile
      ...
    end Common;
```

where we have given Atomic for Flag. As mentioned above, Atomic implies Volatile so it is not necessary to give both. However, if we do have to give two aspects, it is much neater that the one aspect specification does this whereas two distinct pragmas would be necessary.

It is said that this change brings the meaning of volatile into line with that in C. However, it has also been said that the definition of volatile in C is unclear.

5.6   Synchronized interfaces and requeue

Ada 2005 introduced interfaces of various kinds: limited, nonlimited, synchronized, task, and protected. These form a hierarchy and in particular task and protected interfaces are forms of synchronized interfaces. The essence of this was to integrate the OO and real-time features of Ada. However, a problem was discovered regarding requeue as described in a paper presented at IRTAW 2007 [23].

Some examples of interfaces will be found in [7] or [15] where various implementations of the readers and writers paradigm are explained.

The operations of a synchronized interface are denoted by subprograms. Thus we might have

```
    package Pkg is
      type Server is synchronized interface;
      procedure Q(S: in out Server; X: in Item) is abstract;
    end Pkg;
```

We can then implement the interface by a task type or by a protected type. This introduces several different ways of implementing the operation Q. It can be by an entry, or by a protected procedure or by a normal procedure. For example using a task type we might have

```
    package TP1 is
      task type TT1 is new Server with
                      -- Q implemented by entry
        entry Q(X: in Item);
      end TT1;
    end TP1;
```

or

```
    package TP2 is
      task type TT2 is new Server with
                      -- Q implemented by a normal procedure
      end TT2;
      procedure Q(S: in out TT2; X: in Item);
    end TP2;
```

Similarly using a protected type we might have

```
    package PP1 is
      protected type PT1 is new Server with
                      -- Q implemented by entry
        entry Q(X: in Item);
        ...
```

```
      end PT1;
   end PP1;
```

or

```
   package PP2 is
      protected type PT2 is new Server with
                        -- Q implemented by a protected procedure
         procedure Q(X: in Item);

         ...
      end PT2;
   end PP2;
```

or

```
   package PP3 is
      protected type PT3 is new Server with
                        -- Q implemented by a normal procedure

         ...
      end PT3;
      procedure Q(X: In out PT3; X: in Item);
   end PP3;
```

So the interface Server could be implemented in many different ways. And as usual we could dispatch to any of the implementations. We could have

```
   Server_Ptr: access Server'Class := ...
   ...
   Server_Ptr.Q(X => An_Item);
```

and this will dispatch to the implementation of Q concerned.

So a call of Q could end up as a call of an entry in a task, an entry in a protected object, a protected procedure in a protected object, or an ordinary procedure.

Two curious situations arise. One concerns timed calls. We could write a timed call such as

```
   select
      Server_Ptr.Q(An_Item);
   or
      delay Seconds(10);
   end select;
```

and this will always be acceptable. It will dispatch to the appropriate operation. If it is an entry then it will be a timed call. But if it is not an entry then no time-out is possible and so by default the call will always go ahead.

The other curious situation concerns requeue. In this case there is no obvious default action. It is not possible to requeue a procedure call since there is no queue on which to hang it.

The first proposal to do something about this was simply not to allow requeue at all on interfaces. And indeed this was the solution adopted in Ada 2005.

However, this is not really acceptable as explained in [23]. The next idea was to raise some exception if it turned out that the destination was not an entry. But this was considered unsatisfactory.

So it was concluded that if we do a requeue then it must be statically checked that it will dispatch to an entry so that the requeue is possible. The next proposal was that there should be a pragma Implemented giving requirements on the operation. Thus we might have

> **procedure** Q(S: **in out** Server; X: **in** Item) **is abstract**;
> **pragma** Implemented(Q, By_Entry);

and the compiler would ensure that all implementations of the interface Server did indeed implement Q by an entry so that requeue would always work. The other possible values for the pragma were By_Protected_Procedure and By_Any.

The world changed when the notion of an aspect was invented and so after much discussion the final solution is that we there is now an aspect Synchronization so we write

> **procedure** Q(S: **in out** Server; X: **in** Item) **is abstract**
> **with** Synchronization => By_Entry;

and we are now assured that we are permitted to do a requeue on Q for any implementation of Server. The other possible values for the aspect Synchronization are By_Protected_Procedure and Optional.

In summary, if the property is By_Entry then the procedure must be implemented by an entry, if the property is By_Protected_Procedure then the procedure must be implemented by a protected procedure, and if the property is Optional then it can be implemented by an entry, procedure or protected procedure. Naturally enough, the aspect cannot be given for a function.

There are a number of rules regarding consistency. The aspect Synchronization can be applied to a task interface or protected interface as well as to a synchronized interface. However, if it is applied to a task interface then the aspect cannot be specified as By_Protected_Procedure for obvious reasons. If a type or interface is created by inheritance from other interfaces then any Synchronization properties are also inherited and must be consistent. Thus if one is By_Entry then the others must also be By_Entry or Optional.

A final minor improvement mentioned in the Introduction concerns renaming. Since the days of Ada 83 it has been possible to rename an entry as a procedure thus

> **procedure** Write(X: **in** Item) **renames** Buffer.Put;

where Put is an entry in a task Buffer. But in Ada 83 it was not possible to do a timed call using Write. This was corrected in Ada 2005 which allows a timed call on a renaming. Similarly, when requeue was introduced in Ada 95, it was not possible to do a requeue using Write. This anomaly is corrected in Ada 2012. So now both timed calls and requeue are permitted using a renaming of an entry.

6 Iterators, Pools, etc.

This chapter describes various improvements in a number of general areas in Ada 2012.

There are some minor but perhaps surprising changes concerning matters such as the placement of pragmas and labels.

There are important new features regarding indexing and accessing largely introduced to simplify iterating over containers.

There are also a number of additional Restrictions identifiers many related to the introduction of aspect specifications.

The functionality of access types and storage management is made more flexible by the introduction of subpools.

Finally, a number of minor additions and corrections are made to a range of topics such as generics.

6.1 Overview of changes

The areas mentioned in this chapter are not specifically mentioned in the WG9 guidance document [1] other than under the request to remedy shortcomings and improve the functionality of access types and dynamic storage management.

The following Ada Issues cover the relevant changes and are described in detail in this chapter.

6 Nominal subtypes for all names

71 Class-wide operations for formal subprograms

95 Address of intrinsic subprograms

100 Placement of pragmas

111 Subpools, allocators & control of finalization

119 Package Calendar, Daylight Saving Time and UTC_Offset

123 Composability of equality

139 Syntactic sugar for access, containers & iterators

148 Accessibility of anonymous access stand-alone objects

149 Access type conversion and membership

152 Restriction No_Anonymous_Allocators

163 Pragmas in place of null

173 Testing of tags representing abstract types

179 Labels at end of a sequence of statements

189 Restriction No_Standard_Allocators_After_Elaboration

190 Global storage pool control

193 Alignment of allocators

212 Accessors and iterators for Ada.Containers

241 Aspect-related restrictions

242 No_Implementation_Units restriction

246 Restrictions No_Implementation_Identifiers and Profile No_Implementation_Extensions

252 Questions on subpools

253 Accessibility of allocators for anonymous access of an object

255 User-defined iterators and quantified expressions

272 Pragma and attribute restrictions

292 Terminology: indexable type is confusing

These changes can be grouped as follows.

First there are some minor changes to elementary matters such as the placement of pragmas, labels and null statements (100, 163, 179).

An important addition is the introduction of more user-friendly mechanisms for iterating over structures such as arrays and containers (139, 212, 255, 292).

Further flexibility for storage management is provided by the introduction of subpools of storage pools (111, 190, 252). A number of issues concerning anonymous access types and allocators are also resolved (148, 149, 193, 253).

A number of new Restrictions identifiers have been added. They include No_Coextensions, No_Standard_Allocators_After_Elaboration, No_Anonymous_Allocators, No_Implementation_Units, and No_Implementation_Identifiers. A blanket new profile covering a number of restrictions, No_Implementation_Extensions, is also added (152, 189, 241, 242, 246, 272).

Finally, there are a number of minor unrelated improvements. Four are actually classed as binding interpretations and so apply to Ada 2005 as well; they concern nominal subtypes (6), address of intrinsic subprograms (95), time in the package Calendar (119), and class wide operations on formal generic subprograms (71). The other miscellaneous issues concern the composability of equality (123), and tags of abstract types (173).

6.2 Position of pragmas and labels

It is surprising that basic stuff such as where one can place a pragma should be the subject of discussion thirty years after Ada became an ANSI standard.

However, there is a real problem in this area which one could imagine might have led to headlines in the Wall Street Journal and Financial Times such as

> **Collapse of NY Stock Market because of Safety Fears in Avionic Applications after Discovery that Ada is Illegal**

Indeed, it seems that the package Ada in Ada 2005 might be illegal. This surprising conclusion was triggered by the consideration of

```
task type TT is
   pragma Priority(12);
end TT;
```

The rules in Ada 83, Ada 95 and Ada 2005 concerning the position of pragmas say

Pragmas are only allowed at the following places in a program:

- After a semicolon delimiter, but not within a formal part or discriminant part.

- At any place where the syntax rules allow a construct defined by a syntactic category whose name ends with "declaration", "statement", "clause", or "alternative"; or one of the syntactic categories variant or exception_handler; but not in place of such a construct. Also at any place where a compilation_unit would be allowed.

Now the syntax for task_definition in Ada 2005 is

> task_definition ::=
>   {task_item}
> **[private**
>   {task_item}]
> **end** [*task*_identifier]

There are at least two problems. The key one here is that the list of categories in the rule does not include "item". The other concerns the words "not in place of". It seems that the intent was that if at least one instance of the construct is required (as in a sequence of statements) then the pragma cannot be given in place of a single statement. So it looks as if the task type TT is not legal.

It has probably been permitted because task_item itself splits down into aspect_clause or entry_declaration and they seem to be allowed. But if none is present then we cannot tell which category is permitted!

Note rather scarily that the package Ada is given as

> **package** Ada **is**
>   **pragma** Pure(Ada);
> **end** Ada;

and the same problem applies.

The entities in a package specification are of the category basic_declarative_item and again although it splits down into things ending _clause or _declaration we don't know which.

The fear concerning package Ada made one member of the ARG concerned that the sky might be falling in. Of course, we don't ever have to submit a package Ada in our file (on punched cards, paper tape or whatever media we are using). The package Ada is just in the mind of the compiler so that it behaves as if she were declared. The same applies to Standard. They are sort of synthesized and not actually declared.

Anyway, the upshot is that in Ada 2012, the description of the placement of pragmas is corrected by adding "item" to the list and clarifying the meaning of not in place of.

A further discussion considered sequences of statements. In a structure such as an if statement the syntax is

> if_statement ::=
>   **if** condition **then**
>   sequence_of_statements
>   ...

where

> sequence_of_statements ::= statement {statement}

The important point is that a sequence_of_statements must have at least one statement. Moreover, the rules for placing pragmas in Ada 2005 do not allow a pragma in place of a construct so we cannot write

> **if** B **then**
>   **pragma** Assert(...);   -- *illegal in Ada 2005*
> **else** ...

but have to include at least one statement (such as a null statement) by writing perhaps

```
if B then
   pragma Assert( ... ); null;
else ...
```

or

```
if B then
   null; pragma Assert( ... );
else ...
```

On reflection this seemed irritating so the rules for the placement of pragmas are further amended to include another bullet

- In place of a statement in a sequence_of_statements

A useful note on a language definition principle is added to the AARM which is that if all pragmas are treated as unrecognized then a program should remain legal.

Incidentally, there are other places in the language where at least one item is required such as in a component list. Again if we don't want any components we have to write a null component as in

```
type Nothing is
   record
      null;
   end record;
```

One might have thought that we could similarly now allow one to write

```
type T is
   record
      pragma Page;
   end record;
```

Indeed, it might have been thought that we could simply say that in general a pragma can be given "in place of" an entity. But this doesn't work in some cases. For example, an asynchronous select statement can take the form of a series of statements in its triggering alternative thus

```
select
   S1( ... );
   S2( ... );
   S3( ... );
then abort
   ...
end select;
```

Now the call of S1 is the triggering statement and has a different status to S2 and S3. It would be very confusing to be able to replace the call of S1 by a pragma. So such generalization was dismissed as leading to trouble.

The final topic in this vein concerns the position of labels. This was triggered by the consideration of the problem of quitting one iteration of a loop if it proves unsuccessful and then trying the next iteration. As described in the Introduction this can be done by writing

```
for I in Some_Range loop
   ...
   if not OK then goto End_Of_Loop; end if;
   ...                              -- lots of other code
```

```
    <<End_Of_Loop> null;          -- try another iteration
    end loop;
```

Of course, maybe we should avoid the goto and write

```
    for I in Some_Range loop
        ...
        if OK then
            ...                    -- lots of other code
        end if;
                                   -- try another iteration
    end loop;
```

At first sight the latter structure looks nicer. However, if the "lots of other code" encounters several situations which mean that the iteration has to be abandoned then we quickly get a deeply nested structure which is not easy to understand and becomes heavily indented.

Much consideration was given to the introduction of a continue statement but it was felt that this would obscure the existence of the transfer of control. Although the goto may be deprecated as obscure, the corresponding obvious label in its aggressive double angle brackets is a strong clue to the existence of the transfer of control.

In the end it was decided that the only sensible improvement was to remove the need for the null statement at the end of the loop.

This is achieved by changing the syntax for a sequence of statements to

```
    sequence_of_statements ::= statement {statement} {label}
```

where (as before)

```
    statement ::= {label} simple_statement | {label} compound_statement
```

so that as well as being permitted before a statement, a label can also follow a sequence of statements. In addition, a rule is added to the effect that if one or more labels end a sequence of statements then an implicit null statement is inserted after the labels. This rule is necessary because the effect of the goto statement is described in terms of going to the statement after the label. So the loop example can now be written as

```
    for I in Some_Range loop
        ...
        if not OK then goto End_Of_Loop; end if;
        ...                            -- lots of other code
        <<End_Of_Loop>                 -- try another iteration
    end loop;
```

More generally we can write

```
    if B then
        S1;  S2;  <<My_Label>>
    end if;
```

as well as giving the null explicitly thus

```
    if B then
        S1;  S2;  <<My_Label>> null;
    end if;
```

but we still cannot write

```
if B then
  <<My_Label>>                        -- illegal
end if;
```

since a sequence of statements must still include at least one statement. Of course, we could never jump to such a label anyway since control cannot be transferred into a structure.

6.3 Iteration

Iteration and subprogram calls are in some sense the twin cornerstones of programming. We are all familiar with the ubiquitous nature of statements such as

```
for I in A'Range loop
  A(I) := 0;
end loop;
```

which in one form or another exist in all (normal) programming languages.

The detail of giving the precise description of the iteration and the indexing is really a violation of abstraction by revealing unnecessary detail. All we want to say is "assign zero to each element of the set A".

However, although it's not too much of a hassle with arrays, the introduction of containers revealed that detailed iteration could be very heavy-handed. Thus, as mentioned in the Introduction, suppose we are dealing with a list, perhaps a list of the type Twin declared as

```
type Twin is
  record
    P, Q: Integer;
  end record;
```

To manipulate every element of the list in Ada 2005, we have to write something like

```
C := The_List.First;               -- C declared as of type Cursor
loop
  exit when C = No_Element;
  E := Element(C);                 -- E is of type Twin
  if Is_Prime(E.P) then
    Replace_Element(The_List, C, (E.P, E.Q + X));
  end if;
  C := Next(C);
end loop;
```

This reveals the gory details of the iterative process whereas all we want to say is "add X to the component Q for all members of the list whose component P is prime".

There is another way in Ada 2005 and that is to use the procedure Iterate. In that case the details of what we are doing have to be placed in a distinct subprogram called perhaps Do_It. Thus we can write

```
declare
  procedure Do_It(C: in Cursor) is
  begin
    E := Element(C);               -- E is of type Twin
    if Is_Prime(E.P) then
      Replace_Element(The_List, C, (E.P, E.Q + X));
    end if;
  end Do_It;
```

```
begin
   The_List.Iterate(Do_It'Access);
end;
```

This avoids the fine detail of calling First and Next but uses what some consider to be a heavy infrastructure.

However, in Ada 2012 we can simply say

```
for E of The_List loop
   if Is_Prime(E.P) then
      E.Q := E.Q + X;
   end if;
end loop;
```

Not only is this just five lines of text rather than nine or eleven, the key point is that the possibility of making various errors of detail is completely removed.

The mechanisms by which this magic abstraction is achieved are somewhat laborious and it is anticipated that users will take a cookbook approach (show us how to do it, but please don't explain why – after all, this is the approach taken with boiling an egg, we can do it without deep knowledge of the theory of coagulation of protein material).

We will start by looking at the process using arrays. Rather than

```
for I in A'Range loop
   if A(I) /= 0 then
      A(I) := A(I) + 1;
   end if;
end loop;
```

we can write

```
for E of A loop
   if E /= 0 then
      E := E + 1;
   end if;
end loop;
```

In the case of a two-dimensional array, instead of

```
for I in AA'Range(1) loop
   for J in AA'Range(2) loop
      A(I, J) := 0.0;
   end loop;
end loop;
```

we can write

```
for EE of AA loop
   EE := 0.0;
end loop;
```

In Ada 2005 (and indeed in Ada 95 and Ada 83), the syntax for a loop is given by

```
loop_statement ::= [loop_statement_identifier :]
                [iteration_scheme] loop
                    sequence_of_statements
                end loop [loop_identifier] ;
```

iteration_scheme ::= **while** condition
       | **for** loop_parameter_specification

loop_parameter_specification ::= defining_identifier **in**
       [**reverse**] discrete_subtype_definition

This is all quite familiar. In Ada 2012, the syntax for loop_statement remains the same but iteration_scheme is extended to give

iteration_scheme ::= **while** condition
       | **for** loop_parameter_specification
       | **for** iterator_specification

Thus the new form iterator_specification is introduced which is

iterator_specification ::=
       defining_identifier **in** [**reverse**] *iterator*_name
       | defining_identifier [: subtype_indication] **of** [**reverse**] *iterable*_name

The first production defines a *generalized iterator* whereas the second defines an *array component iterator* or a *container element iterator*. For the moment we will just consider the second production which has **of** rather than **in**. The *iterable*_name can refer to an array or a container. Suppose it is an array such as A or AA in the examples above.

We note that we can optionally give the subtype of the loop parameter. Suppose that the type A is given as

    type A **is array** (index) **of** Integer;

then the subtype of the loop parameter (E in the example) if not given will just be that of the component which in this case is simply Integer. If we do give the subtype of the loop parameter then it must cover that of the component. This could be useful with tagged types.

Note carefully that the loop parameter does not have the type of the index of the array as in the traditional loop but has the type of the component of the array. So on each iteration it denotes a component of the array. It iterates over all the components of the array as expected. If **reverse** is not specified then the components are traversed in ascending index order whereas if **reverse** is specified then the order is descending. In the case of a multidimensional array then the index of the last dimension varies fastest matching the behaviour of AA in the expanded traditional version as shown (and which incidentally is the order used in streaming). However, if the array has convention Fortran then it is the index of the first dimension that varies fastest both in the case of the loop and in streaming.

There are other obvious rules. If the array A or AA is constant then the loop parameter E or EE is also constant. So it all works much as expected. But do note carefully the use of the reserved word **of** (rather than **is**) which distinguishes this kind of iteration from the traditional form using an index.

As another array example suppose we have the following

    type Artwin **is array** (1 .. N) **of** Twin;

    The_Array: Artwin;

which is similar to the list example above. In the traditional way we might write

```
for K in Artwin'Range loop
  if Is_Prime(The_Array(K).P) then
    The_Array(K).Q := The_Array(K).Q + X;
  end if;
end loop;
```

Using the new notation this can be simplified to

```
for E: Twin of The_Array loop
  if Is_Prime(E.P) then
    E.Q := E.Q + X;
  end if;
end loop;
```

where we have added the subtype Twin to clarify the situation. Similarly, in the simple list example we could write

```
for E: Twin of The_List loop
  if Is_Prime(E.P) then
    E.Q := E.Q + X;
  end if;
end loop;
```

Note the beautiful similarity between these two examples. The only lexical difference is that The_Array is replaced by The_List showing that arrays and containers can be treated equivalently.

We now have to consider how the above can be considered as behaving like the original text which involves C of type Cursor, and subprograms First, No_Element, Element, Replace_Element and Next.

This magic is performed by several new features. One is a generic package whose specification is

```
generic
  type Cursor;
  with function Has_Element(Position: Cursor) return Boolean;
package Ada.Iterator_Interfaces is
  pragma Pure(Iterator_Interfaces);

  type Forward_Iterator is limited interface;
  function First(Object: Forward_Iterator) return Cursor is abstract;
  function Next(Object: Forward_Iterator; Position: Cursor) return Cursor is abstract;

  type Reversible_Iterator is limited interface and Forward_Iterator;
  function Last(Object: Reversible_Iterator) return Cursor is abstract;
  function Previous(Object: Reversible_Iterator;
                    Position: Cursor) return Cursor is abstract;

end Ada.Iterator_Interfaces;
```

This generic package is used by the various container packages such as Ada.Containers.Doubly_Linked_Lists. Its actual parameters corresponding to the formal parameters Cursor and Has_Element come from the container which includes an instantiation of Ada.Iterator_Interfaces. The instantiation then exports the various required types and functions. Thus in outline the relevant part of the list container now looks like

```
with Ada.Iterator_Interfaces;
generic
  type Element_Type is private;
  with function "=" (Left, Right: Element_Type) return Boolean is <>;
package Ada.Containers.Doubly_Linked_Lists is

  ...

  type List is tagged private ...

  ...

  type Cursor is private;
```

```
      ...
      function Has_Element(Position: Cursor) return Boolean;
      package List_Iterator_Interfaces is
         new Ada.Iterator_Interfaces(Cursor, Has_Element);
      ...

      ...
   end Ada.Containers.Doubly_Linked_Lists;
```

The entities exported from the generic package Ada.Iterator_Interfaces are the two interfaces Forward_Iterator and Reversible_Iterator. The interface Forward_Iterator has functions First and Next whereas the Reversible_Iterator (which is itself descended from Forward_Iterator) has functions First and Next inherited from Forward_Iterator plus additional functions Last and Previous.

Note carefully that a Forward_Iterator can only go forward but a Reversible_Iterator can go both forward and backward. Hence it is reversible and not Reverse_Iterator.

The container packages also contain some new functions which return objects of the type Reversible_Iterator'Class or Forward_Iterator'Class. In the case of the list container they are

```
      function Iterate(Container: in List) return
                        List_Iterator_Interfaces.Reversible_Iterator'Class;
      function Iterate(Container: in List; Start: in Cursor) return
                        List_Iterator_Interfaces.Reversible_Iterator'Class;
```

These are new functions and are not to be confused with the existing procedures Iterate and Reverse_Iterate which enable a subprogram to be applied to every element of the list but are somewhat cumbersome to use as shown earlier. The function Iterate with only one parameter is used for iterating over the whole list whereas that with two parameters iterates starting with the cursor value equal to Start.

Now suppose that the list container is instantiated with the type Twin followed by the declaration of a list

```
      package Twin_Lists is
         new Ada.Containers.Doubly_Linked_Lists(Element_Type => Twin);

      The_List: Twin_Lists.List;
```

So we have now declared The_List which is a list of elements of the type Twin. Suppose we want to do something to every element of the list. As we have seen we might write

```
      for E: Twin of The_List loop
         ...                              -- do something to E
      end loop;
```

However, it might be wise at this point to introduce the other from of iterator_specification which is

```
         defining_identifier in [reverse] iterator_name
```

This defines a generalized iterator and uses the traditional in rather than of used in the new array component and container element iterators. Using this generalized form we can write

```
      for C in The_List.Iterate loop
         ...                              -- do something via cursor C
      end loop;
```

In the body of the loop we manipulate the elements using cursors in a familiar way. The reader might wonder why there are these two styles, one using is and the other using of. The answer is that the generalized iterator is more flexible; for example it does not need to iterate over the whole structure. If we write

for C **in** The_List.Iterate(S) **loop**

then the loop starts with the cursor value equal to S; this is using the version of the function Iterate with two parameters. On the other hand, the new array component and container element iterators using **of** are more succinct where applicable.

The generalized iterators for the list container use reversible iterators because the functions Iterate return a value of the type Reversible_Iterator'Class. The equivalent code generated uses the functions First and Next exported from List_Iterator_Interfaces created by the instantiation of Ada.Iterator_Interfaces with the actual parameters The_List.Cursor and The_List.Has_Element. The code then behaves much as if it were (see paragraph 13/3 of subclause 5.5.2 of the RM)

```
C: The_List.Cursor;
E: Twin;
F: Forward_Iterator'Class := The_List.Iterate;
...
C := F.First;
loop
  exit when not The_List.Has_Element(C);
  E := The_List.Element(C);
  ...                          -- do something to E
  C := F.Next(C);
end loop;
```

Of course, the user does not need to know all this in order to use the construction. Note that the functions First and Next used here (which operate on the class Forward_Iterator and are inherited by the class Reversible_Iterator) are not to be confused with the existing functions First and Next which act on the List and Cursor respectively. The existing functions are retained for compatibility and for use in complex situations.

It should also be noted that the initialization of F is legal since the result returned by Iterate is a value of Reversible_Iterator'Class and this is a subclass of Forward_Iterator'Class.

If we had written

```
for C in reverse The_List.Iterate loop
  ...                 -- do something via cursor C
end loop;
```

then the notional code would have been similar but have used the functions Last and Previous rather than First and Next.

Another point is that the function call F.First will deliver the very first cursor value if we had written The_List.Iterate but the value S if we had written The_List.Iterate(S). Remember that we are dealing with interfaces so there is nothing weird here; the two functions Iterate return different types in the class and these have different functions First so the notional generated code calls different functions.

If we use the form

```
for E: Twin of The_List loop
  ...                 -- do something to E
end loop;
```

then the generated code is essentially the same. However, since we have not explicitly mentioned an iterator, a default one has to be used. This is given by one of several new aspects of the type List which actually now is

```
type List is tagged private
   with Constant_Indexing => Constant_Reference,
        Variable_Indexing => Reference,
        Default_Iterator => Iterate,
        Iterator_Element => Element_Type;
```

The aspect we need at the moment is the one called Default_Iterator which as we see has the value Iterate (this is the one without the extra parameter). So the iterator F is initialized with this default value and once more we get

```
C: The_List.Cursor;
E: Twin;
F: Forward_Iterator'Class := The_List.Iterate;
   ...
```

The use of the other aspects will be explained in a moment.

Lists, vectors and ordered maps and sets can be iterated in both directions. They all have procedures Reverse_Iterate as well as Iterate and the two new functions Iterate return a value of Reversible_Iterator'Class.

However, it might be recalled that the notion of iterating in either direction makes no sense in the case of hashed maps and hashed sets. Consequently, there is no procedure Reverse_Iterate for hashed maps and hashed sets and there is only one new function Iterate which (in the case of hashed maps) is

```
function Iterate(Container: in Map) return
                  Map_Iterator_Interfaces.Forward_Iterator'Class;
```

and we note that this function returns a value of Forward_Iterator'Class rather than Reversible_Iterator'Class in the case of lists, vectors, ordered maps, and ordered sets.

Naturally, we cannot put **reverse** in an iterator over hashed maps and hashed sets nor can we give a starting value. So the following are both illegal

```
for C in The_Hash_Map.Iterate(S) loop     -- illegal
```

```
for E of reverse The_Hash_Map loop     -- illegal
```

The above should have given the reader a fair understanding of the mechanisms involved in setting up the loops using the new iterator forms. We now turn to considering the bodies of the loops, that is the code marked *"do something via cursor C "* or *"do something to E "*.

In the Ada 2005 example we wrote

```
if Is_Prime(E.P) then
   Replace_Element(The_List, C, (E.P, E.Q + X));
end if;
```

It is somewhat tedious having to write Replace_Element when using a container whereas in the case of an array we might directly write

```
if Is_Prime(A(I).P) then
   A(I).Q := A(I).Q + X;
end if;
```

The trouble is that Replace_Element copies the whole new element whereas in the array example we just update the one component. This doesn't matter too much in a case where the components are small such as Twin but if they were giant records it would clearly be a problem. To overcome this Ada 2005 includes a procedure Update_Element thus

```
procedure Update_Element(Container: in out List;
                         Position: in Cursor;
                         Process: not null access procedure (Element: in out Element_Type));
```

To use this we have to write a procedure Do_It say thus

```
procedure Do_It(E: in out Twin) is
begin
  E.Q := E.Q + X;
end Do_It;
```

and then

```
if Is_Prime(E.P) then
  Update_Element(The_List, C, Do_It'Access);
end if;
```

This works fine because E is passed by reference and no giant copying occurs. However, the downside is that the distinct procedure Do_It has to be written so that the overall text is something like

```
declare
  procedure Do_It(E: in out Twin) is
  begin
    E.Q := E.Q + X;
  end Do_It;
begin
  if Is_Prime(E.P) then
    Update_Element(The_List, C, Do_It'Access);
  end if;
end;
```

which is a bit tedious.

But of course, the text in the body of Do_It is precisely what we want to say. Using the historic concepts of left and right hand values, the problem is that The_List(C).Element cannot be used as a left hand value by writing for example

```
The_List(C).Element.Q := ...
```

The problem is overcome in Ada 2012 using a little more magic by the introduction of generalized reference types and various aspects. In particular we find that the containers now include a type Reference_Type and a function Reference which in the case of the list containers are

```
type Reference_Type(Element: not null access Element_Type) is private
  with Implicit_Dereference => Element;

function Reference(Container: aliased in out List;
                   Position: in Cursor) return Reference_Type;
```

Note the aspect Implicit_Dereference applied to the type Reference_Type with discriminant Element.

There is also a type Constant_Reference_Type and a function Constant_Reference for use when the context demands read-only access.

The alert reader will note the inclusion of **aliased** for the parameter Container of the function Reference. As discussed in Section 4.2 on Subprogram parameters, this ensures that the parameter is passed by reference (it always is for tagged types anyway); it also permits us to apply 'Access to the parameter Container within the function and to return that access value.

It might be helpful to say a few words about the possible implementation of Reference and Reference_Type although these need not really concern the user.

The important part of the type Reference_Type is its access discriminant. The private part might contain housekeeping stuff but we can ignore that. So in essence it is simply a record with just one component being the access discriminant

```
type Reference_Type(E: not null access Element_Type) is null record;
```

and the body of the function might be

```
function Reference(Container: aliased in out List;
                   Position: in Cursor) return Reference_Type is
begin
  return (E => Container.Element(Position)'Access);
end Reference;
```

The rules regarding parameters with **aliased** (which we gloss over) ensure that no accessibility problems should arise. Note also that it is important that the discriminant of Reference_Type is an access discriminant since the lifetime of the discriminant is then just that of the return object.

Various aspects are given with the type List which as shown earlier now is

```
type List is tagged private
  with Constant_Indexing => Constant_Reference,
       Variable_Indexing => Reference,
       Default_Iterator => Iterate,
       Iterator_Element => Element_Type;
```

The important aspect here is Variable_Indexing. If this aspect is supplied then in essence an object of the type can be used in a left hand context by invoking the function given as the value of the aspect. In the case of The_List this is the function Reference which returns a value of type Reference_Type. Moreover, this reference type has a discriminant which is of type **access** Element_Type and the aspect Implicit_Dereference with value Element and so gives direct access to the value of type Element.

We can now by stages transform the raw text. So using the cursor form we can start with

```
for C in The_List.Iterator loop
  if Is_Prime(The_List.Reference(C).Element.all.P) then
    The_List.Reference(C).Element.all.Q :=
      The_List.Reference(C).Element.all.Q + X;
  end if;
end loop;
```

This is the full blooded version even down to using **all**.

Omitting the **all** and using the dereferencing with the aspect Implicit_Dereference we can omit the mention of the discriminant Element to give

```
for C in The_List.Iterator loop
  if Is_Prime(The_List.Reference(C).P) then
    The_List.Reference(C).Q := The_List.Reference(C).Q + X;
  end if;
end loop;
```

Remember that Reference is a function with two parameters. It might be clearer to write this without prefix notation which gives

```
for C in Iterator(The_List) loop
  if Is_Prime(Reference(The_List, C).P) then
    Reference(The_List, C).Q := Reference(The_List, C).Q + X;
  end if;
end loop;
```

Now because the aspect Variable_Indexing for the type List has value Reference, the explicit calls of Reference can be omitted to give

```
for C in The_List.Iterator loop
  if Is_Prime(The_List(C).P) then
    The_List(C).Q := The_List(C).Q + X;
  end if;
end loop;
```

It should now be clear that the cursor C is simply acting as an index into The_List. We can compare this text with

```
for C in The_Array'Range loop
  if Is_Prime(The_Array(C).P) then
    The_Array(C).Q := The_Array(C).Q + X;
  end if;
end loop;
```

which shows that 'Range is analogous to .Iterator.

Finally, to convert to the element form using E we just replace The_List(C) by E to give

```
for E of The_List loop
  if Is_Prime(E.P) then
    E.Q := E.Q + X;
  end if;
end loop;
```

The reader might like to consider the transformations in the reverse direction to see how the final succinct form transforms to the expanded form using the various aspects. This is indeed what the compiler has to do.

This underlying technique which transforms the sequence of statements of the container element iterator can be used quite generally. For example, we might not want to iterate over the whole container but just manipulate a particular element given by a cursor C. Rather than calling Update_Element with another subprogram Do_Something, we can write

```
The_List.Reference(C).Q := ...
```

or simply

```
The_List(C).Q := ...
```

Moreover, although the various aspects were introduced into Ada 2012 primarily to simplify the use of containers they can be used quite generally.

The reader may feel that these new features violate the general ideas of a language with simple building blocks. However, it should be remembered that even the traditional form of loop such as

```
for Index in T range L .. U loop
   ...                              -- statements
end loop;
```

is really simply a shorthand for

```
declare
  Index: T;
begin
  if L <= U then
    Index := L;
    loop
       ...                          -- statements
       exit when Index = U;
       Index := T'Succ(Index);
    end loop;
  end if;
end;
```

Without such shorthand, programming would be very tedious and very prone to errors. The features described in this section are simply a further step to make programming safer and simpler.

Further examples of the use of these new features with containers will be given in Chapter 8 dedicated to containers.

The mechanisms discussed above rely on a number of new aspects, a summary of which follows and might be found useful. It is largely based on extracts from the RM.

Dereferencing

The following aspect may be specified for a discriminated type T.

Implicit_Dereference   This aspect is specified by a name that denotes an access discriminant of the type T.

A type with a specified Implicit_Dereference aspect is a *reference type*. The Implicit_Dereference aspect is inherited by descendants of type T if not overridden.

A generalized_reference denotes the object or subprogram designated by the discriminant of the reference object.

Indexing

The following aspects may be specified for a tagged type T.

Constant_Indexing   This aspect is specified by a name that denotes one or more functions declared immediately within the same declaration list in which T is declared. All such functions shall have at least two parameters, the first of which is of type T or T'Class, or is an access-to-constant parameter with designated type T or T'Class.

Variable_Indexing   This aspect is specified by a name that denotes one or more functions declared immediately within the same declaration list in which T is declared. All such functions shall have at least two parameters, the first of which is of type T or T'Class, or is an access parameter with designated type T or T'Class. All such functions shall have a return type that is a reference type, whose reference discriminant is of an access-to-variable type.

These aspects are inherited by descendants of T (including T'Class). The aspects shall not be overridden, but the functions they denote may be.

An *indexable container type* is a tagged type with at least one of the aspects Constant_Indexing or Variable_Indexing specified.

An important difference between Constant_Indexing and Variable_Indexing is that the functions for variable indexing must return a reference type so that it can be used in left hand contexts such as the destination of an assignment. Note that, in both cases, the name can denote several overloaded functions; this is useful, for example, with maps to allow indexing both with cursors and with keys.

Both Constant_Indexing and Variable_Indexing can be provided since the constant one might be more efficient whereas the variable one is necessary in left hand contexts. But we are not obliged to give both, just Variable_Indexing might be enough for some applications.

Iterating

An iterator type is a type descended from the Forward_Iterator interface.

The following aspects may be specified for an indexable container type T.

Default_Iterator   This aspect is specified by a name that denotes exactly one function declared immediately within the same declaration list in which T is declared, whose first parameter is of type T or T'Class or an access parameter whose designated type is type T or T'Class, whose other parameters, if any, have default expressions, and whose result type is an iterator type. This function is the *default iterator function* for T.

Iterator_Element   This aspect is specified by a name that denotes a subtype. This is the *default element subtype* for T.

These aspects are inherited by descendants of type T (including T'Class).

An *iterable container type* is an indexable container type with specified Default_Iterator and Iterator_Element aspects.

The Constant_Indexing and Variable_Indexing aspects (if any) of an iterable container type T shall denote exactly one function with the following properties:

- the result type of the function is covered by the default element type of T or is a reference type with an access discriminant designating a type covered by the default element type of T;

- the type of the second parameter of the function covers the default cursor type for T;

- if there are more than two parameters, the additional parameters all have default expressions.

These functions (if any) are the *default indexing functions* for T.

The reader might care to check that the aspects used in the examples above match these definitions and are used correctly. Note for example that the Default_Iterator and Iterator_Element aspects are only needed if we use the **of** form of iteration (and both are needed in that case, giving one without the other would be foolish).

This section has largely been about the use of iterators with loop statements. However, there is one other use of them and that is with quantified expressions which are also new to Ada 2012. Quantified expressions were discussed in some detail in Section 3.4 of the chapter on Expressions so all we need here is to consider a few examples which should clarify the use of iterators.

Instead of

>   B := (**for all** K **in** A'Range => A(K) = 0);

which assigns true to B if every component of the array A has value 0, we can instead write

>   B := (**for all** E **of** A => E = 0);

Similarly, instead of

>   B := (**for some** K **in** A'Range => A(K) = 0);

which assigns true to B if some component of the array A has value 0, we can instead write

>   B := (**for some** E **of** A => E = 0);

In the case of a multidimensional array, instead of

>   B := (**for all** I **in** AA'Range(1) => (**for all** J **in** AA'Range(2) => AA(I, J) = 0));

we can write

>   B := (**for all** E **of** AA => E = 0);

which iterates over all elements of the array AA however many dimensions it has.

We can also use these forms with the list example. Suppose we are interested in checking whether some element of the list has a prime component P. We can write

>   B := (**for some** E **of** The_List => Is_Prime(E.P));

or perhaps

>   B := (**for some** C **in** The_List.Iterator => Is_Prime(The_List(C).P));

which uses the explicit iterator form.

6.4 Access types and storage pools

A significant change in Ada 2005 was the introduction of anonymous access types. It is believed that the motivation was to remove the feeling that Ada 95 was unnecessarily pedantic in requiring the introduction of lots of named access types whereas in languages such as C one can just place a star on the identifier of the type being referenced in order to introduce a pointer type.

However, anonymous access types raised more complex accessibility check problems which did not arise with named access types. Most of these problems were resolved in the definition of Ada 2005 but one remained concerning stand-alone objects of anonymous access types. Interestingly, such stand-alone objects were added to Ada 2005 late in the development process; perhaps hastily as it turned out.

In Ada 2005, local stand-alone objects take the accessibility level of the master in which they are declared.

Consider an attempt to use a local stand-alone object in an algorithm to reverse a list. We assume that the list comprises nodes of the following type

```
type Node is
  record
     ...
    Next: access Node;
  end record;
```

and we write

```
function Reverse(List: access Node) return access Node is
   Result: access Node := null;
   This_Node: access Node := List;
   Next_Node: access Node := null;
begin
   while This_Node /= null loop
      Next_Node := This_Node.Next;
      This_Node.Next := Result;              -- access failure in 2005
      Result := This_Node;
      This_Node := Next_Node;
   end loop;
   return Result;                            -- access failure in 2005
end Reverse;
```

This uses the obvious algorithm of working down the list and rebuilding it. However, in Ada 2005 there are two accessibility failures associated with the variable Result. The assignment to This_Node.Next fails because Result might be referring to something local and we cannot assign that to a node of the list since the list itself lies outside the scope of Reverse_List. Similarly, attempting to return the value in Result fails.

The problem with returning a result can sometimes be solved by using an extended return statement as illustrated in [7]. But this is not a general remedy. The problem is solved in Ada 2012 by treating stand-alone access objects rather like access parameters so that they carry the accessibility of the last value assigned to them as part of their value.

Another reason for introducing anonymous access types in Ada 2005 was to reduce the need for explicit type conversions (note that anonymous access types naturally have no name to use in an explicit conversion). However, it turns out that in practice it is convenient to use anonymous access types in some contexts (such as the component Next of type Node) but in other contexts we might find it logical to use a named access type such as

```
type List is access Node;
```

In Ada 2005, explicit conversions are often required from anonymous access types to named access types and this has been considered to be irritating. Accordingly, the rule has been changed in Ada 2012 to say that an explicit conversion is only required if the conversion could fail.

This relaxation covers both accessibility checks and tag checks. For example we might have

```
type Class_Acc is access T'Class;         -- named type
type Rec is
   record
      Comp: access T'Class;               -- anon type
   end record;

R: Rec;
```

and then some code somewhere

```
Z: Class_Acc;
...
Z := R.Comp;                              -- OK in Ada 2012
```

The conversion from the anonymous type of Comp to the named type Class_Acc of Z on the assignment to Z cannot fail and so does not require an explicit conversion whereas it did in Ada 2005. However, a conversion from a stand-alone access object or an access parameter always requires an explicit conversion to check the accessibility level carried as part of the value as explained above since such a check could fail.

With regard to tag checks, if it is statically known that the designated type of the anonymous access type is covered by the designated type of the named access type then there is no need for a tag check and so an explicit conversion is not required.

It will be recalled that there is a fictitious type known as *universal_access* (much as *universal_integer*, *root_Integer* and so on). For example, the literal **null** is of this universal type. Moreover, there is a function "=" used to compare *universal_access* values. Permitting implicit conversions requires the introduction of a preference rule for the equality operator of the universal type. Suppose we have

```
type A is access Integer;
R, S: access Integer;
...
if R = S then
```

Now since we can do an implicit conversion from the anonymous access type of R and S to the type A, there is confusion as to whether the comparison uses the equality operator of the type *universal_access* or that of the type A. Accordingly, there is a preference rule that states that in the case of ambiguity there is a preference for equality of the type *universal_access*. Similar preference rules already apply to *root_integer* and *root_real*.

A related topic concerns membership tests which were described in Section 3.6 of the chapter on Expressions.

If we want to ensure that a conversion from perhaps Integer to Index will work and not raise Constraint_Error we can write

```
subtype Index is Integer range 1 .. 20;
I: Index;
K: Integer;
...
if K in Index then
  I := Index(K);              -- bound to work
else
  ...                        -- remedial action
end if;
```

This is much neater than attempting the conversion and then handling Constraint_Error.

However, in Ada 2005, there is no similar facility for testing to see whether an access type conversion would fail. So membership tests in Ada 2012 are extended to permit such a test. So if we have

```
type A is access T1;
X: A;
...
type Rec is
  record
    Comp: access T2;
  end record;

R: Rec;
Y: access T2;
```

we can write

```
if R.Comp in A then
   X := A(R.Comp)                    -- conversion bound to work
else ...
```

The membership test will return true if the type T1 covers T2 and the accessibility rules are satisfied so that the conversion is bound to work. Note that the converted expression (R.Comp in this case) can be an access parameter or a stand-alone access object such as Y; in these cases a dynamic test may be required.

We now turn to consider various features concerning allocation and storage pools.

It will be recalled that if we write our own storage pools then we have to declare a pool type derived from the type Root_Storage_Pool in the package System.Storage_Pools. So we might write

```
package My_Pools is
   type Pond(Size: Storage_Count) is new Root_Storage_Pool with private;
   ...
```

where the discriminant gives the size of the pool. We then have to provide procedures Allocate and Deallocate for our own pool type Pond corresponding to those for Root_Storage_Pool. The procedures Allocate and Deallocate both have four parameters. For example, the procedure Allocate is

```
procedure Allocate(Pool: in out Root_Storage_Pool;
                    Storage_Address: out Address;
                    Size_In_Storage_Elements;
                    Alignment: in Storage_Count) is abstract;
```

When we declare our own Allocate we do not have to use the same names for the formal parameters. So we might more simply write

```
procedure Allocate(Pool: in out Pond;
                    Addr: out Address;
                    SISE: in Storage_Count;
                    Align: in Storage_Count);
```

As well as Allocate and Deallocate we also have to write a function Storage_Size and procedures Initialize and Finalize. However, the key procedures are Allocate and Deallocate which give the algorithms for determining how the storage in the pool is manipulated.

Two parameters of Allocate give the size and alignment of the space to be allocated. However, it is possible that the particular algorithm devised might need to know the worst case values in determining an appropriate strategy. The attribute Max_Size_In_Storage_Elements gives the worst case for the storage size in Ada 2005 but there is no corresponding attribute for the worst case alignment.

This is overcome in Ada 2012 by the provision of the attribute Max_Alignment_For_Allocation. There are various reasons for possibly requiring a different alignment to that expected. For example, the raw objects might simply be byte aligned but the algorithm might decide to append dope or monitoring information which is integer aligned.

The collector of Ada curiosities might remember that Max_Size_In_Storage_Elements is the attribute with most characters in Ada 2005 (28 of which 4 are underlines). Curiously, Max_Alignment_For_Allocation also has 28 characters of which only 3 are underlines.

There are problems with anonymous access types and allocation. Consider

```
package P is
  procedure Proc(X: access Integer);
end P;

with P;
procedure Try_This is
begin
  P.Proc(new Integer'(10));
end Try_This;
```

The procedure Proc has an access parameter X and the call of Proc in Try_This does an allocation with the literal 10. Where does it go? Which pool? Can we do Unchecked_Deallocation? There are special rules for allocators of anonymous access types which aim to answer such questions. The pool is "created at the point of the allocator" and so on.

But various problems arise. An important one is that it is not possible to do unchecked deallocation because the access type has no name; this is particularly serious with library level anonymous access types. An example of such a type might be that of the component Next if the record type Node discussed earlier had been declared at library level.

Consequently, it was concluded that it is best to use named access types if allocation is to be performed. We can always convert to an anonymous type if desired after the allocation has been performed.

In order to avoid encountering such problems a new restriction identifier is introduced. So writing

```
pragma Restrictions(No_Anonymous_Allocators);
```

prevents allocators of anonymous access types and so makes the call of the procedure Proc in the procedure Try_This illegal.

Many long-lived control programs have a start-up phase in which various storage structures are established and which is then followed by the production phase in which various restrictions may be imposed. Ada 2012 has a number of features that enable this to be organized and monitored.

One such feature is the new restriction

```
pragma Restrictions(No_Standard_Allocators_After_Elaboration);
```

This specifies that an allocator using a standard storage pool shall not occur within a parameterless library subprogram or within the statements of a task body. In essence this means that all such allocation must occur during library unit elaboration. Storage_Error is raised if allocation occurs afterwards.

However, it is expected that systems will permit some use of user-defined storage pools. To enable the writers of such pools to monitor their use some additional functions are added to the package Task_Identification so that it now takes the form

```
package Ada.Task_Identification is
  ...

  type Task_Id is private;

  ...

  function Current_Task return Task_Id;
  function Environment_Task return Task_Id;
  procedure Abort_Task(T: in Task_Id);

  function Is_Terminated(T: Task_Id) return Boolean;
  function Is_Callable(T: Task_Id) return Boolean;
  function Activation_Is_Complete(T: Task_Id) return Boolean;
```

private

  ...

end Ada.Task_Identification;

The new function Environment_Task returns the identification of the environment task. The function Activation_Is_Complete returns true if the task concerned has finished activation. Moreover, if Activation_Is_Complete is applied to the environment task then it indicates whether all library items of the partition have been elaborated.

A major new facility is the introduction of subpools. This is an extensive subject so we give only an overview. The general idea is that one wants to manage heaps with different lifetimes. It is often the case that an access type is declared at library level but various groups of objects of the type are declared and so could be reclaimed at a more nested level. This is done by splitting a pool into separately reclaimable subpools. This is far safer and often cheaper than trying to associate lifetimes with individual objects.

A new child package of System.Storage_Pools is declared thus

```
package System.Storage_Pools.Subpools is
  pragma Preelaborate(Subpools);

  type Root_Storage_Pool_With_Subpools is abstract new Root_Storage_Pool with private;

  type Root_Subpool is abstract tagged limited private;

  type Subpool_Handle is access all Root_Subpool'Class;
    for Subpool_Handle'Storage_Size use 0;

  function Create_Subpool(Pool: in out Root_Storage_Pool_With_Subpools)
                             return not null Subpool_Handle is abstract;

  function Pool_Of_Subpool (Subpool: not null Subpool_Handle) return access
                             Root_Storage_Pool_With_Subpools'Class;

  procedure Set_Pool_Of_Subpool(Subpool: not null Subpool_Handle;
                             To: in out Root_Storage_Pool_With_Subpools'Class);

  procedure Allocate_From_Subpool(Pool: in out Root_Storage_Pool_With_Subpools;
                             Storage_Address: out Address;
                             Size_In_Storage_Elements: in Storage_Count;
                             Alignment: in Storage_Count;
                             Subpool: in not null Subpool_Handle) is abstract
    with Pre'Class => Pool_Of_Subpool(Subpool) = Pool'Access;

  procedure Deallocate_Subpool(Pool: in out Root_Storage_Pool_With_Subpools;
                             Subpool: in out Subpool_Handle) is abstract
    with Pre'Class => Pool_Of_Subpool(Subpool) = Pool'Access;

  function Default_Subpool_For_Pool(Pool: in out Root_Storage_Pool_With_Subpools)
                             return not null Subpool_Handle;

  overriding
  procedure Allocate(Pool: in out Root_Storage_Pool_With_Subpools;
                    Storage_Address: out Address;
                    Size_In_Storage_Elements: in Storage_Count;
                    Alignment: in Storage_Count);

  overriding
  procedure Deallocate( ... ) is null;
```

```
    overriding
    function Storage_Size(Pool: Root_Storage_Pool_With_Subpools) return Storage_Count is
            (Storage_Count'Last);

private
        ...          -- not specified by the language
    end System.Storage_Pools.Subpools;
```

If we wish to declare a storage pool that can have subpools then rather than declare an object of the type Root_Storage_Pool in the package System.Storage_Pools we have to declare an object of the derived type Root_Storage_Pool_With_Subpools declared in the child package.

The type Root_Storage_Pool_With_Subpools inherits operations Allocate, Deallocate and Storage_Size from the parent type. Remember that Allocate and Deallocate are automatically called by the compiled code when items are allocated and deallocated. In the case of subpools we don't need Deallocate to do anything so it is null. The function Storage_Size determines the value of the attribute Storage_Size and is given by a function expression.

Subpools are separately reclaimable parts of a storage pool and are identified and manipulated by objects of the type Subpool_Handle (these are access values). We can create a subpool by a call of Create_Subpool. So we might have (assuming appropriate with and use clauses)

```
    package My_Pools is
        type Pond(Size: Storage_Count) is new Root_Storage_Pool_With_Subpools with private;

        subtype My_Handle is Subpool_Handle;

        ...
```

and then

```
        My_Pool: Pond(Size => 1000);

        Puddle: My_Handle := Create_Subpool(My_Pool);
```

The implementation of Create_Subpool should call

```
        Set_Pool_Of_Subpool(Puddle, My_Pool);
```

before returning the handle. This enables various checks to be made.

In order to allocate an object of type T from a subpool, we have to use a new form of allocator. But first we must ensure that T is associated with the pool itself. So we might write

```
    type T_Ptr is access T;
    for T_Ptr'Storage_Pool use My_Pool;
```

And then to allocate an object from the subpool identified by the handle Puddle we write

```
    X := new (Puddle) T'( ... );
```

where the subpool handle is given in parentheses following new.

Of course we don't have to allocate all such objects from a specified subpool since we can still write

```
    Y := new T'( ... );
```

and the object will be allocated from the parent pool My_Pool. It is actually allocated from a default subpool in the parent pool and this is determined by writing a suitable body for the function Default_Subpool_For_Pool and this is called automatically by the allocation mechanism. Note that in effect the whole of the pool is divided into subpools one of which may be the default subpool. If we don't provide an overriding body for Default_Subpool_For_Pool then Program_Error is raised. (Note that this function has a parameter of mode in out for reasons that need not bother us.)

The implementation carries out various checks. For example, it will check that a handle refers to a subpool of the correct pool by calling the function Pool_Of_Subpool. Both this function and Set_Pool_Of_Subpool are provided by the Ada implementation and typically do not need to be overridden by the implementer of a particular type derived from Root_Storage_Pool_ With_Subpools.

In the case of allocation from a subpool, the procedure Allocate_From_Subpool rather than Allocate is automatically called. Note the precondition to check that all is well.

It will be recalled that for normal storage pools, Deallocate is automatically called from an instance of Unchecked_Deallocation. In the case of subpools the general idea is that we get rid of the whole subpool rather than individual items in it. Accordingly, Deallocate does nothing as mentioned earlier and there is no Deallocate_From_Subpool. Instead we have to write a suitable implementation of Deallocate_Subpool. Note again the precondition to check that the subpool belongs to the pool.

Deallocate_Subpool is called automatically as a consequence of calling the following library procedure

```
with System.Storage_Pools.Subpools;
use System.Storage_Pools.Subpools;
procedure Ada.Unchecked_Deallocate_Subpool(Subpool: in out Subpool_Handle);
```

So when we have finished with the subpool Puddle we can write

```
Unchecked_Dellocate_Subpool(Puddle);
```

and the handle becomes null. Appropriate finalization also takes place.

In summary, the writer of a subpool implementation typically only has to provide Create_Subpool, Allocate_From_Subpool and Deallocate_Subpool since the other subprograms are provided by the Ada implementation of the package System.Storage_Pools.Subpools and can be inherited unchanged.

An example of an implementation will be found in subclause 13.11.6 of the RM. This shows an implementation of a Mark/Release pool in a package MR_Pool. Readers are invited to create variants called perhaps Miss_Pool and Dr_Pool!

Further control over the use of storage pools (nothing to do with subpools) is provided by the ability to define our own default storage pool as mentioned in the Introduction. Thus we can write (and completing our Happy Family of Pools)

```
pragma Default_Storage_Pool(Master_Pool);
```

and then all allocation within the scope of the pragma will be from Master_Pool unless a different specific pool is given for a type. This could be done by using an attribute definition clause thus

```
type Cell_Ptr is access Cell;
   for Cell_Ptr'Storage_Pool use Cell_Ptr_Pool;
```

or by using an aspect specification thus

```
type Cell_Ptr is access Cell
   with Storage_Pool => Cell_Ptr_Pool;
```

A pragma Default_Storage_Pool can be overridden by another one so that for example all allocation in a package (and its children) is from another pool.

The default pool can be specified as **null** thus

```
pragma Default_Storage_Pool(null);
```

and this prevents any allocation from standard pools.

Allocation normally occurs from the default pool unless a specific pool has been given for a type. But there are two exceptions, one concerns access parameter allocation and the other concerns coextensions; in these cases allocation uses a pool that depends upon the context.

Thus in the case of the procedure Proc discussed above, a call such as

```
P.Proc(new Integer'(10));
```

might allocate the space in a secret pool created on the fly and that secret pool might be placed on the stack.

Such allocation can be prevented by two more specific restrictions. They are

pragma Restriction(No_Access_Parameter_Allocators);

and

pragma Restriction(No_Coextensions);

These two pragmas plus using the restriction Default_Storage_Pool with **null** ensure that all allocation is from user-defined pools.

6.5 Restrictions

Restrictions provide a valuable way of increasing security. Ada is a rich language and even richer with Ada 2012 and although individual features are straightforward, certain combinations can cause problems.

The new restrictions introduced into Ada 2012 have already been described in this or earlier chapters such as the Introduction. However, for convenience here is a complete list giving the annex where appropriate.

The new Restrictions identifiers are

No_Access_Parameter_Allocators	High-Integrity
No_Anonymous_Allocators	High-Integrity
No_Coextensions	High-Integrity
No_Implementation_Aspect_Specifications	
No_Implementation_Identifiers	
No_Implementation_Units	
No_Specification_Of_Aspect	
No_Standard_Allocators_After_Elaboration	Real-Time
No_Use_Of_Attribute	
No_Use_Of_Pragma	

Some of the new Restrictions identifiers are in the High-Integrity annex. They are

pragma Restrictions(No_Access_Parameter_Allocators);

pragma Restrictions(No_Anonymous_Allocators);

pragma Restrictions(No_Coextensions);

and these were discussed in the previous section.

In a similar vein there is one new restriction in the Real-Time annex, namely

pragma Restrictions(No_Standard_Allocators_After_Elaboration);

and this was also discussed in the previous section.

A number of restrictions prevent the use of implementation-defined features. They are

pragma Restrictions(No_Implementation_Aspect_Specifications);

pragma Restrictions(No_Implementation_Identifiers);

pragma Restrictions(No_Implementation_Units);

These do not apply to the whole partition but only to the compilation or environment concerned. This helps us to ensure that implementation dependent areas of a program are identified. They were discussed in the Introduction and join similar restrictions No_Implementation_Attributes and No_Implementation_Pragmas introduced in Ada 2005.

The restrictions on implementation-defined aspect specifications, attributes and pragmas are obvious but some clarification of what is meant by the restrictions on units and identifiers might be helpful.

It will be recalled that the predefined packages are Ada, System and Interfaces plus various children. In the so-called standard mode, implementations are not permitted to add their own child packages of Ada but can add grandchildren. Thus an implementation might add an additional container package called perhaps Ada.Containers.Slopbucket. If a program were to use this grandchild then clearly it would be unlikely to be portable to other implementations. Accordingly, giving the restriction No_Implementation_Units prevents such potential difficulties. Similarly, this restriction prevents the use of implementation-defined child units of System and Interfaces.

The restriction No_Implementation_Identifiers is more subtle. It will be recalled that several predefined packages are permitted to add implementation-defined identifiers. They are

Standard, System, Ada.Command_Line, Interfaces.C, Interfaces.C.Strings,
Interfaces.C.Pointers, Interfaces.COBOL, and Interfaces.Fortran.

Moreover, the following predefined packages only contain implementation-defined identifiers

Interfaces, System.Machine_Code, Ada.Directories.Information, Ada.Directories.Names,
and the packages Implementation nested in the queue containers.

The restriction No_Implementation_Identifiers prevents the use of any of these.

There is a slight subtlety regarding Long_Integer and Long_Float in Standard. The types Integer and Float must be provided. Types such as Short_Integer and Long_Long_Float may be provided but are definitely considered to be implementation-defined and so excluded by the restriction on implementation identifiers. However, Long_Integer and Long_Float should be provided (if the hardware is capable) and so are considered to be predefined and not covered by the restriction. Nevertheless, an implementation on a specialized small machine might not provide them.

Finally, there are restrictions preventing the use of particular facilities

pragma Restrictions(No_Specification_Of_Aspect => X);

pragma Restrictions(No_Use_Of_Attribute => X);

pragma Restrictions(No_Use_Of_Pragma => X);

where X is the name of a specific aspect, attribute or pragma respectively. They are similar to the restriction No_Dependence introduced in Ada 2005. They apply to a complete partition.

Note that No_Specification_Of_Aspect prevents the specification of an aspect by any means. Remember that some aspects can be specified by an aspect specification or by a pragma or by an attribute definition clause. Thus we mentioned above that a storage pool could be given by an attribute definition clause thus

```
    type Cell_Ptr is access Cell;
      for Cell_Ptr'Storage_Pool use Cell_Ptr_Pool;
```

or by using an aspect specification thus

```
    type Cell_Ptr is access Cell
      with Storage_Pool => Cell_Ptr_Pool;
```

Writing

```
    pragma Restrictions(No_Specification_Of_Aspect => Storage_Pool);
```

prevents both of these whereas

```
    pragma Restrictions(No_Use_Of_Attribute => Strorage_Pool);
```

prevents only the first. Naturally, No_Use_Of_Attribute prevents both setting an attribute and reading it whereas No_Specification_Of_Aspect prevents just setting it. Thus we might want to read 'Size but prevent setting it.

Similarly

```
    pragma Restrictions(No_Specification_Of_Aspect => Pack);
```

prevents both

```
    type Flags is array (1 .. 8) of Boolean
      with Pack;
```

and

```
    type Flags is array (1 .. 8) of Boolean;
    pragma Pack(Flags);
```

whereas

```
    pragma Restrictions(No_Use_Of_Pragma => Pack);
```

prevents only the latter.

In summary, No_Specification_Of_Aspect does not mean No_Aspect_Specification (which does not exist).

Remember that several restrictions can be given in one pragma, so we might have

```
    pragma Restrictions(No_Use_Of_Pragma => P,
                        No_Use_Of_Attribute  => A);
```

As mentioned in the Introduction there is also a new profile No_Implementation_Extensions. This is specified by

```
    pragma Profile(No_Implementation_Extensions);
```

and is equivalent to writing

```
    pragma Restrictions(No_Implementation_Aspect_Specifications,
                        No_Implementation_Attributes,
                        No_Implementation_Identifiers,
                        No_Implementation_Pragmas,
                        No_Implementation_Units);
```

thus providing blanket security against writing programs that use language extensions. This profile is defined in the core language. The only other profile defined in Ada 2012 is Ravenscar which was introduced in Ada 2005 and is in the Real-Time systems annex. Remember that the pragma Profile is a configuration pragma.

Finally, those of a recursive nature might note that writing

    pragma Restrictions(No_Use_Of_Pragma => Restrictions);

is illegal (this prevents the risk that the compiler might melt down). More curiously, there is not a restriction No_Implementation_Restrictions. This might be because of similar concern regarding what would happen with its recursive use.

6.6 Miscellanea

A number of improvements do not neatly fit into any other section of this book and so are lumped together here.

The first four are in fact binding interpretations and thus apply to Ada 2005 as well.

First, nominal subtypes are defined for enumeration literals and attribute references so that all names now have a nominal subtype.

This is clearly a matter for the language lawyer rather than the happy programmer. Consider the following weird example

    subtype S **is** Integer **range** 1 .. 10;

    ...

    case S'Last **is**
      when 0 =>   -- ????

This is clearly nonsense. However, Ada 2005 does not define a nominal subtype for attributes such as S'Last and so we cannot determine whether 0 is allowed as a discrete choice. The language definition is tidied up to cover such cases.

The second gap in Ada 2005 concerns intrinsic subprograms. Remember that intrinsic subprograms are functions such as "+" on the type Integer that only exist in the mind of the compiler. Clearly they have no address. The following is added to the RM:

    The prefix of X'Address shall not statically denote a subprogram that has convention Intrinsic. X'Address raises Program_Error if X denotes a subprogram that has convention Intrinsic.

The dynamic check is needed because of the possibility of passing an intrinsic operation as a generic parameter.

The third of these binding gems concerns the package Ada.Calendar. The problem is that Calendar.Time is not well-defined when a time zone change occurs as for example when Daylight Saving Time is introduced or removed. Thus operations involving several time values (such as subtraction) might give the "correct" answer or might be an hour adrift. The conclusion reached was simply to admit that it is not defined so the wording is slightly changed.

Another problem with the wording in Ada 2005 is that the sign of the difference between local time and UTC as returned by UTC_Offset is not clearly defined. The sign is clarified so that for example UTC_Offset is negative in the American continent.

There is another problem with the package Calendar which will need to be addressed at some time (probably long after the author is dead). Much effort was exerted in Ada 2005 to cope with leap seconds. These arise because the angular velocity of rotation of the Earth is gradually slowing down. In earlier epochs when measurements of time were not accurate this did not matter. However, we now have atomic clocks and the slowdown is significant so that clocks are adjusted by one second as necessary and these are known as leap seconds.

But leap seconds are under threat. There is a move to suggest that tiny adjustments of one second are not worth the effort and that we should wait until the time is a whole hour wrong. A simple adjustment similar to that with which we are familiar with Daylight Saving changes is all that is needed. In other words we will have a leap hour every now and then. Indeed, if leap seconds occur about once a year as they have done on average since 1972 then a leap hour will be needed sometime in the 37th century. This will probably need to be addressed in Ada 3620 or so.

The final binding interpretation concerns class wide types and generics. An annoyance was recently discovered concerning the use of indefinite container packages such as

```
generic
  type Index_Type is range <>;
  type Element_Type(<>) is private;
  with function "=" (Left, Right: Element_Type) return Boolean is <>;
package Ada.Containers.Indefinite_Vectors is
  ...
```

We can instantiate this with an indefinite type such as String by writing perhaps

```
package String_Vectors is
  new Containers.Indefinite_Vectors(Positive, String);
```

The third actual parameter can be omitted because the predefined operation "=" on the type String exists and does what we want.

Class wide types are another example of indefinite types. Thus we might like to create a vector container whose elements are a mixture of objects of types Circle, Square, Triangle and so on. Assuming these are all descended from the abstract type Object we want to instantiate with the class wide type Object'Class.

However, unlike String, class wide types such as Object'Class do not have a predefined equals (class wide types do not themselves have any predefined primitive operations). This is annoying since the derived types Circle, Square, and Triangle (being just records) do have a predefined equals.

So we have to write something like

```
function Equal(L, R: Object'Class) is
begin
  return L = R;
end Equal;
```

Note that this will dispatch to the predefined equals of the type of the objects passed as parameters. They both must be of the same type of course; we cannot compare a Circle to a Triangle (anymore than we can compare Thee to a Summer's Day).

So we can now instantiate thus

```
package Object_Vectors is
  new Containers.Indefinite_Vectors(Positive, Object'Class, Equal);
```

Note irritatingly that we cannot write Equal as just "=" because this causes ambiguities.

This is all a bit annoying and so in Ada 2012, the required "=" is automatically created, we do not have to declare Equal, and the instantiation can simply be

```
package Object_Vectors is
  new Containers.Indefinite_Vectors(Positive, Object'Class);
```

This improvement is also a binding interpretation and so applies to Ada 2005 as well.

A more serious matter is the problem of the composability of equality. In Ada 2005, tagged record types compose but untagged record types do not. If we define a new type (a record type, array type or a derived type) then equality is defined in terms of equality for its various components. However, the behaviour of components which are records is different in Ada 2005 according to whether they are tagged or not. If a component is tagged then the primitive operation is used (which might have been redefined), whereas for an untagged type, predefined equality is used even though it might have been overridden.

Consider

```ada
type Tagrec is tagged
  record
    X1: Integer;
    X2: Integer;
  end record;

type Untagrec is
  record
    Y1: Integer;
    Y2: Integer;
  end record;

type Index is range 0 .. 64;

...

function "=" (L, R: Tagrec) return Boolean is
begin
  return L.X1 = R.X1;            -- compare only first component
end;

function "=" (L, R: Untagrec) return Boolean is
begin
  return L.Y1 = R.Y1;           -- compare only first component
end;

function "=" (L, R: Index) return Boolean is
begin
  raise Havoc;
  return False;
end;

...

type Mixed is
  record
    T: Tagrec;
    U: Untagrec;
    Z: Index;
  end record;
```

Here we have a type Mixed whose components are of a tagged record type Tagrec, an untagged record type Untagrec, and an elementary type Index. Moreover, we have redefined equality for these types.

In Ada 2005, the equality for the type Mixed uses the redefined equality for the component T but the predefined equality for U and Z. Thus it compares T.X1, U.Y1 and U.Y2 and does not raise Havoc.

In Ada 83, the predefined equality always emerged for the components of arrays and records. One reason was to avoid confusion if an inconsistency arose between "=", "<" and "<=". Remember that many elementary types and certain array types have predefined "<" as well as "=" and to get the relationship messed up would have been confusing.

However, Ada 95 introduced tagged record types and inheritance of operations became an important feature. So it seemed natural that if a structure (array or record) had components of a tagged type and equality for that tagged type had been redefined then it would be natural to expect that equality for the structure should use the redefined equality. But, fearful of introducing an incompatibility, the rule for untagged record types was left unchanged so that predefined equality reemerges.

On reflection, this difference between tagged and untagged records was surprising and so has been changed in Ada 2012 so that all record types behave the same way and use the primitive operation. This is often called composability of equality so we can say that in Ada 2012, record types always compose for equality. Remember that this only applies to records; components which are of array types and elementary types continue to use predefined equality. So in Ada 2012, equality for Mixed only compares T.X1 and U.Y1 but not U.Y2 and still does not raise Havoc.

Concern for incompatibility and inconsistency has been allayed by a deep analysis of a number of programs. No nasties were revealed and in the only cases where it made a difference it was clear that the original behaviour was in fact wrong.

The final miscellaneum (singular of miscellanea?) concerns tags.

The package Ada.Tags defines various functions operating on tags. For example

> **function** Parent_Tag(T: Tag) **return** Tag;

returns the tag of the parent unless the type has no parent in which case it returns No_Tag.

A type can be abstract or concrete. The key property of abstract types is that we cannot have an object of an abstract type. If we wish to create an object using Generic_Dispatching_Constructor and the tag passed as a parameter represents an abstract type then Tag_Error is raised. It would, of course, be far better to check whether a tag represents an abstract type before using Generic_Dispatching_Constructor.

However, given a tag, there is no sensible way in Ada 2005 to find out whether it represents an abstract type. We could attempt to create an object and see if it raises Tag_Error. If it doesn't then we know that it was not abstract but we have also created an object we maybe didn't want; if it does raise Tag_Error then it might or might not have been abstract since there are other reasons for the exception being raised. Either way this is madness.

In Ada 2012, we can test the tag using the new function

> **function** Is_Abstract(T: Tag) **return** Boolean;

which is added near the end of the package Ada.Tags just before the declaration of the exception Tag_Error.

7 Predefined library

This chapter describes various relatively minor improvements to the predefined library in Ada 2012. The major changes concerning the container library will be described in the chapter.

7.1 Overview of changes

The WG9 guidance document [1] does not specifically identify problems in this area other than through a general exhortation to remedy shortcomings.

We have already discussed the additional library packages in the area of tasking and real-time in Chapter 5. There are also many additional library packages concerning containers and these will be discussed in the next chapter. The following Ada issues cover the relevant changes in other areas and are described in detail in this chapter:

   1   Bounded containers and other container issues

   31   Add a From parameter to Find_Token

   49   Extend file name processing in Ada.Directories

   127   Adding locale capabilities

   137   String encoding package

   185   Wide_Character and Wide_Wide_Character classification and folding

   233   Questions on locales

   266   Use latest version of ISO/IEC 10646

   283   Stream_IO should be preelaborated

   285   Defaulted environment variable queries

   286   Internationalization of Ada

These changes can be grouped as follows.

A number of enhancements concern strings and characters. These include comprehensive new packages to support conversions between strings (and wide strings and wide-wide strings) and the UTF-8 and UTF-16 encodings (137). It is important to note that Ada 2012 directly supports source code in UTF-8 (286). Additional facilities are also provided for the classification of characters and new packages added for similar operations on wide characters and wide wide characters (185, 266). A minor change is the provision of a further procedure Find_Token with an additional parameter giving the start of the search (31).

The file name processing in Ada.Directories is enhanced to overcome some shortcomings (49).

A new package is added to enable a program to identify the locale in which it is being used (127, 233).

There are a number of additional facilities regarding hashing and case insensitive comparisons. The hashing issues really relate to containers but are briefly mentioned here for completeness (1, 286).

Finally, other improvements are that the package Ada.Streams.Stream_IO is now preelaborated (283) and that an additional function Value is added to the package Ada.Environment_Variables (285).

7.2   Strings and characters

Ada 95 added a number of packages for manipulating strings and characters. Three child packages of Ada.Strings enable the manipulation of fixed length, bounded and unbounded strings. They are Ada.Strings.Fixed, Ada.Strings.Bounded and Ada.Strings.Unbounded. The packages have many subprograms with similar facilities.

In particular there are functions Index and Index_Non_Blank which search through a string and return the index of the first character satisfying some criteria and procedures Find_Token which search through a string and find the first instance of a slice satisfying some other criteria.

As originally defined in Ada 95 these subprograms all started the search at the beginning of the string. This proved to be somewhat inconvenient and so in Ada 2005, versions of the functions Index and Index_Non_Blank with an extra parameter From were added to enable the search to be started at any position. However, the fact that versions of the procedures Find_Token with an extra parameter From should also have been added was overlooked. This is remedied in Ada 2012.

So in Ada 2012 corresponding additional subprograms Find_Token are added to the appropriate packages. They are

```
procedure Find_Token(Source: in String;
                     Set: in Maps.Character_Set;
                     From: in Positive;
                     Test: in Membership;
                     First: out Positive;
                     Last: out Natural);

procedure Find_Token(Source: in Bounded_String;
                     Set: in Maps.Character_Set;
                     From: in Positive;
                     Test: in Membership;
                     First: out Positive;
                     Last: out Natural);

procedure Find_Token(Source: in Unbounded_String;
                     Set: in Maps.Character_Set;
                     From: in Positive;
                     Test: in Membership;
                     First: out Positive;
                     Last: out Natural);
```

Note also that the wording for Find_Token is modified to make it clear that the values of First and Last identify the longest possible slice starting at From. If no characters satisfy the criteria then First is set to From and Last is set to zero.

The existing procedures Find_Token are now defined as calls of the new ones with From set to Source'First.

The encodings UTF-8 and UTF-16 are now widely used but Ada 2005 provides no mechanisms to convert between these encodings and the types String, Wide_String, and Wide_Wide_String.

The encoding UTF-8 works in terms of raw bytes and is straightforward; it is defined in Annex D of ISO/IEC 10646. However, UTF-16 comes in two forms according to whether the arrangement of two bytes into a 16-bit word uses big-endian or little-endian packing. So there are two forms UTF-16BE and UTF-16LE; they are defined in Annex C of ISO/IEC 10646.

The different encodings can be distinguished by a special value known as a BOM (Byte Order Mark) at the start of the string. So we have BOM_8, BOM_16BE, BOM_16LE, and just BOM_16 (for wide strings).

To support these encodings, Ada 2012 includes the following five new packages

Ada.Strings.UTF_Encoding
Ada.Strings.UTF_Encoding.Conversions
Ada.Strings.UTF_Encoding.Strings
Ada.Strings.UTF_Encoding.Wide_Strings
Ada.Strings.UTF_Encoding.Wide_Wide_Strings

The first package declares items that are used by the other packages. It is

```
package Ada.Strings.UTF_Encoding is
  pragma Pure(UTF_Encoding);

  type Encoding_Scheme is (UTF_8, UTF_16BE, UTF_16LE);

  subtype UTF_String is String;
  subtype UTF_8_String is String;
  subtype UTF_16_Wide_String is Wide_String;

  Encoding_Error: exception;

  BOM_8: constant UTF_8_String :=
                      Character'Val(16#EF#) &
                      Character'Val(16#BB#) &
                      Character'Val(16#BF#);

  BOM_16BE: constant UTF_String :=
                      Character'Val(16#FE#) &
                      Character'Val(16#FF#);

  BOM_16LE: constant UTF_String :=
                      Character'Val(16#FF#) &
                      Character'Val(16#FE#);

  BOM_16: constant UTF_16_Wide_String := (1 => Wide_Character'Val(16#FEFF#);

  function Encoding(Item: UTF_String; Default: Encoding_Scheme := UTF_8)
                                             return Encoding_Scheme;

end Ada.Strings.UTF_Encoding;
```

Note that the encoded forms are actually still held in objects of type String or Wide_String. However, in order to aid understanding, the subtypes UTF_String, UTF_8_String and UTF_16_Wide_String are introduced and these should be used when referring to objects holding the encoded forms.

The type Encoding_Scheme defines the various schemes. Note that an encoded string might or might not start with the identifying BOM; it is optional. The function Encoding takes a UTF_String (that is a plain old string), checks the BOM if present and returns the value of Encoding_Scheme identifying the scheme. If there is no BOM then it returns the value of the parameter Default which itself by default is UTF_8.

Note carefully that the function Encoding does not do any encoding – that is done be functions Encode in the other packages which will be described in a moment. Note also that there is no corresponding function Encoding for wide strings; that is because there is only one relevant scheme corresponding to UTF_16_Wide_String, namely that with BOM_16.

We will now look at the other packages. The package UTF_Encoding.Strings contains functions Encode and Decode which convert between the raw type String and the UTF forms. Similar packages apply to wide and wide wide strings. The package UTF_Encoding.Conversions contains functions Convert which convert between the various UTF forms.

The package for the type String is

```
package Ada.Strings.UTF_Encoding.Strings is
  pragma Pure(Strings);

  function Encode(Item: String; Output_Scheme: Encoding_Scheme;
                        Output_BOM: Boolean := False) return UTF_String;

  function Encode(Item: String; Output_BOM: Boolean := False) return UTF_8_String;

  function Encode(Item: String; Output_BOM: Boolean := False)
                                                    return UTF_16_Wide_String;

  function Decode(Item: UTF_String; Input_Scheme: Encoding_Scheme) return String;

  function Decode(Item: UTF_8_String) return String;

  function Decode(Item: UTF_16_Wide_String) return String;

end Ada.Strings.UTF_Encoding.Strings;
```

The functions Encode take a string and return it encoded. The first function has a parameter Output_Scheme which determines whether the encoding is to be to UTF_8, UTF_16BE or UTF_16LE. The second function is provided as a convenience for the common case of encoding to UTF_8 and the third function is necessary for encoding to UTF_16_Wide_String. In all cases there is a final optional parameter indicating whether or not an appropriate BOM is to be placed at the start of the encoded string.

The functions Decode do the reverse. Thus the first function takes a value of subtype UTF_String and a parameter Input_Scheme giving the scheme to be used and returns the decoded string. If a BOM is present which does not match the Input_Scheme, then the exception Encoding_Error is raised. The second function is a convenience for the common case of decoding from UTF_8 and the third function is necessary for decoding from UTF_16_Wide_String; again, if a BOM is present that does not match the expected scheme then Encoding_Error is raised.

In all cases all the strings returned have a lower bound of 1.

The packages UTF_Encoding.Wide_Strings and UTF_Encoding.Wide_Wide_Strings are identical except that the type String is replaced by Wide_String or Wide_Wide_String throughout.

Finally, the package for converting between the various UTF forms is as follows

```
package Ada.Strings.UTF_Encoding.Conversions is
  pragma Pure(Conversions);

  function Convert(Item: UTF_String;
              Input_Scheme: Encoding_Scheme
              Output_Scheme: Encoding_Scheme;
              Output_BOM: Boolean := False) return UTF_String;

  function Convert(Item: UTF_String;
              Input_Scheme: Encoding_Scheme
              Output_BOM: Boolean := False) return UTF_16_Wide_String;

  function Convert(Item: UTF_8_String;
              Output_BOM: Boolean := False) return UTF_16_Wide_String;
```

```
    function Convert(Item: UTF_16_Wide_String;
                      Output_Scheme: Encoding_Scheme;
                      Output_BOM: Boolean := False) return UTF_String;

    function Convert(Item: UTF_16_Wide_String;
                      Output_BOM: Boolean := False) return UTF_8_String;

  end Ada.Strings.UTF_Encoding.Conversions;
```

The purpose of these should be obvious. The first converts between encodings held as strings with parameters indicating both the Input_Scheme and the Output_Scheme. If the input string has a BOM that does not match the Input_Scheme then the exception Encoding_Error is raised. The final optional parameter indicates whether or not an appropriate BOM is to be placed at the start of the converted string.

The other functions convert between UTF encodings held as strings and wide strings. Two give the explicit Input_Scheme or Output_Scheme and two are provided for convenience for the common case of UTF_8.

The final topic in this section concerns the classification and conversion of characters and strings. The package Ada.Characters.Handling was introduced in Ada 95; this contains various classification functions such as Is_Lower, Is_Digit and so on. This package also contains functions such as To_Upper and To_Lower which convert characters to upper case or lower case.

These facilities are extended in Ada 2012 by the addition of a few more classification functions in the package Ada.Characters.Handling plus similar packages named Ada.Wide_Characters.Handling for dealing with wide characters and Ada.Wide_Wide_Characters.Handling for dealing with wide wide characters.

It should be noticed that these new packages are children of Ada.Wide_Characters and Ada.Wide_Wide_Characters respectively. These packages were introduced in Ada 2005 but are empty other than for pragmas Pure.

The additional character classification functions in Ada.Characters.Handling are

```
    function Is_Line_Terminator ...
    function Is_Mark(Item: Character) return Boolean;
    function Is_Other ...
    function Is_Punctuation_Connector ...
    function Is_Space ...
```

In each case they have a single parameter Item of type Character and return a result of type Boolean.

The meanings are as follows

Is_Line_Terminator – returns True if Item is one of Line_Feed (10), Line_Tabulation (11), Form_Feed (12), Carriage_Return (13), or Next_Line (133).

Is_Mark – always returns False.

Is_Other_Format – returns True if Item is Soft_Hyphen (171).

Is_Punctuation_Connector – returns True if Item is Low_Line (95); this is often known as Underscore.

Is_Space – returns True if Item is Space (32) or No_Break_Space (160).

Readers might feel that Is_Mark is a foolish waste of time. However, it is introduced because the corresponding functions in the new packages for wide and wide wide characters can return True.

An important point is that these classifications enable a compiler to analyze Ada source code without direct reference to the definition of ISO/IEC 10646. Note further that case insensitive text comparison which is useful for the analysis of identifiers is now provided by new functions described in Section 5 below.

The new package Wide_Characters.Handling is very similar to the package Characters.Handling (as modified by the additional functions just described) with Character and String everywhere replaced by Wide_Character and Wide_String. However, there are no functions corresponding to Is_Basic, Is_ISO_646, To_Basic and To_ISO_646. In the case of Is_Basic this is because there is no categorization of Basic in 10646. In the case of ISO-646 it is not really necessary because it would seem rather unlikely that one would want to check a wide character WC to see if it was one of the 7-bit ISO-646 set. In any event, one could always write

> WC in Wide_Characters'POS(0) .. Wide_Characters'POS(127)

The package Wide_Characters.Handling also has the new function Character_Set_Version thus

> **function** Character_Set_Version **return** String;

The string returned identifies the version of the character set standard being used. Typically it will include either "10646:" or "Unicode". The reason for introducing this function is because the categorization of some wide characters depends upon the version of 10646 or Unicode being used. So rather than specifying that the package uses a particular set (which might be a nuisance in the future if the character set standard changes), it seemed more appropriate to enable the program to find out exactly which version is being used. For most programs, it won't matter at all of course.

Note that there is no corresponding function in Ada.Characters.Handling. This is because the set used for the type Character is frozen as at 1995 and the classification functions defined for the type Character are frozen as well (and so do not now exactly match 10646 which has since evolved). It might be that classifications for wide and ever wider characters might change in the future for some obscure characters but the programmer can rest assured that Character is for ever reliable.

So Wide_Characters.Handling in essence is

```
package Ada.Wide_Characters.Handling is
  pragma Pure(Handling);

  function Character_Set_Version return String;

  function Is_Control(Item: Wide_Character) return Boolean;

  ...        -- and so on

  function To_Upper(Item: Wide_String) return Wide_String);

end Ada.Wide_Characters.Handling;
```

The new package Wide_Wide_Characters.Handling is the same as Wide_Characters.Handling with Wide_Character and Wide_String replaced by Wide_Wide_Character and Wide_Wide_String throughout.

7.3 Directories

The package Ada.Directories was introduced in Ada 2005. However, experience with its use has revealed a number of shortcomings which are rectified in Ada 2012.

Three specific problems are mentioned in AI-49.

First, it is not possible to concatenate a root directory such as "/tmp" with a relative pathname such as "public/file.txt" using the procedure Compose thus

The_Path: String := Compose("/tmp", "public/file.txt");

This is because the second parameter of Compose has to be a simple name such as just "file" if there is no extension parameter. If we supply the extension parameter thus

The_Path: String := Compose("/tmp", "public/file", "txt");

then the second parameter has to be just a base name such as "public".

Another problem is that there is no sensible way to check for a root directory. Thus suppose the string S is a directory name and we want to see whether it is just a root such as "/" in Unix then the only thing that we can do is write

Containing_Directory(S)

which will raise Use_Error which is somewhat ugly.

We could write **if** S ="/" **then** but this would not be portable from Unix to other systems. Indeed, the whole purpose of providing file name operations in Ada.Directories is so that file names can be manipulated in an abstract manner without fiddling with text strings.

The third problem concerns case sensitivity. At the moment it is not possible to write portable programs because operating systems differ in their approach to this issue.

This last problem is solved by adding an enumeration type Name_Case_Kind and a function Name_Case_Equivalence to the file and directory name operations of the package Ada.Directories. So in outline we now have

```
with Ada.IO_Exceptions;  with Ada.Calendar;
package Ada.Directories is

   ...

   -- File and directory name operations:

   function Full_Name(Name: String) return String;
   function Simple_Name(Name: String) return String;
   function Containing_Directory(Name: String) return String;
   function Extension(Name: String) return String;
   function Base_Name(Name: String) return String;
   function Compose(Containing_Directory: String := "";
                    Name: String;
                    Extension: String := "") return String;

   type Name_Case_Kind := (Unknown, Case_Sensitive, Case_Insensitive, Case_Preserving);
   function Name_Case_Equivalence(Name: String) return Name_Case_Kind;

   -- File and directory queries:

   -- and so on

end Ada.Directories;
```

The function Name_Case_Equivalence returns the file name equivalence rule for the directory containing Name. It raises Name_Error if Name is not a Full_Name.

It returns Case_Sensitive if file names that differ only in the case of letters are considered to be different. If file names that differ only in the case of letters are considered to be the same, then it returns Case_Preserving if the name has the case of the file name used when a file is created and Case_Insensitive otherwise. It returns Unknown if the name equivalence rule is not known.

We thus see that Unix and Linux are **Case_Sensitive**, Windows is **Case_Preserving**, and historic systems such as CP/M and early MS/DOS were **Case_Insensitive**.

The other problems are solved by the introduction of an optional child package for dealing with systems with hierarchical file names. Its specification is

package Ada.Directories.Hierarchical_File_Names **is**

> **function** Is_Simple_Name(Name: String) **return** Boolean;
> **function** Is_Root_Directory_Name(Name: String) **return** Boolean;
> **function** Is_Parent_Directory_Name(Name: String) **return** Boolean;
> **function** Is_Current_Directory_Name(Name: String) **return** Boolean;
> **function** Is_Full_Name(Name: String) **return** Boolean;
> **function** Is_Relative_Name(Name: String) **return** Boolean;
>
> **function** Simple_Name(Name: String) **renames** Ada.Directories.Simple_Name;
> **function** Containing_Directory(Name: String)
>   **renames** Ada.Directories.Containing_Directory;
>
> **function** Initial_Directory(Name: String) **return** String;
> **function** Relative_Name(Name: String) **return** String;
>
> **function** Compose(Directory: String := "";
>   Relative_Name: String;
>   Extension: String := "") **return** String;

end Ada.Directories.Hierarchical_File_Names;

Note that the six functions, Full_Name, Simple_Name, Containing_Directory, Extension, Base_Name and Compose in the existing package Ada.Directories just manipulate strings representing file names and do not in any way interact with the actual external file system. The same applies to many of the new functions such as Is_Simple_Name.

In particular, Is_Root_Directory_Name returns true if the string is syntactically a root and so cannot be decomposed further. It therefore solves the second problem mentioned earlier. Thus

Is_Root_Directory_Name("/")

returns true for Unix. In the case of Windows "C:\" and "\\Computer\Share" are roots.

The function Is_Parent_Directory_Name returns true if and only if the Name is ".." for both Unix and Windows.

The function Is_Current_Directory_Name returns true if and only if Name is "." for both Unix and Windows.

The function Is_Full_Name returns true if the leftmost part of Name is a root whereas Is_Relative_Name returns true if Name allows identification of an external file but is not a full name. Note that relative names include simple names as a special case.

The functions Simple_Name and Containing_Directory are just renamings of those in the parent package and are provided for convenience.

Finally, the functions Initial_Directory, Relative_Name and Compose provide the ability to manipulate relative file names and so solve the problem with Compose mentioned at the beginning of this section.

Thus Initial_Directory returns the leftmost directory part of Name and Relative_Name returns the entire full name apart from the initial directory portion.

If we apply Relative_Name to a string that is just a single part of a name then Name_Error is raised. In particular this happens if Relative_Name is applied to a name which is a Simple Name, a Root Directory Name, a Parent Directory Name or a Current Directory Name.

The function Compose is much like Compose in the parent package except that it takes a relative name rather than a simple name. It therefore allows us to write

```
The_Path: String := Compose("/tmp", "public/file.txt");
```

as required.

The result of calling Compose is a full name if Is_Full_Name(Directory) is true and otherwise is a relative name.

7.4 Locale

When writing portable software it is often necessary to know the locality in which the software is to be run. Two key items are the country and the language (human language that is, not programming language).

To enable this to be done, Ada 2012 includes the following package

```
package Ada.Locales is
    pragma Preelaborate(Locales);
    pragma Remote_Types(Locales);

    type Language_Code is array (1 .. 3) of Character range 'a' .. 'z';

    type Country_Code is array (1 .. 2) of Character range 'A' .. 'Z';

    Language_Unknown: constant Language_Code := "und";
    Country_Unknown: constant Country_Code := "ZZ";

    function Language return Language_Code;
    function Country return Country-Code;

end Ada.Locales;
```

The various country codes and language codes are defined in ISO/IEC 3166-1:2006 and ISO/IEC 639-3:2007 respectively.

Knowledge of the locale is important for writing programs where the convention for certain information varies. Thus in giving a date we might want to add the name of the day of the week and clearly in order to do this we need to know what language to use. An earlier (really grotesque) attempt at providing this information introduced a host of packages addressing many issues. However, it was decided that for simplicity and indeed reliability all that is really needed is to know the language to use and the country.

Canada is interesting in that it has just one country code ("CA") but two language codes ("eng" and "fra"). In Quebec, a decimal value for a million dollars and one cent is written as $1.000.000,01 whereas in English language parts it is written as $1,000,000.01 with the comma and stop interchanged.

Sometimes, several locales might be available on a target. Some environments define a system locale and a locale for the current user. In the case of an Ada program the active locale is the one associated with the partition of the current task.

Finally, note that subsequent to ISO standardization, some serious difficulty was found in the practical use of the types Language_Code and Country_Code. Accordingly, they have been changed as described in Section 9.5 of the Epilogue.

7.5 Hashing and comparison

New library functions are added for case insensitive comparisons and hashing. Thus we have

> **function** Ada.Strings.Equal_Case_Insensitive(Left, Right: String) **return** Boolean;
> **pragma** Pure(Ada.Strings.Equal_Case_Insensitive);

This simply compares the strings Left and Right for equality but ignoring case. Thus

> Equal_Case_Insensitive("Pig", "PIG")

is true.

The function Ada.Strings.Fixed.Equal_Case_Insensitive is a renaming of the above. There are also similar functions Ada.Strings.Bounded.Equal_Case_Insensitive for bounded strings and Ada.Strings.Unbounded.Equal_Case_Insensitive for unbounded strings. And, as expected, there are similar functions for wide and wide wide versions.

Note that the comparison for strings can be phrased as convert to lower case and then compare. But this does not always work for wide and wide wide strings. The proper terminology is "apply locale-independent case folding and then compare".

Although it comes to the same thing for Latin-1 characters there are problems with some character sets where there is not a one-one correspondence between lower case and upper case. This used to apply to English with the two forms of lower case S and still applies to the corresponding letters in Greek where the upper case character is Σ and there are two lower case versions namely σ and ς. So

> Ada.Wide_Strings.Equal_Case_Insensitive("ΣΟΣ", "σος")

returns true. Note that if we just convert to lower case first rather than applying case folding then it would not be true.

Furthermore there is also

> **function** Ada.Strings.Less_Case_Insensitive(Left, Right: String) **return** Boolean;
> **pragma** Pure(Ada.Strings.Less_Case_Insensitive);

which does a lexicographic comparison.

As expected there are similar functions for fixed, bounded and unbounded strings and, naturally, for wide and wide wide versions.

Ada 2005 has functions for hashing such as

> **with** Ada.Containers;
> **function** Ada.Strings.Hash(Key: String) **return** Containers.Hash_Type;

Ada 2012 adds case insensitive versions as well such as

> **with** Ada.Containers;
> **function** Ada.Strings.Hash_Case_Insensitive(Key: String) **return** Containers.Hash_Type;

There are also fixed, bounded and unbounded versions and the inevitable wide and wide wide ones as well.

7.6 Miscellanea

The first item is that the package Stream_IO should be marked as preelaborated. So in Ada 2012 it now begins

> **with** Ada.IO_Exceptions;
> **package** Ada.Streams.Stream_IO **is**

> **pragma** Preelaborate(Stream_IO);
>
> ...

The reason for making this change concerns the use of input–output in preelaborated packages. The normal input–output packages such as Text_IO are not preelaborated and so cannot be used in packages that are themselves preelaborated. This makes preelaborated packages awkward to debug since they cannot do straightforward output for monitoring purposes. To make packages such as Text_IO preelaborated is essentially impossible because they involve local state. However, no such problem exists with Stream_IO, and so making it preelaborated means that it can be used to implement simple logging facilities in other preelaborated packages.

In principle, there is a similar problem with pure units. But they cannot change state anyway and so cannot do output since that changes the state of the environment. They just have to be written correctly in the first place.

(I have been told that there are naughty ways around this with pure packages but I will not contaminate innocent minds with the details.)

The package Ada.Environment_Variables was introduced in Ada 2005 as follows

> **package** Ada.Environment_Variables **is**
> **pragma** Preelaborate(Environment_Variables);
>
> **function** Value(Name: String) **return** String;
> **function** Exists(Name: String) **return** Boolean;
> **procedure** Set(Name: **in** String; Value: **in** String);
> **procedure** Clear(Name: **in** String);
> **procedure** Clear;
>
> **procedure** Iterate(Process: **not null access procedure** (Name, Value: **in** String));
>
> **end** Ada.Environment_Variables;

If we do not know whether an environment variable exists then we can check by calling Exists prior to accessing the current value. Thus a program might be running in an environment where we might expect an environment variable "Ada" whose value indicates the version of Ada currently supported.

So as in [7] we might write

> **if not** Exists("Ada") **then**
> **raise** Horror;
> **end if**;
> Put("Current Ada is ");
> Put_Line(Value("Ada"));

But this raises a possible race condition. After determining that Ada does exist some malevolent process (such as another Ada task or an external human agent) might execute Clear("Ada"); and then the call of Value("Ada") will raise Constraint_Error.

The other race condition might arise as well. Having decided that Ada does not exist and so taking remedial action some kindly process might have created Ada.

These problems are overcome in Ada 2012 by the introduction of an additional function Value with a default parameter

> **function** Value(Name: String; Default: String);

Calling this version of Value returns the value of the variable if it exists and otherwise returns the value of Default.

8 Containers

This chapter describes improvements to the predefined container library in Ada 2012.

8.1 Overview of changes

The WG9 guidance document [1] specifically says that attention should be paid to

improving the use and functionality of the predefined containers.

The predefined containers were introduced in Ada 2005 and experience with their use revealed a number of areas where they could be improved.

The following Ada Issues cover the relevant changes and are described in detail in this chapter.

1 Bounded containers and other container issues

69 Holder container

136 Multiway tree container

139 Syntactic sugar for access, containers & iterators

159 Queue containers

184 Compatibility of streaming of containers

212 Accessors and iterators for Ada.Containers

251 Problems with queue containers

These changes can be grouped as follows.

The existing containers are unbounded and generally require dynamic storage management to be performed behind the scenes. However, for high-integrity systems, such dynamic management is often unacceptable. Accordingly, bounded versions of all the existing containers are added (1).

A number of facilities are added to make important operations on containers more elegant. These are the updating of individual elements of a container and iteration over a container (139, 212).

Ada 2005 introduced containers for the manipulation of lists and it was expected that this would provide a basis for manipulating trees. However, this proved not to be the case, so specific containers are added for the manipulation of multiway trees (136). There are versions for unbounded indefinite and unbounded definite trees and for bounded definite trees.

A further new kind of container is just for single indefinite objects and is known as the holder container (69).

A range of containers are added for manipulating queues with defined behaviour regarding multiple task access to the queues (159, 251).

The Ada 2005 container library also introduced sorting procedures for constrained and unconstrained arrays. An additional more general sorting mechanism is added in Ada 2012 (1).

Finally, an oversight regarding the streaming of containers is corrected (184).

8.2 Bounded and unbounded containers

It is perhaps worth starting this discussion by summarizing the containers introduced in Ada 2005. First, there is a parent package Ada.Containers which simply declares the types Hash_Type and Count_Type.

Then there are six containers for definite objects, namely (abbreviating the prefix Ada.Containers to just A.C)

A.C.Vectors
A.C.Doubly_Linked_Lists
A.C.Hashed_Maps
A.C.Ordered_Maps
A.C.Hashed_Sets
A.C.Ordered_Sets

The declarations of these six containers all start with

generic
    ...
    type Element_Type **is private**;
    ...
    package Ada.Containers.XXX...

and we see that the type Element_Type has to be definite. There are also containers for the manipulation of indefinite types whose names are

A.C.Indefinite_Vectors
A.C.Indefinite_Doubly_Linked_Lists
A.C.Indefinite_Hashed_Maps
A.C.Indefinite_Ordered_Maps
A.C.Indefinite_Hashed_Sets
A.C.Indefinite_Ordered_Sets

and these are very similar to the definite containers except that the formal type Element_Type is now declared as

    type Element_Type(<>) **is private**;

so that the actual type can be indefinite such as String.

Finally, there are two generic packages for sorting arrays namely

A.C.Generic_Array_Sort
A.C.Generic_Constrained_Array_Sort

which apply to unconstrained and constrained arrays respectively.

The first change in Ada 2012 is that the parent package Ada.Containers now includes the declaration of the exception Capacity_Error so that it becomes

package Ada.Containers **is**
    pragma Pure(Containers);

    type Hash_Type **is mod** *implementation-defined*;
    type Count_Type **is range** 0 .. *implementation-defined*;
    Capacity_Error: **exception**;

end Ada.Containers;

The names of the new containers with bounded storage capacity are

A.C.Bounded_Vectors
A.C.Bounded_Doubly_Linked_Lists
A.C.Bounded_Hashed_Maps
A.C.Bounded_Ordered_Maps

A.C.Bounded_Hashed_Sets
A.C.Bounded_Ordered_Sets

The facilities of the bounded containers are almost identical to those of the original unbounded ones so that converting a program using one form to the other is relatively straightforward. The key point of the bounded ones is that storage management is guaranteed (implementation advice really) not to use features such as pointers or dynamic allocation and therefore can be used in high-integrity or safety-critical applications.

The major differences between the packages naturally concern their capacity. In the case of the bounded packages the types such as Vector have discriminants thus

type Vector(Capacity: Count_Type) **is tagged private**;

whereas in the original packages the type Vector is simply

type Vector **is tagged private**;

The other types in the bounded packages are

type List(Capacity: Count_Type) **is tagged private**;

type Map(Capacity: Count_Type; Modulus: Hash_Type) **is tagged private**;

type Map(Capacity: Count_Type) **is tagged private**;

type Set(Capacity: Count_Type; Modulus: Hash_Type) **is tagged private**;

type Set(Capacity: Count_Type) **is tagged private**;

Note that the types for hashed maps and sets have an extra discriminant to set the modulus; this will be explained in a moment.

Remember that the types Count_Type and Hash_Type are declared in the parent package Ada.Containers shown above.

When a bounded container is declared, its capacity is set once and for all by the discriminant and cannot be changed. If we subsequently add more elements to the container than it can hold then the exception Capacity_Error is raised.

If we are using a bounded container and want to make it larger then we cannot. But what we can do is create another bounded container with a larger capacity and copy the values from the old container to the new one. Remember that we can check the number of items in a container by calling the function Length.

So we might have a sequence such as

```
My_List: List(100);
   ...                                -- use my list
if Length(My_List) > 90 then         -- Gosh, nearly full
   ...
   declare
      My_Big_List: List := Copy(My_List, 200);
   begin
      ...
```

The specification of the function Copy is

function Copy(Source: List; Capacity: Count_Type := 0) **return** List;

If the parameter Capacity is not specified (or is given as zero) then the capacity of the copied list is the same as the length of Source.

If the given value of Capacity is larger than (or equal to) the length of the Source (as in our example) then the returned list has this capacity and the various elements are copied. If we foolishly supply a value which is less than the length of Source then Capacity_Error is naturally raised. Remember that a discriminant can be set by an initial value.

Note that if we write

```
declare
  My_Copied_List: List := My_List;
begin
```

then My_Copied_List will have the same capacity as My_List because discriminants are copied as well as the contents.

In order to make it easier to move from the bounded form to the unbounded form, a function Copy is added to the unbounded containers as well although it does not need a parameter Capacity in the case of lists and ordered maps and sets. So in the case of the list container it is simply

```
function Copy(Source: List) return List;          -- unbounded
```

Similar unification between bounded and unbounded forms occurs with assignment. In Ada 2005, if we have two lists L and M, then we can simply write

```
L := M;
```

and the whole structure is copied (including all its management stuff). Note that this will almost certainly require that the value of L be finalized which might be a nuisance. Such an assignment with discriminated types needs to check the discriminants as well (and raises Constraint_Error if they are different). This is a nuisance because although the capacities might not be the same, the destination L might have plenty of room for the actual elements in the source M.

This is all rather bothersome and so procedures Assign are added to both unbounded and bounded containers which simply copy the element values. Thus in both case we have

```
procedure Assign(Target: in out List; Source: in List);
```

In the bounded case, if the length of Source is greater than the capacity of Target, then Capacity_Error is raised. In the unbounded case, the structure is automatically extended.

It might be recalled that in Ada 2005, lists and ordered maps and sets do not explicitly have a notion of capacity. It is in their very nature that they automatically extend as required. However, in the case of vectors and hashed maps and sets (which have a notion of indexing) taking a purely automatic approach could lead to lots of extensions and copying so the notion of capacity was introduced. The capacity can be set by calling

```
procedure Reserve_Capacity(Container: in out Vector; Capacity: in Count_Type);
```

and the current value of the capacity can be ascertained by calling

```
function Capacity(Container: Vector) return Count_Type;
```

which naturally returns the current capacity. Note that Length(V) cannot exceed Capacity(V) but might be much less.

If we add items to a vector whose length and capacity are the same then no harm is done. The capacity will be expanded automatically by effectively calling Reserve_Capacity internally. So the user does not need to set the capacity although not doing so might result in poorer performance.

The above refers to the existing unbounded forms and is unchanged in Ada 2012. For uniformity the new bounded forms for vectors and hashed maps and sets also declare a procedure Reserve_Capacity. However, since the capacity cannot be changed for the bounded forms it simply checks that the value of the parameter Capacity does not exceed the actual capacity of the container; if it does then Capacity_Error is raised and otherwise it does nothing. There is of course also a function Capacity for bounded vectors and hashed maps and sets which simply returns the fixed value of the capacity.

Many operations add elements to a container. For unbounded containers, they are automatically extended as necessary as just explained. For the bounded containers, if an operation would cause the capacity to be exceeded then Capacity_Error is raised.

There are a number of other differences between the unbounded and bounded containers. The original unbounded containers have pragma Preelaborate whereas the new bounded containers have pragma Pure.

The bounded containers for hashed maps and hashed sets are treated somewhat differently to those for the corresponding unbounded containers regarding hashing.

In the case of unbounded containers, the hashing function to be used is left to the user and is provided as an actual generic parameter. For example, in the case of hashed sets, the package specification begins

```
generic
  type Element_Type is private;
  with function Hash(Element: Element_Type) return Hash_Type;
  with function Equivalent_Elements(Left, Right: Element_Type) return Boolean;
  with function "=" (Left, Right: Element_Type) return Boolean is <>;
package Ada.Containers.Hashed_Sets is
  pragma Preelaborate(Hashed_Sets);
```

What the implementation actually does with the hash function is entirely up to the implementation The value returned is in the range of Hash_Type which is a modular type declared in the root package Ada.Containers. The implementation will typically then map this value onto the current range of the capacity in some way. If the unbounded container becomes nearly full then the capacity will be automatically extended and a new mapping will be required; this in turn is likely to require the existing contents to be rehashed. None of this is visible to the user.

In the case of the new bounded containers, these problems do not arise since the capacity is fixed. Moreover, the modulus to be used for the mapping is given when the container is declared since the type has discriminants thus

```
type Set(Capacity: Count_Type; Modulus: Hash_Type) is tagged private;
```

The user can then choose the modulus explicitly or alternatively can use the additional function Default_Modulus whose specification is

```
function Default_Modulus(Capacity: Count_Type) return Hash_Type;
```

This returns an implementation defined value for the number of distinct hash values to be used for the given capacity. Thus we can write

```
My_Set: Set(Capacity => My_Cap; Modulus => Default_Modulus(My_Cap));
```

Moreover, for these bounded hashed maps and sets, the function Copy has an extra parameter thus

```
function Copy(Source: Set; Capacity: Count_Type := 0; Modulus: Hash_Type := 0)
                                                        return Set;
```

If the capacity is given as zero then the newly returned set has the same capacity as the length of Source as mentioned above. If the modulus is given as zero then the value to be used is obtained by applying Default_Modulus to the new capacity.

As mentioned in Section 7.5 on Hashing and comparison, Ada 2012 introduces additional functions for hashing strings (fixed, bounded and unbounded) to provide for case insensitive, wide and wide wide situations.

Finally, note that there are no bounded containers for indefinite types. This is because the size of an object of an indefinite type (such as String) is generally not known and so indefinite types need some dynamic storage management. However, the whole point of introducing bounded containers was to avoid such management.

8.3   Iterating and updating containers

This topic was largely covered in Chapter 6 on Iterators and Pools which introduced the generic package Ada.Iterator.Interfaces whose specification is

```
generic
  type Cursor;
  with function Has_Element(Position: Cursor) return Boolean;
package Ada.Iterator_Interfaces is
  pragma Pure(Iterator_Interfaces);

  type Forward_Iterator is limited interface;
  function First(Object: Forward_Iterator) return Cursor is abstract;
  function Next(Object: Forward_Iterator; Position: Cursor) return Cursor is abstract;

  type Reversible_Iterator is limited interface and Forward_Iterator;
  function Last(Object: Reversible_Iterator) return Cursor is abstract;
  function Previous(Object: Reversible_Iterator; Position: Cursor) return Cursor is abstract;

end Ada.Iterator_Interfaces;
```

This generic package is used by both existing and new container packages. For illustration we consider the list container Ada.Containers.Doubly_Linked_Lists. Here is its specification giving all new and changed material in full (marked -- 12) and identifying most existing entities by comment only.

```
with Ada.Iterator_Interfaces;                                                    -- 12
generic
  type Element_Type is private;
  with function "=" (Left, Right: Element_Type) return Boolean is <>;
package Ada.Containers.Doubly_Linked_Lists is
  pragma Preelaborate(Doubly_Linked_Lists);
  pragma Remote_Types(Doubly_Linked_Lists)                                       -- 12

  type List is tagged private                                                    -- 12
    with Constant_Indexing => Constant_Reference,
         Variable_Indexing => Reference,
         Default_Iterator => Iterate,
         Iterator_Element => Element_Type;
  pragma Preelaborable_Initialization(List);
  type Cursor is private;
  pragma Preelaborable_Initialization(Cursor);
  Empty_List: constant List;
  No_Element: constant Cursor;

  function Has_Element(Position: Cursor) return Boolean;                         -- moved 12
```

```
      package List_Iterator_Interfaces is                                -- 12
         new Ada.Iterator_Interfaces(Cursor, Has_Element);

      ...      -- functions "=", Length, Is_Empty, Clear, Element
      ...      -- procedures Replace_, Query_, Update_Element

      type Constant_Reference_Type                                       -- 12
                   (Element: not null access constant Element_Type) is private
         with Implicit_Dereference => Element;

      type Reference_Type                                                -- 12
                   (Element: not null access Element_Type) is private
         with Implicit_Dereference => Element;

      function Constant_Reference                                        -- 12
                   (Container: aliased in List; Position: in Cursor)
                                      return Constant_Reference_Type;

      function Reference                                                 -- 12
                   (Container: aliased in out List; Position: in Cursor)
                                      return Reference_Type;

      procedure Assign(Target: in out List; Source: in List);            -- 12

      function Copy(Source: List) return List;                           -- 12

      ...      -- Move, Insert, Prepend, Append,
      ...      -- Delete, Delete_First, Delete_Last,
      ...      -- Reverse_Elements, Swap, Swap_Links, Splice,
      ...      -- First, First_Element, Last, Last_Element,
      ...      -- Next, Previous, Find, Reverse_Find,
      ...      -- Contains, Iterate, Reverse_Iterate

      function Iterate(Container: in List)                               -- 12
                   return List_Iterator_Interfaces.Reversible_Iterator'Class;

      function Iterate(Container: in List; Start: in Cursor)             -- 12
                   return List_Iterator_Interfaces.Reversible_Iterator'Class;

      ...      -- generic package Generic_Sorting
   private
      ... -- not specified by the language
   end Ada.Containers.Doubly_Linked_Lists;
```

Note that the function Has_Element has been moved. In Ada 2005 it was declared towards the end between Contains and Iterate. It has been moved so that it can be used as an actual parameter in the declaration of List_Iterator_Interfaces using the instantiation of Ada.Iterator_Interfaces.

It will be recalled from Section 6.3 on Iteration, that in Ada 2012 we can simply write

```
   for C in The_List.Iterate loop
      ...                              -- do something via cursor C
   end loop;
```

or even

```
   for E of The_List loop
      ...                              -- do something to Element E
   end loop;
```

rather than the laborious and error prone

```
C: The_List.Cursor;
E: Twin;
F: Forward_Iterator'Class := The_List.Iterate;
   ...
C := F.First;
loop
  exit when not The_List.Has_Element(C);
  E := The_List.Element(C);
     ...                           -- do something to E
  C := F.Next(C);
end loop;
```

Note that in the case of

```
for C in The_List.Iterate loop
   ...                            -- do something via cursor C
end loop;
```

we are not permitted to assign to C since that would upset the mechanism of the loop. There is an analogy with the traditional loop statement. If we write

```
for K in A'Range loop
  A(K) := 0;
end loop;
```

then the language prevents us from making a direct assignment to the loop parameter K.

If we write

```
for E of The_List loop
   ...                            -- do something to Element E
end loop;
```

then we can change the element E unless The_List has been declared as constant.

It will be recalled that subprograms Replace_Element, Query_Element and Update_Element are defined for all containers in Ada 2005. Query_Element and Update_Element permit *in situ* operations. Thus in order to find the value of some component Q of an element of The_List identified by cursor C we can write either

```
X := Element(C).Q;
```

or we can first declare a slave procedure

```
procedure Get_Q(E: in Element_Type) is
begin
  X := E.Q;
end Get_Q;
```

and then call Query_Element thus

```
Query_Element(C, Get_Q'Access);
```

The advantage of the former is that it is easy but it could be slow because it copies the whole element which could be enormous. The advantage of the latter is that it does not copy the element; its disadvantage is that it is somewhat incomprehensible.

In Ada 2012, we can do much better. The type List now has new functions Reference and Constant_Reference, so we can write for example

    X := The_List.Constant_Reference(C).Q;

This works because the function Constant_Reference returns a value of Constant_Reference_Type and this moreover has aspect Implicit_Dereference whose value is Element.

However, we can simplify this even more because the type List has aspects Constant_Indexing and Variable_Indexing which refer to the functions Constant_Reference and Reference. The result is that we can simply write

    X := The_List(C).Q;   -- *gosh that's better*

which is a lot better than calling Query_Element.

Similarly, if we just want to update the component Q of some element given by a cursor C, then in Ada 2005 we either have to create a whole new element with the new value for Q and then use Replace_Element thus

    Temp: E_Type := Element(C);
    ...
    Temp.Q := X;
    Replace_Element(The_List, C, Temp);

or declare a slave procedure and use Update_Element thus

    procedure Put_Q(E: **in out** Element_Type) **is**
    begin
      E.Q := X;
    end Put_Q;
    Update_Element(The_List, C, Put_Q'Access);

Again the first is slow, the second is gruesome (well, they are both gruesome really).

In Ada 2012 we simply write

    The_List(C).Q := X;   -- *gosh again*

which implicitly uses the aspect Variable_Indexing to call the function Reference which gives access to the element.

It will be remembered that there are dire warnings in Ada 2005 about tampering with elements and cursors. Thus we must not use Update_Element (that is via Put_Q in the example above) to do other things such as add new elements.

Although tampering is still possible in Ada 2012; the new features discourage it. Thus if we write

    The_List(C).Q := X;

rather than calling Update_Element then no tampering can occur (unless X is some gruesome function).

Similarly if we write

    for C **in** My_Container **loop**
      ...
      Delete(My_Container, Position => C);   --*illegal*
      ...
    end loop;

then we are prevented from madness since the parameter Position of Delete is of mode **in out** and this is not matched by the loop parameter C which is a constant. However, if we write the loop out using First and Next as illustrated earlier then we could get into trouble.

8.4 Multiway tree containers

Three new containers are added for multiway trees; two correspond to the existing unbounded definite and unbounded indefinite forms for existing structures such as Lists and Maps in Ada 2005. There is also a bounded form corresponding to the newly introduced bounded containers for the existing structures discussed above. As expected their names are

A.C.Multiway_Trees
A.C.Indefinite_Multiway_Trees
A.C.Bounded_Multiway_Trees

These containers have all the operations required to operate on a tree structure where each node can have multiple child nodes to any depth. Thus there are operations on subtrees, the ability to find siblings, to insert and remove children and so on. It will be noted that many of the operations on trees are similar to corresponding operations on lists.

We will look in detail at the unbounded definite form by giving its specification interspersed with some explanation. It starts with the usual generic parameters.

```
with Ada.Iterator_Interfaces;
generic
  type Element_Type is private;
  with function "=" (Left, Right: Element_Type) return Boolean is <>;
package Ada.Containers.Multiway_Trees is
  pragma Preelaborate(Multiway_Trees);
  pragma Remote_Types(Multiway_Trees);

  type Tree is tagged private
    with Constant_Indexing => Constant_Reference,
         Variable_Indexing => Reference,
         Default_Iterator => Iterate,
         Iterator_Element => Element_Type;
  pragma Preelaborable_Initialization(Tree);
  type Cursor is private;
  pragma Preelaborable_Initialization(Cursor);
  Empty_Tree: constant Tree;
  No_Element: constant Cursor;

  function Has_Element(Position: Cursor) return Boolean;
  package Tree_Iterator_Interfaces is
    new Ada.Iterator_Interfaces(Cursor, Has_Element);
```

This is much as expected and follows the same pattern as the start of the list container in the previous section.

```
  function Equal_Subtree(Left_Position: Cursor; Right_Position: Cursor) return Boolean;
  function "=" (Left, Right: Tree) return Boolean;

  function Is_Empty(Container: Tree) return Boolean;

  function Node_Count(Container: Tree) return Count_Type;
  function Subtree_Node_Count(Position: Cursor) return Count_Type;

  function Depth(Position: Cursor) return Count_Type;
```

function Is_Root(Position: Cursor) **return** Boolean;
function Is_Leaf(Position: Cursor) **return** Boolean;
function Root(Container: Tree) **return** Cursor;
procedure Clear(Container: **in out** Tree);

A tree consists of a set of nodes linked together in a hierarchical manner. Nodes are identified as usual by the value of a cursor. Nodes can have one or more child nodes; the children are ordered so that there is a first child and a last child. Nodes with the same parent are siblings. One node is the root of the tree. If a node has no children then it is a leaf node.

All nodes other than the root node have an associated element whose type is Element_Type. The whole purpose of the tree is of course to give access to these element values in a structured manner.

The function "=" compares two trees and returns true if and only if they have the same structure of nodes and corresponding nodes have the same values as determined by the generic parameter "=" for comparing elements. Similarly, the function Equal_Subtree compares two subtrees.

The function Node_Count gives the number of nodes in a tree. All trees have at least one node, the root node. The function Is_Empty returns true only if the tree consists of just this root node. Note that A_Tree = Empty_Tree, Node_Count(A_Tree) = 1 and Is_Empty(A_Tree) always have the same value. The function Subtree_Node_Count returns the number of nodes in the subtree identified by the cursor. If the cursor value is No_Element then the result is zero.

The functions Is_Root and Is_Leaf indicate whether a node is the root or a leaf respectively. If a tree is empty and so consists of just a root node then that node is both the root and a leaf so both functions return true.

The function Depth returns 1 if the node is the root, and otherwise indicates the number of ancestor nodes. Thus a node which is an immediate child of the root has depth equal to 2. The function Root returns the cursor designating the root of a tree. The procedure Clear removes all elements from the tree so that it consists just of a root node.

function Element(Position: Cursor) **return** Element_Type;

procedure Replace_Element(Container: **in out** Tree;
                               Position: **in** Cursor;
                               New_Item: **in** Element_Type);

procedure Query_Element(Position: **in** Cursor;
          Process : **not null access procedure** (Element: **in** Element_Type));

procedure Update_Element(Container: **in out** Tree; Position: **in** Cursor;
          Process: **not null access procedure** (Element: **in out** Element_Type));

These subprograms have the expected behaviour similar to other containers.

type Constant Reference_Type(Element: **not null access constant** Element_Type)
                                                                      is private
    with Implicit_Dereference => Element;

type Reference_Type(Element: **not null access** Element_Type) **is private**
    with Implicit_Dereference => Element;

function Constant_Reference(Container: **aliased in** Tree; Position: **in** Cursor)
                                                return Constant_Reference_Type;

function Reference(Container: **aliased in out** Tree; Position: **in** Cursor)
                                                return Reference_Type;

These types and functions are similar to those for the other containers and were explained in Section 6.4 on Iteration and also in the previous section.

>   **procedure** Assign(Target: **in out** Tree; Source: **in** Tree);

>   **function** Copy(Source: Tree) **return** Tree;

>   **procedure** Move(Target: **in out** Tree; Source: **in out** Tree);

The subprograms Assign and Copy behave as expected and were explained in Section 8.2 on Bounded and unbounded containers. The procedure Move moves all the nodes from the source to the target after first clearing the target; it does not make copies of the elements so after the operation the source only has a root node.

>   **procedure** Delete_Leaf(Container: **in out** Tree; Position: **in out** Cursor);

>   **procedure** Delete_Subtree(Container: **in out** Tree; Position: **in out** Cursor);

>   **procedure** Swap(Container: **in out** Tree; I, J: **in** Cursor);

The procedures Delete_Leaf and Delete_Subtree check that the cursor value designates a node of the container and raise Program_Error if it does not. Program_Error is also raised if Position designates the root node and so cannot be removed. In the case of Delete_Leaf, if the node has any children then Constraint_Error is raised. The appropriate nodes are then deleted and Position is set to No_Element.

The procedure Swap interchanges the values in the two elements denoted by the two cursors. The elements must be in the given container (and must not denote the root) otherwise Program_Error is raised.

>   **function** Find(Container: Tree; Item: Element_Type) **return** Cursor;

>   **function** Find_In_Subtree(Item: Element_Type; Position: Cursor) **return** Cursor;

>   **function** Ancestor_Find(Item: Element_Type; Position: Cursor) **return** Cursor;

>   **function** Contains(Container: Tree; Item: Element_Type) **return** Boolean;

These search for an element in the container with the given value Item. The function Contains returns false if the item is not found; the other functions return No_Element if the item is not found. The function Find searches the whole tree starting at the root node, Find_In_Subtree searches the subtree rooted at the node given by Position including the node itself; these searches are in depth-first order. The function Ancestor_Find searches upwards through the ancestors of the node given by Position including the node itself.

Depth-first order is explained at the end of the section.

>   **procedure** Iterate(Container: **in** Tree;
>   Process: **not null access procedure** (Position: **in** Cursor));

>   **procedure** Iterate_Subtree(Position: **in** Cursor;
>   Process: **not null access procedure** (Position: **in** Cursor));

These apply the procedure designated by the parameter Process to each element of the whole tree or the subtree. This includes the node at the subtree but not at the root; iteration is in depth-first order.

>   **function** Iterate(Container: **in** Tree) **return** Tree_Iterator_Interfaces.Forward_Iterator'Class;

>   **function** Iterate_Subtree(Position: **in** Cursor)
>   **return** Tree_Iterator_Interfaces.Forward_Iterator'Class;

The first of these is called if we write

```
    for C in The_Tree.Iterate loop
        ...                          -- do something via cursor C
    end loop;
```

and iterates over the whole tree in the usual depth-first order. In order to iterate over a subtree we write

```
    for C in The_Tree.Iterate(S) loop
        ...                          -- do something via cursor C
    end loop;
```

and this iterates over the subtree rooted at the cursor position given by S.

If we use the other new form of loop using **of** thus

```
    for E of The_Tree loop
        ...                          -- do something to element E
    end loop;
```

then this also calls Iterate since the aspect Default_Iterator of the type Tree (see above) is Iterate. However, we cannot iterate over a subtree using this mechanism.

```
    function Child_Count(Parent: Cursor) return Count_Type;

    function Child_Depth(Parent, Child: Cursor) return Count_Type;
```

The function Child_Count returns the number of child nodes of the node denoted by Parent. This count covers immediate children only and not grandchildren.

The function Child_Depth indicates how many ancestors there are from Child to Parent. If Child is an immediate child of Parent then the result is 1; if it is a grandchild then 2 and so on.

```
    procedure Insert_Child(Container: in out Tree;
                           Parent: in Cursor;
                           Before: in Cursor;
                           New_Item: in Element_Type;
                           Count: in Count_Type := 1);

    procedure Insert_Child(Container: in out Tree;
                           Parent: in Cursor;
                           Before: in Cursor;
                           New_Item: in Element_Type;
                           Position: out Cursor;
                           Count: in Count_Type := 1);

    procedure Insert_Child(Container: in out Tree;
                           Parent: in Cursor;
                           Before: in Cursor;
                           Position: out Cursor;
                           Count: in Count_Type := 1);
```

These three procedures enable one or more new child nodes to be inserted. The parent node is given by Parent. If Parent already has children then the new nodes are inserted before the child node identified by Before; if Before is No_Element then the new nodes are inserted after all existing children. The second procedure is similar to the first but also returns a cursor to the first of the added nodes. The third is like the second but the new elements take their default values. Note the default value of one for the number of new nodes.

```
procedure Prepend_Child(Container: in out Tree;
                        Parent: in Cursor;
                        New_Item: in Element_Type;
                        Count: in Count_Type := 1);

procedure Append_Child(Container: in out Tree;
                       Parent: in Cursor;
                       New_Item: in Element_Type;
                       Count: in Count_Type:= 1);
```

These insert the new children before or after any existing children.

```
procedure Delete_Children(Container: in out Tree;
                          Parent: in Cursor);
```

This procedure simply deletes all the children, grandchildren, and so on of the node designated by Parent.

```
procedure Copy_Subtree(Target: in out Tree;
                       Parent: in Cursor;
                       Before: in Cursor;
                       Source: in Cursor);
```

This copies the complete subtree rooted at Source into the tree denoted by Tree as a subtree of Parent at the place denoted by Before using the same rules as Insert_Child. Note that this makes a complete copy and creates new nodes with values equal to the corresponding existing nodes. Note also that Source might be within Tree but might not. There are the usual various checks.

```
procedure Splice_Subtree(Target: in out Tree;
                         Parent: in Cursor;
                         Before: in Cursor;
                         Source: in out Tree;
                         Position: in out Cursor);

procedure Splice_Subtree(Container: in out Tree;
                         Parent: in Cursor;
                         Before: in Cursor;
                         Position: in Cursor);

procedure Splice_Children(Target: in out Tree;
                          Target_Parent: in Cursor;
                          Before: in Cursor;
                          Source: in out Tree;
                          Source_Parent: in Cursor);

procedure Splice_Children(Container: in out Tree;
                          Target_Parent: in Cursor;
                          Before: in Cursor;
                          Source_Parent: in Cursor);
```

These are similar to the procedures Splice applying to lists. They enable nodes to be moved without copying. The destination is indicated by Parent or Target_Parent together with Before as usual indicating where the moved nodes are to be placed with respect to existing children of Parent or Target_Parent.

The first Splice_Subtree moves the subtree rooted at Position in the tree Source to be a child of Parent in the tree Target. Note that Position is updated to be the appropriate element of Target. We can use this procedure to move a subtree within a tree but an attempt to create circularities raises Program_Error.

The second Slice_Subtree is similar but only moves a subtree within a container. Again, circularities cannot be created.

The procedures Splice_Children are similar but move all the children and their descendants of Source_Parent to be children of Target_Parent.

```
function Parent(Position: Cursor) return Cursor;

function First_Child(Parent: Cursor) return Cursor;
function First_Child_Element(Parent: Cursor) return Element_Type;
function Last_Child(Parent: Cursor) return Cursor;
function Last_Child_Element(Parent: Cursor) return Element_Type;

function Next_Sibling(Position: Cursor) return Cursor;
function Previous_Sibling(Position: Cursor) return Cursor;
procedure Next_Sibling(Position: in out Cursor);
procedure Previous_Sibling(Position: in out Cursor);
```

Hopefully, the purpose of these is self-evident.

```
procedure Iterate_Children(Parent: in Cursor;
                    Process: not null access procedure (Position: in Cursor));

procedure Reverse_Iterate_Children(Parent : in Cursor;
                    Process: not null access procedure (Position: in Cursor));
```

These apply the procedure designated by the parameter Process to each child of the node given by Parent. The procedure Iterate_Children starts with the first child and ends with the last child whereas Reverse_Iterate_Children starts with the last child and ends with the first child. Note that these do not iterate over grandchildren.

```
function Iterate_Children(Container: in Tree; Parent: in Cursor) return
                    Tree_Iterator_Interfaces.Reversible_Iterator'Class;
```

This is called if we write

```
for C in Parent.Iterate_Children loop
    ...                            -- do something via cursor C
end loop;
```

and iterates over all the children from Parent.First_Child to Parent.Last_Child. Note that we could also insert **reverse** thus

```
for C in reverse Parent.Iterate_Children loop
    ...                            -- do something via cursor C
end loop;
```

in which case the iteration goes in reverse from Parent.Last_Child to Parent.First_Child. The observant reader will note that this function returns Reversible_Iterator'Class and so can go in either direction whereas the functions Iterate and Iterate_Subtree described earlier use Forward_Iterator'Class and cannot be reversed.

```
private
    ...                            -- not specified by the language
end Ada.Containers.Multiway_Trees;
```

The above descriptions have not described all the situations in which something can go wrong and so raise Constraint_Error or Program_Error. Generally, the former is raised if a source or target is No_Element; the latter is raised if a cursor does not belong to the appropriate tree. In particular, as mentioned above, an attempt to create an illegal tree such as one with circularities using Splice_Subtree raises Program_Error. Remember also that every tree has a root node but the root node has no element value; attempts to remove the root node or read its value or assign a value similarly raise Program_Error.

The containers for indefinite and bounded trees are much as expected.

In the case of the indefinite tree container the generic formal type is

```
type Element_Type(<>) is private;
```

The other significant difference is that the procedure Insert_Child without the parameter New_Item is omitted; this is because indefinite types do not have a default value.

In the case of the bounded tree container the changes are similar to those for the other containers. One change is that the package has pragma Pure; the other changes concern the capacity. The type Tree is

```
type Tree(Capacity: Count_Type) is tagged private;
```

and the function Copy is

```
function Copy(Source: Tree; Capacity: Count_Type := 0) return Tree;
```

And of course the exception Capacity_Error is raised in various circumstances.

Applications of trees are usually fairly complex. The tree structure for depicting the analysis of a program for a whole language such as even Ada 83 has an enormous variety of nodes corresponding to the various syntactic structures. And trees depicting human relationships are complex because of multiple marriages, divorces, illegitimacy and so on. So we content ourselves with a couple of small examples.

A tree representing a simple algebraic expression involving just the binary operations of addition, subtraction, multiplication and division applied to simple variables and real literals is straightforward. Nodes are of three kinds, those representing operations have two children giving the two operands, and those representing variables and literals have no children and so are leaf nodes.

We can declare the element type thus

```
type Operator is ('+', '–', '×', '/');
type Kind is (Op, Var, Lit);

type El(K: Kind) is
  record
    case K is
      when Op =>
        Fn: Operator;
      when Var =>
        V: Character;
      when Lit =>
        Val: Float;
    end case;
  end record;
```

Note that the variables are (as typically in mathematics) represented by single letters.

So the expression

$$(x + 3) \times (y - 4)$$

is represented by nodes with elements such as

(Op, 'x')
(Var, 'x')
(Lit, 3.0)

So now we can declare a suitable tree thus

package Expression_Trees **is**
  new Ada.Containers.Multiway_Trees(El);

use Expression_Trees;

My_Tree: Tree := Empty_Tree;

C: Cursor;

and then build it by the following statements

C := Root(My_Tree);

Insert_Child(Container => My_Tree,
           Parent => C,
           Before => No_Element,
           New_Item => (Op, 'x'),
           Position => C);

This puts in the first real node as a child of the root which is designated by the cursor C. There are no existing children so Before is No_Element. The New_Item is as mentioned earlier. Finally, the cursor C is changed to designate the position of the newly inserted node.

We can then insert the two children of this node which represent the mathematical operations + (plus) and – (minus).

Insert_Child(My_Tree, C, No_Element, (Op, '+'));
Insert_Child(My_Tree, C, No_Element, (Op, '–'));

These calls are to a different overloading of Insert_Child and have not changed the cursor. The second call also has Before equal to No_Element and so the second child goes after the first child.

We now change the cursor to that of the first newly inserted child and then insert its children which represent x and 3. Thus

C := First_Child(C);
Insert_Child(My_Tree, C, No_Element, (Var, 'x'));
Insert_Child(My_Tree, C, No_Element, (Lit, 3.0));

And then we can complete the tree by inserting the final two nodes thus

C := Next_Sibling(C);
Insert_Child(My_Tree, C, No_Element, (Var, 'y'));
Insert_Child(My_Tree, C, No_Element, (Lit, 4.0));

Of course a compiler will do all this recursively and keep track of the cursor rather more neatly than we have in this manual illustration.

The resulting tree should be as in Figure 1.

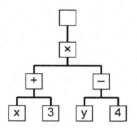

Figure 1   The expression tree

We can assume that the variables are held in an array which might be as follows

     subtype Variable_Name **is** Character **range** 'a' .. 'z';

     Variables: **array** (Variable_Name) **of** Float;

We can then evaluate the tree by a recursive function such as

```
function Eval(C: Cursor) return Float is
  E: El := Element(C);
  L, R: Float
begin
  case E.K is
    when Op =>
      L := Eval(First_Child(C));
      R := Eval(Last_Child(C));
      case E.Fn is
        when '+' => return (L+R);
        when '−' => return (L−R);
        when '×' => return (L*R);
        when '/' => return (L/R);
      end case;
    when Var =>
      return Variables(E.V);
    when Lit =>
      return E.Val;
  end case;
end Eval;
```

Finally, we obtain the value of the tree by

     X := Eval(First_Child(Root(My_Tree)));

Remember that the node at the root has no element so hence the call of First_Child.

An alternative approach would be to use tagged types with a different type for each kind of node rather than the variant record. This would be much more flexible and would have required the use of the unbounded indefinite container Ada.Containers.Indefinite_Multiway_Trees.

As a more human example we can consider the family tree of the Tudor Kings and Queens of England. We start with Henry VII, who had four children, Arthur, Margaret, Henry VIII and Mary. See Figure 2.

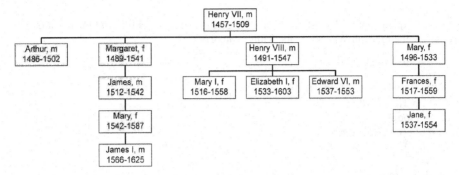

Figure 2   The Tudor tree

Arthur died young, Margaret married James IV of Scotland and had James (who was thus James V of Scotland), Henry VIII had three children, namely Edward VI, Mary I and Elizabeth I. And Mary had Frances. Henry VII was succeeded by Henry VIII and he was succeeded by his three children.

Remember the rules of primogeniture. The heir is the eldest son if there are sons; if not then the heir is the eldest daughter. If there are no offspring at all then we go back a generation and try again. Hence Edward VI became king despite being younger than Mary.

Since Edward, Mary and Elizabeth had no children we go back to the descendants of the other children of Henry VII. Margaret, her son James, and his daughter Mary Queen of Scots were all dead by then, so the throne of England went to the son of Mary who became James I of England and VI of Scotland and thus united the two thrones. So the Tudor line died with Elizabeth (Good Queen Bess).

Incidentally, Frances, the daughter of Mary, the fourth child of Henry VII, had a daughter, Lady Jane Grey; she was Queen for 9 days but lost her head over a row with Mary I.

Representing this is tricky, especially with people such as Henry VIII having so many wives. But the essence could be represented by a tree with a simple element type thus

```
type Person is
  record
    Name: String(1 .. 10);
    Sex: Gender;
    Birth: Date;
    Death: Date;
  end record;
```

With such a structure and the dates, starting from Henry VII and using the rules of primogeniture, one should be able to trace the monarchs (apart from poor Lady Jane Grey who would I am sure much rather not have been involved).

The overall tree structure is shown in Figure 2.

With the obvious connections we can define useful functions such as

```
function Are_Cousins(A, B: Cursor) return Boolean is
  (Parent(A) /= Parent (B) and then Parent(Parent(A)) = Parent(Parent(B)));
```

More of a challenge is to define a function Is_Successor using the rules described above. The reader can contemplate these and other family relationships and attempt to construct the Tudor tree.

Finally, an explanation of depth-first order. The general principle is that child nodes are visited in order before their parent. We can symbolically write this as

```
procedure Do_Node(N) is
begin
  for CN in N.First_Child .. N.Last_Child loop
    Do_Node(CN);
  end loop;
  if not N.Is_Root then
    Do_Element(N);
  end if;
end Do_Node;
```

and the whole thing is triggered by calling **Do_Node(Root)**. Remember that the root node has no element. The result is that the first element to be processed is that of the leftmost leaf.

Thus in the tree illustrated below in Figure 3, the elements are visited in order A, B, C, D, and so on. Note that the root has no element and so is not visited.

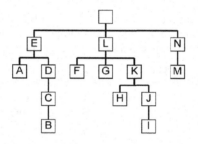

Figure 3   A tree showing depth-first order

8.5   The holder container

As mentioned in the Introduction, it is not possible to declare an object of an indefinite type that can hold any value of that type since the object becomes constrained by the mandatory initial value. Thus we can write

Pet: String := "dog";

We can assign "cat" to Pet but we cannot assign "rabbit" because it is too long.

This is overcome in Ada 2012 by the introduction of the holder container which can hold a single indefinite object. Its specification is

```
generic
  type Element_Type(<>) is private;
  with function "=" (Left, Right: Element_Type) return Boolean is <>;
package Ada.Containers.Indefinite_Holders is
  pragma Preelaborate(Indefinite_Holders);
  pragma Remote_Types(Indefinite_Holders);

  type Holder is tagged private;
  pragma Preelaborable_Initialization(Holder);
```

```
Empty_Holder: constant Holder;

function "=" (Left, Right: Holder) return Boolean;

function To_Holder(New_Item: Element_Type) return Holder;

function Is_Empty(Container: Holder) return Boolean;

procedure Clear(Container: in out Holder);

function Element(Container: Holder) return Element_Type;

procedure Replace_Element(Container: in out Holder; New_Item: in Element_Type);

procedure Query_Element(Container: in Holder;
            Process: not null access procedure (Element: in Element_Type));

procedure Update_Element(Container: in out Holder;
            Process: not null access procedure (Element: in out Element_Type));

type Constant_Reference_Type(Element: not null access constant Element_Type)
                                                        is private
    with Implicit_Dereference => Element;

type Reference_Type(Element: not null access Element_Type) is private
    with Implicit_Dereference => Element;

function Constant_Reference(Container: aliased in Holder)
                                    return Constant_Reference_Type;

function Reference(Container: aliased in out Holder) return Reference_Type;

procedure Assign(Target: in out Holder; Source: in Holder);

function Copy(Source: Holder) return Holder;

procedure Move(Target: in out Holder; Source: in out Holder);

private
    ...                      -- not specified by the language
end Ada.Containers.Indefinite_Holders;
```

Hopefully, the purpose of the facilities provided by this container are obvious given an understanding of the use of the existing containers. It would be possible to use a list container with just a single element to act as a holder but it seems better to have an explicit container with probably less overhead and risk of confusion.

A trivial example of its use might be to provide a holder for pets. We write

```
package Strings is
   new Ada.Containers.Indefinite_Holders(String);

Kennel: Strings.Holder := To_Holder("cat");
```

This declares an object Kennel which is a wrapper for a string and initializes it with the string "cat". We can replace the cat with a rabbit by writing

```
Kennel := To_Holder("rabbit");
```

However, using To_Holder in this way could be a bit slow since this will create a new object which has to be destroyed after the assignment. It is better to write

```
Replace_Element(Kennel, "rabbit");
```

If we want to print out the contents of the kennel we just write

Put(Element(Kennel));

Operations such as Update_Element are provided partly for uniformity but also because the object might be large so that it is better to update it *in situ*. Alternatively, we can use the functions such as Reference as explained earlier.

8.6 Queue containers

When the goals of the revision to Ada 2005 were discussed, one of the expectations was that it would be possible to improve the containers, or maybe introduce variants, that would be task safe. However, further investigation revealed that this would not be practicable because the number of ways in which several tasks could interact with a container such as a list or map was large.

However, one data structure that is amenable to controlled access by several tasks is the queue. One or more tasks can place objects on a queue and one or more can remove them. Moreover, the existing container library did not include queues as such so we were not tied to any existing structures.

There are in fact four different queue containers in Ada 2012. These are all for elements of a definite type. Two are bounded and two are unbounded. And there are priority and synchronized queues. The names are

A.C.Unbounded_Synchronized_Queues
A.C.Bounded_Synchronized_Queues
A.C.Unbounded_Priority_Queues
A.C.Bounded_Priority_Queues

At one stage it was also planned to have unbounded containers for elements of an indefinite type. This would then have been similar to the other containers which have unbounded definite, unbounded indefinite and bounded definite forms. However, there were significant problems with the Dequeue operation to remove an indefinite object related to the fact that Ada does not have entry functions. This is easily overcome by making the elements of the queue a holder container as described in the previous section.

These four different queue containers are all derived from a single synchronized interface declared in a generic package whose specification is as follows

```
generic
   type Element_Type is private;              -- definite
package A.C.Synchronized_Queue_Interfaces is
   pragma Pure(Synchronized_Queue_Interfaces);

   type Queue is synchronized interface;

   procedure Enqueue(Container: in out Queue; New_Item: in Element_Type) is abstract
      with Synchronization => By_Entry;

   procedure Dequeue(Container: in out Queue; Element: out Element_Type) is abstract
      with Synchronization => By_Entry;

   function Current_Use(Container: Queue) return Count_Type is abstract;
   function Peak_Use(Container: Queue) return Count_Type is abstract;
end A.C.Synchronized_Queue_Interfaces;
```

This generic package declares the synchronized interface Queue and four operations on queues. These are the procedures Enqueue and Dequeue to add items to a queue and remove items from a queue respectively; note the aspect Synchronization which ensures that all implementations of these abstract procedures must be by an entry. There are also functions Current_Use and Peak_Use which can be used to monitor the number of items on a queue.

The four queue containers are generic packages which themselves declare a type Queue derived in turn from the interface Queue declared in the package above. We will look first at the synchronized queues and then at the priority queues.

The package for unbounded synchronized queues is as follows

```
with System; use System;
with A.C.Synchronized_Queue_Interfaces;
generic
  with package Queue_Interfaces is new A.C.Synchronized_Queue_Interfaces(<>);
  Default_Ceiling: Any_Priority := Priority'Last;
package A.C.Unbounded_Synchronized_Queues is
  pragma Preelaborate(Unbounded_Synchronized_Queues);

  package Implementation is
       ...                   -- not specified by the language
  end Implementation;

  protected type Queue(Ceiling: Any_Priority := Default_Ceiling)
    with Priority => Ceiling
                       is new Queue_Interfaces.Queue with

    overriding
    entry Enqueue(New_Item: in Queue_Interfaces.Element_Type);
    overriding
    entry Dequeue(Element: out Queue_Interfaces.Element_Type);

    overriding
    function Current_Use return Count_Type;
    overriding
    function Peak_Use return Count_Type;

  private
       ...                  -- not specified by the language
  end Queue;

private
     ...                    -- not specified by the language
end A.C.Unbounded_Synchronized_Queues;
```

Note that there are two generic parameters. The first (Queue_Interfaces) has to be an instantiation of the interface generic Synchronized_Queue_Interfaces; remember that the parameter (<>) means that any instantiation will do. The second parameter concerns priority and has a default value so we can ignore it for the moment.

Inside this package there is a protected type Queue which controls access to the queues via its entries Enqueue and Dequeue. This protected type is derived from Queue_Interfaces.Queue and so promises to implement the operations Enqueue, Dequeue, Current_Use and Peak_Use of that interface. And indeed it does implement them and moreover implements Enqueue and Dequeue by entries as required by the aspect Synchronization.

As an example suppose we wish to create a queue of some records such as

```
type Rec is record ... end record;
```

First of all we instantiate the interface package (using named notation for clarity) thus

```
package Rec_Interface is
   new A.C.Synchronized_Queue_Interfaces(Element_Type => Rec);
```

This creates an interface from which we can create various queuing mechanisms for dealing with objects of the type Rec.

Thus we might write

```
package Unbounded_Rec_Package is
   new A.C.Unbounded_Synchronized_Queues(Queue_Interfaces => Rec_Interface);
```

Finally, we can declare a protected object, My_Rec_UQ which is the actual queue, thus

```
My_Rec_UQ: Unbounded_Rec_Package.Queue;
```

To place an object on the queue we can write

```
Enqueue(My_Rec_UQ, Some_Rec);
```

or perhaps more neatly

```
My_Rec_UQ.Enqueue(Some_Rec);
```

And to remove an item from the queue we can write

```
My_Rec_UQ.Dequeue(The_Rec);
```

where The_Rec is some object of type Rec which thereby is given the value removed.

The statement

```
N := Current_Use(My_Rec_UQ);
```

assigns to N the number of items on the queue when Current_Use was called (it could be out of date by the time it gets into N) and similarly Peak_Use(My_Rec_UQ) gives the maximum number of items that have been on the queue since it was declared.

This is all task safe because of the protected type; several tasks can place items on the queue and several, perhaps the same, can remove items from the queue without interference.

It should also be noticed that since the queue is unbounded, we never get blocked by Enqueue since extra storage is allocated as required just as for the other unbounded containers (I suppose we might get Storage_Error).

The observant reader will note the mysterious local package called Implementation. This enables the implementation to declare local types to be used by the protected type. It will be recalled that there is an old rule that one cannot declare a type within a type. These local types really ought to be within the private part of the protected type; maybe this is something for Ada 2020.

The package for bounded synchronized queues is very similar. The only differences (apart from its name) are that it has an additional generic parameter Default_Capacity and the protected type Queue has an additional discriminant Capacity. So its specification is

```
with System; use System;
with A.C.Synchronized_Queue_Interfaces;
generic
   with package Queue_Interfaces is new A.C.Synchronized_Queue_Interfaces(<>);
   Default_Capacity: Count_Type;
   Default_Ceiling: Any_Priority := Priority'Last;
package A.C.Bounded_Synchronized_Queues is
   pragma Preelaborate(Bounded_Synchronized_Queues);
```

```
package Implementation is
        ...             -- not specified by the language
end Implementation;

protected type Queue(Capacity: Count_Type := Default_Capacity,
                     Ceiling: Any_Priority := Default_Ceiling)
    with Priority => Ceiling
         is new Queue_Interfaces.Queue with

        ...                  -- etc as for the unbounded one

end A.C.Bounded_Synchronized_Queues;
```

So using the same example, we can use the same interface package Rec_Interface. Now suppose we wish to declare a bounded queue with capacity 1000, we can write

```
package Bounded_Rec_Package is
  new A.C.Bounded_Synchronized_Queues
        (Queue_Interfaces => Rec_Interface, Default_Capacity => 1000);
```

Finally, we can declare a protected object, My_Rec_BQ which is the actual queue, thus

```
My_Rec_BQ: Bounded_Rec_Package.Queue;
```

And then we can use the queue as before. To place an object on the queue we can write

```
My_Rec_BQ.Enqueue(Some_Rec);
```

And to remove an item from the queue we can write

```
My_Rec_BQ.Dequeue(The_Rec);
```

The major difference is that if the queue becomes full then calling Enqueue will block the calling task until some other task calls Dequeue. Thus, unlike the other containers, Capacity_Error is never raised.

Note that having given a value for Default_Capacity, it can be overridden when the queue is declared, perhaps

```
My_Rec_Giant_BQ: Bounded_Rec_Package.Queue(Capacity => 100000);
```

These packages also provide control over the ceiling priority of the protected type. By default it is Priority'Last. This default can be overridden by our own default when the queue package is instantiated and can be further specified as a discriminant when the actual queue object is declared. So we might write

```
My_Rec_Ceiling_BQ: Bounded_Rec_Package.Queue(Ceiling => 10);
```

In the case of the bounded queue, if we do not give an explicit capacity then the ceiling has to be given using named notation. This does not apply to the unbounded queue which only has one discriminant, so to give that a ceiling priority we can just write

```
My_Rec_Ceiling_UQ: Unbounded_Rec_Package.Queue(10);
```

But clearly the use of the named notation is advisable.

Being able to give default discriminants is very convenient. In Ada 2005, this was not possible if the type was tagged. However, in Ada 2012, it is permitted in the case of limited tagged types and a protected type is considered to be limited. This was explained in detail in Section 4.4 on Discriminants.

If we wanted to make a queue of indefinite objects, then as mentioned above, there is no special container for this because Dequeue would be difficult to use since it is a procedure and not a function. So the actual parameter would have to be constrained which means knowing before the call the value of the discriminant, tag, or bound of the object which is unlikely. However, we can use the holder container to wrap the indefinite type so that it looks definite.

So to create a queue for strings, using the example of the previous section, we can write

```
package Strings is
  new Ada.Containers.Indefinite_Holders(String);

package Strings_Interface is
  new A.C.Synchronized_Queue_Interfaces(Element_Type => Strings.Holder);

package Unbounded_Strings_Package is
  new A.C.Unbounded_Synchronized_Queues(Queue_Interfaces => Strings_Interface);
```

and then finally declare the actual queue

```
My_Strings_UQ: Unbounded_Strings_Package.Queue;
```

To put some strings on this queue, we write

```
My_Strings_UQ.Enqueue(To_Holder("rabbit"));
```

```
My_Strings_UQ.Enqueue(To_Holder("horse"));
```

or even

```
My_Strings_UQ.Enqueue(Element(Kennel));
```

We now turn to considering the two other forms of queue which are the unbounded and bounded priority queues.

Here is the specification of the unbounded priority queue

```
with System; use System;
with A.C.Synchronized_Queue_Interfaces;
generic
  with package Queue_Interfaces is new
          A.C.Synchronized_Queue_Interfaces(<>);

  type Queue_Priority is private;
  with function Get_Priority(Element : Queue_Interfaces.Element_Type)
                                                    return Queue_Priority is <>;
  with function Before(Left, Right : Queue_Priority) return Boolean is <>;

  Default_Ceiling: Any_Priority := Priority'Last;
package A.C.Unbounded_Priority_Queues is
  pragma Preelaborate(Unbounded_Priority_Queues);

  package Implementation is
    ...                    -- not specified by the language
  end Implementation;

  protected type Queue(Ceiling: Any_Priority := Default_Ceiling)
    with Priority => Ceiling
          is new Queue_Interfaces.Queue with

    overriding
    entry Enqueue(New_Item: in Queue_Interfaces.Element_Type);
    overriding
    entry Dequeue(Element: out Queue_Interfaces.Element_Type);
```

not overriding
procedure Dequeue_Only_High_Priority(At_Least: **in** Queue_Priority;
                                                    Element: **in out** Queue_Interfaces.Element_Type;
                                                    Success: **out** Boolean);

overriding
function Current_Use **return** Count_Type;
overriding
function Peak_Use **return** Count_Type;

private
          ...   *-- not specified by the language*
end Queue;

private
          ...   *-- not specified by the language*
end A.C.Unbounded_Priority_Queues;

The differences from the synchronized bounded queue are that there are several additional generic parameters, namely the private type Queue_Priority and the two functions Get_Priority and Before which operate on objects of the type Queue_Priority, and also that the protected type Queue has an additional operation, the protected procedure Dequeue_Only_High_Priority.

The general idea is that elements have an associated priority which can be ascertained by calling the function Get_Priority. The meaning of this priority is given by the function Before.

When we call Enqueue, the new item is placed in the queue taking due account of its priority with respect to other elements already on the queue. So it will go before all less important elements as defined by Before. If existing elements already have the same priority then it goes after them.

As expected Dequeue just returns the first item on the queue and will block if the queue is empty.

The new procedure Dequeue_Only_High_Priority (note that it is marked as **not overriding** unlike the other operations) is designed to enable us to process items only if they are important enough as defined by the parameter At_Least. The priority of the first element E on the queue is P as given by Get_Priority(E). And so if Before(At_Least, P) is false, then the item on the queue is indeed important enough and so is removed from the queue and the Boolean parameter Success is set to true. On the other hand if Before(At_Least, P) is true then the item is not removed and Success is set to false. Note especially that Dequeue_Only_High_Priority never blocks. If the queue is empty, then Success is just set to false; it never waits for an item to be put on the queue.

As an (unrealistic) example, suppose we decide to make the queue of strings into a priority queue and that the priority is given by their length so that "rabbit" takes precedence over "horse". Remember that the type of the elements is Strings.Holder. We can define the priority as given by the attribute Length so we might as well make the actual type corresponding to Queue_Priority as simply Natural. Then we define

function S_Get_Priority(H: Strings.Holder) **return** Natural **is**
  (H.Element'Length);

function S_Before(L, R: Natural) **return** Boolean **is**
  (L > R);

Note the convenient use of expression functions for this sort of thing.

The instantiation now becomes

```
package Unbounded_Priority_Strings_Package is
  new A.C.Unbounded_Priority_Queues(Queue_Interfaces => Strings_Interface,
                                    Queue_Priority => Natural,
                                    Get_Priority => S_Get_Priority,
                                    Before => S_Before);
```

and we then declare a queue thus

```
My_Strings_UPQ: Unbounded_Priority_Strings_Package.Queue;
```

To put some strings on this queue, we write

```
My_Strings_UPQ.Enqueue(To_Holder("rabbit"));
```

```
My_Strings_UPQ.Enqueue(To_Holder("horse"));
```

```
My_Strings_UPQ.Enqueue(To_Holder("donkey"));
```

```
My_Strings_UPQ.Enqueue(To_Holder("gorilla"));
```

The result is that "gorilla" will have jumped to the head of the queue despite having been put on last. It will be followed by "rabbit" and "donkey" and the "horse" is last.

If we do

```
My_Strings_UPQ.Dequeue_Only_High_Priority(7, Kennel, OK);
```

then the "gorilla" will be taken from the queue and placed in the Kennel and OK will be true. But if we then do it again, nothing will happen because the resulting head of the queue (the "rabbit") is not long enough.

Finally, we need to consider bounded priority queues. They are exactly like the unbounded priority queues except that they have the same additional features regarding capacity as found in the synchronized queues. Thus the only differences (apart from the name) are that there is an additional generic parameter Default_Capacity and the protected type Queue has an additional discriminant Capacity.

As a final example we will do a bounded priority queue of records. Suppose the records concern requests for servicing a dishwasher. They might included usual information such as the model number, name and address of owner and so on. They might also have a component indicating degree of urgency, such as

Urgent – machine has vomited dirty water all over floor; housewife/husband having a tantrum,

Major – machine won't do anything; husband refuses to help with washing up,

Minor – machine leaves some dishes unclean, mother-in-law is coming next week,

Routine – machine needs annual service.

So we might have

```
type Degree is (Urgent, Major, Minor, Routine);
```

```
type Dish_Job is
  record
    Urgency: Degree;
    Name: ...

      ...
  end record;
```

First we declare the interface for this type

```
package Dish_Interface is
  new A.C.Synchronized_Queue_Interfaces(Element_Type => Dish_Job);
```

and then we declare the two slave functions for the priority mechanism thus

```
function W_Get_Priority(X: Dish_Job) return Degree is
  (X.Urgency);

function W_Before(L, R: Degree) return Boolean is
  (Degree'Pos(L) < Degree'Pos(R));
```

The instantiation is then

```
package Washer_Package is
  new A.C.Bounded_Priority_Queues(Queue_Interfaces => Dish_Interface,
                                  Queue_Priority => Degree,
                                  Get_Priority => W_Get_Priority,
                                  Before => W_Before,
                                  Default_Capacity => 100);
```

and we declare the queue of waiting calls thus

```
Dish_Queue: Washer_Package.Queue;
```

which gives a queue with the default capacity of 100.

The staff taking requests then place the calls on the queue by

```
Dish_Queue.Enqueue(New_Job);
```

To cope with the possibility that the queue is full, they can do a timed entry call; remember that this is possible because the procedure Enqueue in the interface package has Synchronization => By_Entry.

And then general operatives checking in and taking the next job do

```
Dish_Queue.Dequeue(Next_Job);
```

However, at weekends we can suppose that just one operative is on call and deals with only Urgent and Major calls. He might check the queue from time to time by calling

```
Dish_Queue.Dequeue_Only_High_Priority(Major, My_Job, Got_Job);
```

and if Got_Job is false, he can relax and go back to digging the garden or playing golf.

8.7 Sorting

Ada 2005 provides two containers for sorting arrays; one is for unconstrained array types and one is for constrained array types. The specification of the unconstrained one is

```
generic
  type Index_Type is (<>);
  type Element_Type is private;
  type Array_Type is array (Index_Type range <>) of Element_Type;
  with function "<" (Left, Right: Element_Type) return Boolean is <>;
  procedure Ada.Containers.Generic_Array_Sort(Container: in out Array_Type);
  pragma Pure(Ada.Containers.Generic_Array_Sort);
```

This does the obvious thing. It sorts the array Container so that the components are in the order defined by the generic parameter "<".

We could for example sort the letters in a string into alphabetical order. We would declare

```
procedure String_Sort is
   new Ada.Containers.Generic_Array_Sort(Positive, Character, String);
```

and then if we had a string such as

```
Bigpet: String := "rabbit";
```

we could apply String_Sort to it thus

```
String_Sort(Bigpet);
```

and the value in Bigpet will now be "abbirt".

That is all in Ada 2005. However, sorting doesn't just apply to arrays and Ada 2012 provides a much more flexible approach. An additional container is provided whose specification is

```
generic
   type Index_Type is (<>);
   with function Before(Left, Right: Index_Type) return Boolean;
   with procedure Swap(Left, Right: in Index_Type);
   procedure Ada.Containers.Generic_Sort(First, Last: Index_Type'Base);
   pragma Pure(Ada.Containers.Generic_Sort);
```

This can be used to sort any indexable structure and not just arrays. The generic parameters define the required ordering through the parameter Before much as expected. The cunning trick however, is that the means of interchanging two items in the structure is provided by the parameter Swap.

As an illustration we can use this on the array Bigpet. We can use an expression function for BP_Before and so we write

```
function BP_Before(L, R: Positive) return Boolean is
   (Bigpet(L) < Bigpet(R));

procedure BP_Swap(L, R: in Positive) is
   Temp: Character;
begin
   Temp := Bigpet(L);
   Bigpet(L) := Bigpet(R);
   Bigpet(R) := Temp;
end BP_Swap;

procedure BP_Sort is
   new Ada.Containers.Generic_Sort(Positive, BP_Before, BP_Swap);
```

and then we actually do the sort by

```
BP_Sort(Bigpet'First, Bigpet'Last);
```

That may seem to be rather a struggle but the key point is that the technique can be used to sort items in any indexable structure such as a vector container.

Suppose we have a number of records of a type Score which might be

```
type Score is
   record
      N: Natural := 0;
      OS: Other_Stuff;
   end record;
```

and we declare a vector container to hold such objects thus

```
package Scores is
   new Ada.Containers.Vectors(Natural, Score);
```

```
My_Vector: Scores.Vector;
```

Now assume that we have added various objects of the type Score to our vector and that we decide that we would like them sorted into order determined by their component N.

We write

```
function MV_Before(L, R: Natural) return Boolean is
   (Scores.Element(My_Vector, L).N < Scores.Element(My_Vector, R).N);
```

```
procedure MV_Swap(L, R: in Natural) is
begin
   Scores.Swap(My_Vector, L, R);
end MV_Swap;
```

```
procedure MV_Sort is
   new Ada.Containers.Generic_Sort(Natural, MV_Before, MV_Swap);
```

and then we do the sort by

```
MV_Sort(Scores.First_Index(My_Vector), Scores.Last_Index(My_Vector));
```

Note that the vectors container package conveniently already has a procedure Swap.

This vector example is not very exciting because it might be recalled that the vectors containers already have their own internal generic sort. To use it on this example we would have to write

```
package MV_Sorting is
   new Scores.Generic_Sorting(MV_Before);
```

```
MV_Sorting.Sort(My_Vector);
```

which is somewhat simpler. However, note that this sorts the whole vector. If we only wanted to sort part of it, say from elements in index range P to Q then it cannot be used. But that would be easy with the new one since we would simply write

```
MV_Sort(P, Q);
```

Note that curiously this does not need to mention My_Vector.

8.8 Streaming

Ada 2005 was somewhat unclear regarding streaming values from and to containers. This is clarified in Ada 2012. Thus if V is a vector container then V'Write writes Length(V) elements to the stream concerned.

An important point is that in order to simplify the interchange between containers, we are assured that we can stream between them using 'Write and 'Read. Thus we can stream between a bounded and an unbounded container as well as between two bounded or two unbounded containers provided of course that the elements all have the same subtype.

9 Epilogue

This last chapter summarizes a small number of general issues of importance to the user such as compatibility between Ada 2012 and Ada 2005. It also briefly revisits a number of problems that were considered for Ada 2005 but rejected for various reasons; the important ones have been solved in Ada 2012.

Finally, it discusses a small number of corrections that have been found necessary since the standard was approved.

9.1 Compatibility

There are two main sorts of problems regarding compatibility. These are termed Incompatibilities and Inconsistencies.

An incompatibility is a situation where a legal Ada 2005 program is illegal in Ada 2012. These can be annoying but not a disaster since the compiler automatically detects such situations.

An inconsistency is where a legal Ada 2005 program is also a legal Ada 2012 program but might have a different effect at execution time. These can in principle be really nasty but typically the program is actually wrong anyway (in the sense that it does not do what the programmer intended) or its behaviour depends upon the raising of a predefined exception (which is generally considered poor style) or the situation is extremely unlikely to occur.

As mentioned below in Section 2, during the development of Ada 2012 a number of corrections were made to Ada 2005 and these resulted in some incompatibilities and inconsistencies with the original Ada 2005 standard. These are not considered to be incompatibilities or inconsistencies between Ada 2005 and Ada 2012 and so are not covered in this section.

9.1.1 Incompatibilities with Ada 2005

Each incompatibility listed below gives the AI concerned and the paragraph in the AARM which in some cases will give more information. Where relevant, the section in this rationale where the topic is discussed is also given. Where appropriate the incompatibilities are grouped together.

Note that this list only covers those incompatibilities that might reasonably occur. There are a number of others which are so unlikely that they do not seem worth mentioning.

1 – The word **some** is now reserved. Programs using it as an identifier will need to be changed. (AI-176, 2.9)

Adding new reserved words is a very visible incompatibility. Six were added in Ada 95, three in Ada 2005, and now just one in Ada 2012. Perhaps this is the end of the matter. The word **some** is used in quantified expressions; it already was reserved in SPARK [13] where it is used in quantified expressions in proof contexts.

2 – If a predefined package has additional entities then incompatibilities can arise. Thus suppose the predefined package Ada.Stuff has an additional entity More added to it. Then if an Ada 2005 program has a package P containing an entity More then a program with a use clause for both Ada.Stuff and P will become illegal in Ada 2012 because the reference to More will become ambiguous. This also applies if further overloadings of an existing entity are added.

This can be overcome by adding child packages of course. However, adding lots of child packages can be an inconvenience for the user and so in many cases extending a package seemed more appropriate especially if the identifiers concerned are unlikely to have been used by programmers.

The following packages have been extended with additional entities as listed.

Ada.Characters.Handling – Is_Line_Terminator, Is_Mark, Is_Other_Format, Is_Punctuation_ Connector, Is_Space. (AI-185, A.3.2)

Ada.Containers – Capacity_Error. (AI-1, A.18.1)

Ada.Containers.Vectors – Assign, Copy, Constant_Reference, Constant_Reference_Type, Iterate, Reference, Reference_Type, Vector_Iterator_Interfaces. (AI-1, AI-212, A.18.2)

There are similar additions to the other containers Ada.Containers.Doubly_Linked_Lists etc.

Ada.Directories – Name_Case_Kind, Name_Case_Equivalence. (AI-49, A.16)

Ada.Dispatching – Yield. (AI-166, D.2.1)

Ada.Environment_Variables – Value. (AI-285, A.17)

Ada.Execution_Time – Interrupt_Clocks_Supported, Separate_Interrupt_Clocks_Supported, Clocks_For_Interrupts. (AI-170, D.14)

Ada.Task_Identification – Environment_Task, Activation_ Is_Complete. (AI-189, C.7.1)

Ada.Strings.Fixed – Find_Token. (AI-31, A.4.3)

Ada.Strings.Bounded – Find_Token. (AI-31, A.4.4)

Ada.Strings.Unbounded – Find_Token. (AI-31, A.4.5)

There are similar additions to Ada.Strings.Wide_Fixed, Ada.Strings.Wide_Bounded and Ada.Strings.Wide_Unbounded. (AI-31, A.4.7)

Ada.Tags – Is_Abstract. (AI-173, 3.9)

It seems unlikely that existing programs will be affected by these potential incompatibilities.

3 – Membership tests are no longer allowed as a discrete choice. This is explained in detail in Section 3.6 of the chapter on Expressions. (AI-158, 3.8.1)

4 – Allowing functions to have parameters of all modes led to the introduction of stricter rules on aliasing. It is possible that a program that seemed to work in Ada 2005 is illegal in Ada 2012. See Section 4.2 of the chapter on Structure and Visibility. (AI-144, 6.4.1)

5 – Implicit conversion is now allowed from anonymous access types to general access types. Such conversions can make calls ambiguous in the presence of overloading where only one call was permitted in Ada 2005. Consider

```
type RT is access all T;
function F return RT;
function F return access T;

procedure B(R: RT);
```

and then the call

```
B(F);                    -- ambiguous in Ada 2012
```

The call of B is ambiguous in Ada 2012 because the call could be to either function F. But in Ada 2005, the implicit conversion is not possible and so the call has to be to the first function F. (AI-149, 8.6)

6 – It is now illegal to declare a formal abstract subprogram whose controlling type is incomplete. This is related to various improvements to incomplete types described in Section 4.3 of the chapter on Structure and Visibility. (AI-296, 12.6)

7 – The pragma Controlled has been removed from the language. It was never implemented anyway. (AI-229, 13.11.3)

8 – The package Ada.Dispatching was Pure in Ada 2005 but has been downgraded to Preelaborable because of the addition of Yield. This is unlikely to be a problem. (AI-166, D.2.1)

9.1.2 Inconsistencies with Ada 2005

Note that this list only covers those inconsistencies that might reasonably occur. There are a number of others which are so unlikely that they do not seem worth mentioning.

1 – The definition of character sets can change with time. It is thus possible that the result of character classification functions for obscure characters might be or become inconsistent. (AI-91, AI-227, AI-266, 2.1, 2.3)

2 – User defined untagged record equality is now defined to compose and be used in generics. Code which assumes that predefined equality reemerges in generics and in predefined equals for composite types could fail. However, it is more likely that this change will fix bugs. (AI-123, 4.5.2)

3 – A stand alone object of an anonymous access type now has dynamic accessibility. This is most likely to make illegal programs now legal. However, it is possible that a program that raised Program_Error in Ada 2005 will not do so in Ada 2012. It seems very unlikely that a program would rely on the raising of this exception. (AI-148, 4.6)

4 – There is an obscure interaction between the change to the composability of equality and renaming. Renaming of user-defined untagged record equality is now defined to call the overridden body so long as the overriding occurred before the renames. Consider

```
package P is
   type T is
     record
       ...
     end record;
                    -- (1) consider renaming here
private
   function "=" (L, R: T) return Boolean;
end P;

with P;
package Q is
   function Equals renames P."=";
end Q;
```

In Ada 2005, Equals refers to the predefined equality, whereas in Ada 2012 it refers to the overridden user-defined equality in the private part. This is so that composed equality and explicit calls on "=" give the same answer. However, if the renaming had been at the point (1) then calling Equal would call the predefined equality. Remember that renaming squirrels away the operation so that it can be retrieved. (AI-123, 8.5.4)

5 – A group budget is now defined to work on a single processor. However, it is unlikely that any implementation of Ada 2005 managed to implement this on multiprocessors anyway. (AI-169, D.14.2)

9.2 Retrospective changes to Ada 2005

In the course of the development of Ada 2012, a number of small changes were deemed to apply also to Ada 2005 and thus were classified as binding interpretations rather than amendments. Some were mentioned in previous chapters (including that which ensured that package Ada is legal); see

Sections 6.2 and 6.6 of the chapter on Iterators, Pools etc. Most of these do not introduce incompatibilities or inconsistencies so will not be discussed further.

A few binding interpretations do introduce minor incompatibilities or inconsistencies and will now be briefly discussed.

9.2.1 Incompatibilities with original Ada 2005

There are a small number of incompatibilities between the original Ada 2005 and that resulting from various corrections.

1 – The rules for full conformance have been strengthened; for example, null exclusions must now match. (AI-46, AI-134, AI-207, 6.3.1)

2 – When an inherited subprogram is implemented by a protected function, the first parameter has to be an **in** parameter, but not an access to variable type. Ada 2005 allowed access to variable parameters in this case; the parameter will need to be changed to access to constant by the addition of the **constant** keyword. (AI-291, 9.4)

3 – A missing rule is added that a limited with clause cannot name an ancestor unit. (AI-40, 10.1.2)

4 – Matching of formal access to subprogram types uses subtype conformance in Ada 2012 whereas it only used mode conformance in original Ada 2005. This change was necessary to avoid undefined behaviour in some situations. (AI-288, 12.5.4)

5 – An address attribute with a prefix of a subprogram with convention Intrinsic is now illegal. This is discussed in Section 6.6 of the chapter on Iterators, Pools etc. (AI-95, 13.3)

6 – Stream attributes must be specified by a static subprogram name rather than by a dynamic expression. (AI-39, 13.13.2)

7 – The use of discriminants on Unchecked_Union types is now illegal in record representation clauses. It makes no sense to specify the position of something that is not supposed to exist. (AI-26, B.3.3)

8 – A nonvolatile generic formal derived type precludes a volatile actual type. (AI-218, C.6)

9 – The restriction No_Relative_Delay has been extended to also prohibit a call of Timing_Events.Set_Handler with a Time_Span parameter. (AI-211, D.7)

10 – Various restrictions have been reworded to prevent the bypassing of the restriction by calling the forbidden subprogram via renames. (AI-211, D.7)

9.2.2 Inconsistencies with original Ada 2005

There are a small number of inconsistencies between the original Ada 2005 and that resulting from various corrections.

1 – The description of Dependent_Tag has been changed to say that it must raise Tag_Error if there is more than one type that matches the requirements. (AI-113, 3.9)

2 – A curious omission regarding checking arrays allows a component in an aggregate whose value is given as <> even if the component is outside the bounds. It is now clarified that Constraint_Error is raised. (AI-37, 4.3.3)

3 – The first procedure Split in Ada.Calendar.Formatting raises Time_Error for a value of exactly 86400.0. This was unspecified in Ada 2005. (AI-238, 9.6.1)

4 – An address attribute with a prefix of a generic formal subprogram whose actual parameter has convention Intrinsic now raises Program_Error. (AI-95, 13.3)

5 – User specified external tags that conflict with other external tags now raise Program_Error or are illegal. (AI-113, 13.3)

6 – The definition of Set_Line is corrected. As originally defined in Ada 95 and Ada 2005, Set_Line(1) could call New_Line(0) which would raise Constraint_Error which is unhelpful. This was mentioned right at the end of the Postscript in the Rationale for Ada 2005 [15]. (AI-38, A.10.5)

7 – The definitions of Start_Search, Search, Delete_Directory, and Rename are clarified so that they raise the correct exception if misused. (AI-231, A.16)

8 – If Count = 0 for a container Insert subprogram that has a Position parameter, the Position parameter is set to the value of the Before parameter by the call. The original wording remained silent on this. (AI-257, A.18.3)

9.3 Unfinished topics from Ada 2005

A number of topics which seemed to be good ideas initially were abandoned during the development of Ada 2005 for various reasons. Usually the reason was simply that a good solution could not be produced in the time available and the trouble with a bad solution is that it is hard to put it right later. This section briefly reconsiders these topics which were discussed in the Rationale for Ada 2005 [15]; some have now been solved in Ada 2012; the others were considered unimportant.

9.3.1 Aggregates for private types

The <> notation was introduced in Ada 2005 for aggregates to mean the default value if any. A curiosity is that we can write

```
type Secret is private;

type Visible is
   record
      A: Integer;
      S: Secret;
   end record;

X: Visible := (A => 77; S => <>);
```

but we cannot write

```
S: Secret := <>;                 -- illegal
```

The argument is that this would be of little use since the components take their default values anyway.

For uniformity it was proposed that we might allow

```
S: Secret := (others => <>);
```

for private types and also for task and protected types. One advantage would be that we could then write

```
S: constant Secret := (others => <>);
```

whereas it is not possible to declare a constant of a private type because we are unable to give an initial value.

However, discussion of this issue led into a quagmire in Ada 2005 and so was abandoned. It remains abandoned in Ada 2012!

9.3.2 Partial generic instantiation

Certain attempts to use signature packages led to circularities in Ada 95. Consider

```
generic
  type Element is private;
  type Set is private;
  with function Union(L, R: Set) return Set is <>;
  with function Intersection(L, R: Set) return Set is <>;
  ... -- and so on
package Set_Signature is end;
```

Remember that a signature is a generic package consisting only of a specification. When we instantiate it, the effect is to assert that the actual parameters are consistent and the instantiation provides a name to refer to them as a group.

If we now attempt to write

```
generic
  type Elem is private;
  with function Hash(E: Elem) return Integer;
package Hashed_Sets is
  type Set is private;
  function Union(L, R: Set) return Set;
  function Intersection(L, R: Set) return Set;

  ...
  package Signature is new Set_Signature(Elem, Set);
private
  type Set is
    record

      ...
    end record;
end Hashed_Sets;
```

then we are in trouble. The problem is that the instantiation of Set_Signature tries to freeze the type Set prematurely.

After a number of false starts this problem is partially overcome in Ada 2012 by the introduction of incomplete formal generic parameters. This is discussed in Section 4.3 of the chapter on Structure and Visibility. See also Section 9.4.1 of this chapter.

9.3.3 Support for IEEE 559: 1989

The proposal was to provide full support for all aspects of IEEE 559 arithmetic such as NaNs (a NaN is Not A Number). This would have necessitated adding attributes such as S'Infinity, S'Is_NaN, S'Finite and so on plus a package Ada.Numerics.IEC_559.

The proposal was abandoned because it would have had a big impact on implementers and it was not clear that there was sufficient demand. It was not reconsidered for Ada 2012.

9.3.4 Defaults for generic parameters

Generic subprogram parameters and object parameters of mode in can have defaults. But other parameters such as packages and types cannot. This was considered irksome and untidy and efforts were made to define a suitable notation for all possible generic parameters.

However, it was abandoned partly because an appropriate syntax seemed hard to find and more importantly, it was not felt to be that important. Again, it was not deemed important enough to be reconsidered for Ada 2012.

9.3.5   Pre/post-conditions for subprograms

The original proposal was to add pragmas such as Pre_Assert and Post_Assert. Thus in the case of a subprogram Push on a type Stack we might write

```
procedure Push(S: in out Stack; X: in Item);
pragma Pre_Assert(Push, not Is_Full(S));
pragma Post_Assert(Push, not Is_Empty(S));
```

This was all abandoned in Ada 2005 for various reasons; one being that pragmas are ugly for such an important matter.

However, this is neatly solved in Ada 2012 by the introduction of aspect specifications so we can now write

```
procedure Push(S: in out Stack; X: in Item)
   with
     Pre => not Is_Full(S),
     Post => not Is_Empty(S);
```

which is really excellent; this is discussed in detail in Chapter 2 on Contracts and Aspects.

9.3.6   Type and package invariants

This defined further pragmas similar to those in the previous proposal but concerned with packages and types. Thus the pragma Package_Invariant proposed for Ada 2005 identified a function returning a Boolean result. This function would be implicitly called after the call of each subprogram in the package and if the result were false the behaviour would be as for an Assert pragma that failed.

This proposal was also abandoned for Ada 2005. However, Ada 2012 has introduced type invariants thus

```
type Stack is private
   with Type_Invariant => Is_Unduplicated(Stack);
```

as discussed in Chapter 2 on Contracts and Aspects. On the other hand, package invariants remain abandoned.

9.3.7   Exceptions as types

This proposal originally arose out of a workshop organized by Ada-Europe. It was quite complex and considered far too radical a change and probably expensive to implement. As a consequence it was slimmed down considerably. But having been slimmed down it seemed pointless and was then abandoned. The only part to survive was the idea of raise with message which became a separate AI and was incorporated into Ada 2005.

This was not pursued in Ada 2012.

9.3.8   Sockets operations

This seemed a very good idea at the time but no detailed proposal was forthcoming and so it died. It has been left dead.

9.3.9   In out parameters for functions

The proposal was to allow functions to have parameters of all modes. The rationale for the proposal was well summarized thus "Ada functions can have arbitrary side effects, but are not allowed to announce that in their specifications".

But strangely, this AI was abandoned quite early in the Ada 2005 revision process on the grounds that it was "too late". (Perhaps too late in this context meant 25 years too late.)

However, in Ada 2012, the bullet has been bitten and functions can indeed now have parameters of all modes. See the discussion in Section 4.2 of the chapter on Structure and Visibility.

9.3.10 Application defined scheduling

The International Real-Time Ada Workshops have been a source of suggestions for improvements to Ada. The Workshop at Oporto suggested a number of further scheduling algorithms [24]. Most of these such as Round Robin and EDF were included in Ada 2005. But that for application defined scheduling was not.

No further action on this topic was taken in Ada 2012.

9.4 Unfinished topics for Ada 2012

A number of topics which seemed to be good ideas initially were abandoned during the development of Ada 2012 for various reasons. It is interesting to note that there are far fewer of these loose ends than there were in Ada 2005. The following deserve mention.

9.4.1 Integrated packages (AI-135)

Difficulties sometimes arise with nested packages. Consider for example a package that needs to export a private type T and a container instantiated for that type. We cannot write

```
package P is
  type T is private;
  package T_Set is new Ordered_Sets(T);
private
  ...
end P;
```

because the type T is not frozen. We have to write something like

```
package P is
  package Inner is
    type T is private;
  private
    ...
  end Inner;
  package T_Set is new Ordered_Sets(Inner.T);
end P;
```

What we now want is some way to say that the declarations in Inner are really at the level of P itself after all. In other words we want to integrate the package Inner with the outer package P.

Various attempts were made to solve this by another kind of use clause or perhaps by putting Inner in a <> box. But all attempts led to difficulties so this remains unresolved.

9.4.2 Cyclic fixed point (AI-175)

Measurements in the physical world of Euclid and Newton are either lengths or angles. Angles are cyclic in nature and so can be mapped with a modular type. However, this leaves scaling in the hands of the user and is machine dependent. Consideration was given to the possibility of a cyclic form of fixed point. Sadly, there was much hidden complexity and so no solution was agreed.

One might have thought that it would be easy to use the natural wrap-around hardware. However, with a binary machine, if 180 degrees is held exactly then 60 degrees is not which excludes an exact representation of an equilateral triangle. The whole point about using fixed point is that it is precise but it just doesn't work unless the hardware uses a base with divisibility by 60. The Babylonians would have understood. The text of AI-175 includes a generic which might be useful for many applications.

9.4.3 Global annotations (AI-186)

The idea here was that the specification of a subprogram should have annotations indicating the global objects that it might manipulate. For example a function can have side effects on global variables but this important matter is not mentioned in the specification. This topic has strong synergy with the information given in contracts such as pre- and postconditions. However, it was abandoned perhaps because of the complexity arising from the richness of the full Ada language. It should be noted that such annotations have always featured in SPARK as comments and moreover, at the time of writing, are being considered using the aspect notation in a new version of SPARK.

9.4.4 Shorthand for assignments (AI-187)

Consideration was given to having some short of shorthand for assignments where source and target have commonality as in statements such as

```
A(I) := A(I) + 1;
```

But maybe the thought of C++ was too much. In any event no agreement that it was worthwhile was reached and there was certainly no agreement on what syntax might be acceptable.

9.5 Postscript

It should also be noticed that a few corrections and improvements have been made since Ada 2012 was approved as a standard. The more important of these will now be discussed.

A new form of expression, the raise expression, is added (AI12-22). This means that by analogy with

```
if X < Y then
  Z := +1;
elsif X > Y then
  Z := –1;
else
  raise Error;
end if;
```

we can also write

```
Z := (if X<Y then 1 elsif X>Y then –1 else raise Error);
```

A raise expression is a new form of relation so the syntax for relation (see Section 3.6 of the chapter on Expressions) is extended as follows

```
relation ::=
        simple_expression [relational_operator simple_expression]
        | simple_expression [not] in membership_choice_list
        | raise_expression

raise_expression ::=
        raise exception_name [with string_expression]
```

Since a raise expression is a relation it has the same precedence and so will need to be in parentheses in some contexts. But as illustrated above it does not need parentheses when used in a conditional expression which itself will have parentheses.

Raise expressions will be found useful with pre- and postconditions. Thus if we have

```
procedure Push(S: in out Stack; X: in Item)
  with
    Pre => not Is_Full(S);
```

and the precondition is false then Assertion _Error is raised. But we can now alternatively write

```
procedure Push(S: in out Stack; X: in Item)
  with
    Pre => not Is_Full(S) or else raise Stack_Error;
```

and of course we can also add a message thus

```
Pre => not Is_Full(S) or else raise Stack_Error with "wretched stack is full";
```

On a closely related topic the new syntax for membership tests (also see Section 3.6 of the chapter on Expressions) has been found to cause ambiguities (AI12-39).

Thus

```
A in B and C
```

could be interpreted as either of the following

```
(A in B) and C                    -- or
A in (B and C)
```

This is cured by changing the syntax for relation yet again to

```
relation ::=
        simple_expression [relational_operator simple_expression]
      | tested_simple_expression [not] in membership_choice_list
      | raise_expression
```

and changing

```
membership_choice ::=
                choice_expression | range | subtype_mark
```

to

```
membership_choice ::=
                choice_simple_expression | range | subtype_mark
```

Thus a membership_choice no longer uses a choice_expression. However, the form choice_expression is still used in discrete_choice.

A curious difficulty has been found in attempting to use the seemingly innocuous package Ada.Locales described in Section 7.4 of the chapter on the Predefined Library.

The types Language_Code and Country_Code were originally declared as

```
type Language_Code is array (1 .. 3) of Character range 'a' .. 'z';
```

```
type Country_Code is array (1 .. 2) of Character range 'A' .. 'Z';
```

The problem is that a value of these types is not a string and cannot easily be converted into a string because of the range constraints and so cannot be a simple parameter of a subprogram such as Put. If LC is of type Language_Code then we have to write something tedious such as

```
Put(LC(1));  Put(LC(2));  Put(LC(3));
```

Accordingly, these types are changed so that they are derived from the type String and the constraints on the letters are then imposed by dynamic predicates. So we have

> **type** Language_Code **is new** String(1 .. 3)
> **with** Dynamic_Predicate => (**for all** E **of** Language_Code => E **in** 'a' .. 'z');

with a similar construction for Country_Code (AI12-37).

Readers might like to contemplate whether this is an excellent illustration of some of the new features of Ada 2012 or simply an illustration of static strong or maybe string typing going astray.

AI12-45 notes that pre- and postconditions are allowed on generic units but they are not allowed on instances. See Section 2.3 of the chapter on Contracts and Aspects where this topic should have been mentioned.

Another modification in this area is addressed by AI12-44 which states that type invariants are not checked on **in** parameters of functions but are checked on **in** parameters of procedures. See Section 2.4 of the chapter on Contracts and Aspects. This change was necessary to avoid infinite recursion which would arise if an invariant itself called a function with a parameter of the type. Note also that a class wide invariant could not be used at all without this modification.

A further aspect, Predicate_Failure, is defined by AI12-54-2. The expected type of the expression defined by this aspect is String and gives the message to be associated with a failure. So we can write

> **subtype** Open_File_Type **is** File_Type
> **with**
>   Dynamic_Predicate => Is_Open(Open_File_Type),
>   Predicate_Failure => "File not open";

If the predicate fails then Assertion_Error is raised with the message "File not open". See Section 2.5 of the chapter on Contracts and Aspects.

We can also use a raise expression and thereby ensure that a more appropriate exception is raised. If we write

> Predicate_Failure => **raise** Status_Error **with** "File not open";

then Status_Error is raised rather than Assertion_Error with the given message. We could of course explicitly mention Assertion_Error thus by writing

> Predicate_Failure => **raise** Assertion_Error **with** "A message";

Finally, we could omit any message and just write

> Predicate_Failure => **raise** Status_Error;

in which case the message is null.

A related issue is discussed in AI12-71. If several predicates apply to a subtype which has been declared by a refined sequence then the predicates are evaluated in the order in which they occur. This is especially important if different exceptions are specified by the use of Predicate_Failure since without this rule the wrong exception might be raised. The same applies to a combination of predicates, null exclusions and old-fashioned subtypes.

This can be illustrated by an extension of the above example. Suppose we have

> **subtype** Open_File_Type **is** File_Type
> **with**
>   Dynamic_Predicate => Is_Open(Open_File_Type),
>   Predicate_Failure => **raise** Status_Error;

```
    subtype Read_File_Type is Open_File_Type
      with
        Dynamic_Predicate => Mode(Real_File_Type) = In_File,
        Predicate_Failure => raise Mode_Error with "Can't read file: " & Name(Read_File_Type);
```

The subtype Read_File_Type refines Open_File_Type. If the predicate for it were evaluated first and the file was not open then the call of Mode would raise Status_Error which we would not want to happen if we wrote

```
    if F in Read_File_Type then ...
```

Care is needed with membership tests. The whole purpose of a membership test (and similarly the Valid attribute) is to find out whether a condition is satisfied. So if we write

```
    if X in S then
        ...              -- do this
    else
        ...              -- do that
    end if;
```

we expect the membership test to be true or false. However, if the evaluation of S itself raises some exception then the purpose of the test is violated.

It is important to understand these related topics. Another example might clarify. Suppose we have a very simple predicate as in Section 2.5 of the chapter on Contracts and Aspects such as

```
    subtype Winter is Month
      with Static_Predicate => Winter in Dec | Jan | Feb;
```

where

```
    type Month is (Jan, Feb, Mar, Apr, ..., Nov, Dec);
```

and we declare a variable W thus

```
    W: Winter := Jan;
```

If we now do

```
    W := Mar;
```

then Assertion_Error will be raised because the value Mar is not within the subtype Winter (we assume that the assertion policy is Check). If, however, we would rather have Constraint_Error raised then we can modify the declaration of Winter to

```
    subtype Winter is Month
      with Static_Predicate => Winter in Dec | Jan | Feb,
           Predicate_Failure => raise Constraint_Error;
```

and then obeying

```
    W := Mar;
```

will raise Constraint_Error.

On the other hand suppose we declare a variable M thus

```
    M: Month := Mar;
```

and then do a membership test

```
if M in Winter then
    ...                     -- do this if M is a winter month
else
    ...                     -- do this if M is not a winter month
end if;
```

then of course no exception is raised since this is a membership test and not a predicate check.

Note however, that we could write something odd such as

```
subtype Winter2 is Month
    with Dynamic_Predicate => (if Winter2 in Dec | Jan | Feb then true else raise E);
```

then the very evaluation of the predicate might raise the exception E so that

```
M in Winter2
```

will either be true or raise the exception E but will never be false. Note that in this silly example the predicate has to be a dynamic one because a static predicate cannot include a raise expression.

So this should clarify the reasons for introducing Predicate_Failure. It enables us to give a different behaviour for when the predicate is used in a membership test as opposed to when it is used in a check and it also allows us to add a message.

Finally, it should be noted that the predicate expression might involve the evaluation of some subexpression perhaps through the call of some function. We might have a predicate describing those months that have 30 days thus

```
subtype Month30 is Month
    with Static_Predicate => Month30 in Sep | Apr | Jun | Nov;
```

which mimics the order in the nursery rhyme. However, suppose we decide to declare a function Days30 to do the check so that the subtype becomes

```
subtype Month30 is Month
    with Dynamic_Predicate => Days30(Month30);
```

and for some silly reason we code the function incorrectly so that it raises an exception (perhaps it accidentally runs into its **end** and always raises Program_Error). In this situation if we write

```
M in Month30
```

then we will indeed get Program_Error and not false.

Perhaps this whole topic can be summarized by simply saying that a membership test is not a check. Indeed a membership test is often useful in ensuring that a subsequent check will not fail as was discussed in Section 6.4 of the chapter on Iterators, Pools etc.

On a rather different topic, AI12-28 discusses the import of variadic C functions (that is functions with a variable number of parameters). In Ada 95, it was expected that such functions would use the same calling conventions as normal C functions; however, that is not true for some targets today. Accordingly, this AI adds additional conventions to describe variadic C functions so that the Ada compiler can compile the correct calling sequence.

Finally, an important modification is made to the topic of dispatching domains by AI12-33. See Section 5.3 of the chapter on Tasking and Real-Time.

As defined originally, a dispatching domain consists of a set of processors whose CPU values are contiguous. However, this is unrealistic since CPUs are often grouped together in other ways. Accordingly, the package System.Multiprocessors.Dispatching_Domains is extended by the addition of a type CPU_Set and two further functions thus

```
type CPU_Set is array (CPU range <>) of Boolean;

function Create(Set: CPU_Set) return Dispatching_Domain;
function Get_CPU_Set(Domain: Dispatching_Domain) return CPU_Set;
```

So if we want to create a domain consisting of processors 0, 4, and 8 we can write

```
My_Set: CPU_Set(0 .. 8) := (0 | 4 | 8 => true, others => false);
```

and then

```
My_Domain: Dispatching_Domain := Create(My_Set);
```

and so on. The function Get_CPU_Set can be applied to any domain and returns the appropriate array representing the set of CPUs. Note that this function can be applied to any domain and not just to one created from a CPU_Set.

References

[1] ISO/IEC JTC1/SC22/WG9 N498 (2009) *Instructions to the Ada Rapporteur Group from SC22/WG9 for Preparation of Amendment 2 to ISO/IEC 8652.*

[2] ISO/IEC TR 24718:2004 *Guide for the use of the Ada Ravenscar profile in high integrity systems.*

[3] ISO/IEC 8652:1995/COR 1:2001 *Ada Reference Manual – Technical Corrigendum 1.*

[4] ISO/IEC 8652:1995/AMD 1:2007 *Ada Reference Manual – Amendment 1.*

[5] S. T. Taft et al (eds) (2007) *Ada 2005 Reference Manual*, LNCS 4348, Springer-Verlag.

[6] Jean Ichbiah, John Barnes, Robert Firth, Mike Woodger (1986) *Rationale for the Design of the Ada Programming Language*, Honeywell and Alsys.

[7] John Barnes (2006) *Programming in Ada 2005*, Addison-Wesley.

[8] P. Naur (ed.) *Revised Report on the Algorithmic Language ALGOL 60* (1963) Communications of the Association for Computing Machinery, Vol. 6, p. 1.

[9] D. W. Barron et al (1963) *The main features of CPL*, Computer Journal vol. 6, pp 134-143.

[10] A. van Wijngaarden et al (eds) (1973) *Revised Report on the Algorithmic Language – ALGOL 68*, Springer-Verlag.

[11] K. Jensen and N. Wirth (1975) *Pascal User Manual and Report*, Springer-Verlag.

[12] Defense Advanced Research Projects Agency (1978) *Department of Defense Requirements for High Order Computer Programming Languages – STEELMAN*, USDoD.

[13] John Barnes (2012) *SPARK – The proven approach to High Integrity Software*, Altran Praxis.

[14] D. R. Hofstadter (1980) *Gödel, Escher, Bach: an Eternal Golden Braid*, Basic Books.

[15] John Barnes (2008) *Ada 2005 Rationale*, LNCS 5020, Springer-Verlag.

[16] David Fisher (1976) *A Common Programming Language for the Department of Defense – Background and Technical Requirements*, Institute for Defense Analyses, Arlington, Virginia.

[17] Defense Advanced Research Projects Agency (1977) *Department of Defense Requirements for High Order Computer Programming Languages – Revised IRONMAN*, USDoD.

[18] Jean Ichbiah et al (1978) *Preliminary Reference Manual for the Green Programming Language*, Honeywell Inc.

[19] Jean Ichbiah et al (1979) *Reference Manual for the Green Programming Language*, Honeywell Inc.

[20] ACM (1979) *Preliminary Ada Reference Manual*, Sigplan Notices, Vol 14, No 6.

[21] ANSI / Mil–Std 1815A (1983) *Ada Reference Manual.*

[22] B Higman (1963) *What everybody should know about Algol*, Computer Journal, vol 6, no 1, pp 50-56.

[23] A. Burns and A. Wellings (2007) *Integrating OOP and Tasking – the missing requeue*, Proceedings of the 13th International Real-Time Ada Workshop, Ada Letters, Vol 27, No 2.

[24] ACM (2003) *Proceedings of the 12th International Real-Time Ada Workshop*, Ada Letters, Vol 23, No 4.

Index

A

access type
  conversion 133
Activation_Is_Complete function 137
Ada package 117
Ada Resource Association 1
Ada-Europe 1
Ada.Calendar package 143
Ada.Containers package 160
Ada.Containers.Bounded_Doubly_Linked_Lists
                           package 160
Ada.Containers.Bounded_Hashed_Maps
                           package 160
Ada.Containers.Bounded_Hashed_Sets
                           package 161
Ada.Containers.Bounded_Multiway_Trees
                      package 27, 168
Ada.Containers.Bounded_Ordered_Maps
                           package 160
Ada.Containers.Bounded_Ordered_Sets
                           package 161
Ada.Containers.Bounded_Priority_Queues
                           package 180
Ada.Containers.Bounded_Synchronized_Queues
                           package 180
Ada.Containers.Bounded_Vectors package 160
Ada.Containers.Generic_Array_Sort procedure 187
Ada.Containers.Generic_Sort procedure 188
Ada.Containers.Indefinite_Holders
                      package 27, 178
Ada.Containers.Indefinite_Multiway_Trees
                      package 27, 168
Ada.Containers.Multiway_Trees package 27, 168
Ada.Containers.Synchronized_Queue_Interfaces
                      package 28, 180
Ada.Containers.Unbounded_Priority_Queues
                           package 180
Ada.Containers.Unbounded_Synchronized_Queues
                      package 28, 180
Ada.Directories package 25, 152
Ada.Directories.Hierarchical_File_Names
                      package 26, 154
Ada.Dispatching package 18, 101
Ada.Dispatching.EDF package 102

Ada.Dispatching.Non_Preemptive
                      package 18, 101
Ada.Environment_Variables package 157
Ada.Execution_Time package 20, 108
Ada.Execution_Time.Group_Budgets package 107
Ada.Execution_Time.Interrupts package 21, 109
Ada.Iterator_Interfaces generic package 123, 164
Ada.Locales package 26, 155, 200
Ada.Streams.Stream_IO package 156
Ada.Strings.Hash function 156
Ada.Strings.Hash_Case_Insensitive function 156
Ada.Strings.Less_Case_Insensitive function 156
Ada.Strings.UTF_Encoding package 25, 149
Ada.Strings.UTF_Encoding.Conversions
                      package 25, 150
Ada.Strings.UTF_Encoding.Strings
                      package 25, 150
Ada.Strings.UTF_Encoding.Wide_Strings
                      package 25, 150
Ada.Strings.UTF_Encoding.Wide_Wide_Strings
                      package 25, 150
Ada.Synchronous_Barriers package 19, 103
Ada.Synchronous_Task_Control package 101
Ada.Synchronous_Task_Control.EDF
                      package 19, 102
Ada.Tags package 146
Ada.Task_Identification package 136
Ada.Unchecked_Deallocate_Subpool
                         procedure 139
Ada.Wide_Characters package 151
Ada.Wide_Characters.Handling package 25, 152
Ada.Wide_Wide_Characters package 151
Ada.Wide_Wide_Characters.Handling package 25
Address attribute 143
Algol 60 66, 85
Algol 68 66
aliased
  extended return object 95
aliased parameter 16, 88
anonymous access type 132
array component iterator 122
aspect
  Asynchronous 37
  Atomic 38, 110
  Atomic_Components 38

Attach_Handler 39
Constant_Indexing 130
Convention 37, 38
CPU 19, 39, 104
Default_Component_Value 9, 62
Default_Iterator 131
Default_Value 9, 62
Dispatching_Domain 9, 39
Dynamic_Predicate 8, 56
Elaborate_Body 40
Export 38
External_Name 38
Implicit_Dereference 130
Import 38
Independent 38
Independent_Components 38
Inline 36
Interrupt_Handler 39
Interrupt_Priority 39
Iterator_Element 131
Link_Name 38
No_Return 36
Pack 36
Post 4, 42
Post'Class 6, 42
Pre 4, 42
Pre'Class 6, 42
Predicate_Failure 201
Preelaborate 40
Priority 39
Pure 40
Relative_Deadline 39
Static_Predicate 8, 56
Storage_Size 39
Synchronization 21, 113
Type_Invariant 7, 51
Type_Invariant'Class 8, 54
Unchecked_Union 38
Variable_Indexing 130
Volatile 38, 110
Volatile_Components 38
aspect specification 35
Assert pragma 40
assertion policy 5
Assertion_Policy pragma 40, 43, 51, 58
assignment statement 199
Asynchronous aspect 37
Atomic aspect 38, 110

Atomic_Components aspect 38
Attach_Handler aspect 39
attribute
    Address 143
    First_Valid 60
    Has_Same_Storage 9, 63
    Last_Valid 60
    Max_Alignment_For_Allocation 135
    Max_Size_In_Storage_Elements 135
    Old 6, 42
    Overlaps_Storage 9, 63
    Result 6, 43

B

BOM 149
born obsolescent 39, 105
bounded containers 26, 160
Brukardt
    Randy 1
Byte Order Mark 149

C

C 86
Capacity_Error 160
    raised 161
case expression 11, 70
case sensitivity
    of file names 153
case-insensitive string comparison 156
character set version 152
child node 168
class-wide invariant 54
class-wide postcondition 45
class-wide precondition 45
composability of equality 145
conditional expression 9, 66
constant
    extended return object 96
Constant_Indexing aspect 130
Constant_Reference function 167
container
    bounded 160
    holder 178
    multiway tree 168
    queue 180
container element iterator 122

continue statement 119
contract 4
Controlled pragma 38
Convention aspect 37, 38
conversion of access types 133
CPL 66
CPU
  aspect 104
  pragma 105
  subtype 104
  set 203
CPU aspect 19, 39

D

Daylight Saving Time 143
deadline 19
Decode 150
default element subtype 131
default indexing function 131
default iterator function 131
default storage pool 23, 139
Default_Component_Value aspect 9, 62
Default_Iterator aspect 131
Default_Storage_Pool pragma 23, 139
Default_Value aspect 9, 62
delay statement 100
discriminant
  with a default 92
dispatching domain 20, 105, 203
Dispatching_Domain aspect 19. 39
domain
  dispatching 105, 203
dynamic predicate 56
Dynamic_Predicate aspect 8, 56

E

EDF 19
EDF_Across_Priorities 101
Eiffel 33
Elaborate_Body aspect 40
Encode 150
environment variable 157
Environment_Task function 137
equality of records 145
execution time 108
existential quantifier 72

explicitly aliased parameter 88
Export aspect 38
expression function 13, 73
extended return object
  aliased 95
  constant 96
extended return statement 95
External_Name aspect 38

F

FIFO_Within_Priorities 100
Find_Token 25, 148
First_Valid attribute 60
fixed point
  cyclic 198
formal incomplete type 90
Forward_Iterator interface 124
freezing
  a profile 90
  a profile with a formal incomplete parameter 91
  a subprogram 90
  actual types of an instance 91
function
  Activation_Is_Complete 137
  Ada.Strings.Hash 156
  Ada.Strings.Hash_Case_Insensitive 156
  Ada.Strings.Less_Case_Insensitive 156
  Environment_Task 137
  Is_Abstract 146
  Iterate 124
function result
  having an incomplete type 90

G

generalized iterator 122
generic formal incomplete type 90
generic formal subprogram 143
generic package
  Ada.Iterator_Interfaces 123, 164
global annotation 199
Green Programming Language 85
group budget 107

H

Has_Same_Storage attribute 9, 63

holder container   27, 178

I

Ichbiah
  Jean   1
if expression   10, 66
immutably limited type   95
implicit conversion
  anonymous access   132
Implicit_Dereference aspect   130
Import aspect   38
in out parameter   15, 84
incompatibility
  with Ada 2005   191
incomplete type   88
  as parameter type   89
  completed by private type   89
  generic formal   90
inconsistency
  with Ada 2005   193
Independent aspect   38
Independent_Components aspect   38
indexable container type   131
Inline aspect   36
interface
  Forward_Iterator   124
  Reversible_Iterator   124
interface types   111
interrupt handler
  execution time   108
Interrupt_Handler aspect   39
Interrupt_Priority aspect   39
invariant
  class-wide   54
  specific   51
Ironman   84
Is_Abstract function   146
ISO 10646   148
iterable container type   131
Iterate function   124
iterator
  array component   122
  container   30
  container element   122
  generalized   122
Iterator_Element aspect   131
Iterator_Interfaces generic package   123, 164

K

known to denote the same object   86
known to refer to the same object   86

L

label   118
language
  locale   155
Last_Valid attribute   60
leaf node   169
leap seconds   143
Leroy
  Pascal   1
Link_Name aspect   38
Liskov Substitution Principle   48
List pragma   40
locale   26, 155
LSP   48

M

Max_Alignment_For_Allocation attribute   135
Max_Size_In_Storage_Elements attribute   135
membership test   77, 202
  of an access type   134
mode
  function parameters   84
Moore
  Jim   1
multiple inheritance   48
multiprocessor   103
Multiprocessors package   19
multiway tree container   27, 188
mutable   92

N

No_Access_Parameter_Allocators
           restriction   24, 140
No_Anonymous_Allocators
           restriction   23, 136, 140
No_Coextensions restriction   24, 140
No_Implementation_Aspect_Specifications
           restriction   24, 141
No_Implementation_Extensions profile   24, 142

No_Implementation_Identifiers
                    restriction 24, 141
No_Implementation_Units restriction 24, 141
No_Return aspect 36
No_Specification_of_Aspect restriction 24, 141
No_Standard_Allocators_After_Elaboration
                    restriction 23, 136, 140
No_Use_Of_Attribute restriction 141
No_Use_Of_Pragma restriction 141
node
  child 168
  leaf 169
  root 169
  tree 169
nominal subtype 143
Non_Preemptive_FIFO_Within_Priorities 101

O

Old attribute 6, 42
Optimize pragma 40
order of evaluation
  unspecified 86
Overlaps_Storage attribute 9, 63

P

Pack aspect 36
package
  Ada 117
  Ada.Calendar 143
  Ada.Containers 160
  Ada.Containers.Bounded_Doubly_Linked_Lists
                    160
  Ada.Containers.Bounded_Hashed_Maps 160
  Ada.Containers.Bounded_Hashed_Sets 161
  Ada.Containers.Bounded_Multiway_Trees
                    27, 168
  Ada.Containers.Bounded_Ordered_Maps 160
  Ada.Containers.Bounded_Ordered_Sets 161
  Ada.Containers.Bounded_Priority_Queues 180
  Ada.Containers.Bounded_Synchronized_Queues
                    180
  Ada.Containers.Bounded_Vectors 160
  Ada.Containers.Indefinite_Holders 27, 178
  Ada.Containers.Indefinite_Multiway_Trees
                    27, 168
  Ada.Containers.Multiway_Trees 27, 168

  Ada.Containers.Synchronized_Queue_Interfaces
                    28, 180
  Ada.Containers.Unbounded_Priority_Queues 180
  Ada.Containers.Unbounded_Synchronized_Queues
                    28, 180
  Ada.Directories 25, 152
  Ada.Directories.Hierarchical_File_Names
                    26, 154
  Ada.Dispatching 18, 101
  Ada.Dispatching.EDF 102
  Ada.Dispatching.Non_Preemptive 18, 101
  Ada.Environment_Variables 157
  Ada.Execution_Time 21, 108
  Ada.Execution_Time.Group_Budgets 107
  Ada.Execution_Time.Interrupts 20, 109
  Ada.Iterator_Interfaces generic 123, 164
  Ada.Locales 26, 155, 200
  Ada.Streams.Stream_IO 156
  Ada.Strings.UTF_Encoding 25, 149
  Ada.Strings.UTF_Encoding.Conversions 25, 150
  Ada.Strings.UTF_Encoding.Strings 25, 150
  Ada.Strings.UTF_Encoding.Wide_Strings 25, 150
  Ada.Strings.UTF_Encoding.Wide_Wide_Strings
                    25, 150
  Ada.Synchronous_Barriers 19, 103
  Ada.Synchronous_Task_Control 101
  Ada.Synchronous_Task_Control.EDF 19, 102
  Ada.Tags 146
  Ada.Task_Identification 136
  Ada.Wide_Characters 151
  Ada.Wide_Characters.Handling 25, 152
  Ada.Wide_Wide_Characters 151
  Ada.Wide_Wide_Characters.Handling 25
  System.Multiprocessors 19, 104
  System.Multiprocessors.Dispatching_Domains
                    19, 105, 203
  System.Storage_Pools.Subpools 137
package use clause 93
Page pragma 40
parameter
  aliased 16, 88
  in out 15, 87
  of an incomplete type 89
Pascal 67
Plödereder
  Erhard 1
pool
  default 23, 139

Post aspect 4, 42
Post'Class aspect 6, 42
postcondition 4
  class-wide 45
  specific 42
pragma
  Assert 40
  Assertion_Policy 40, 43, 51, 58
  Controlled 38
  CPU 105
  Default_Storage_Pool 23, 139
  List 40
  Optimize 40
  Page 40
  Preelaborable_Initialization 40
  Profile 142
  Restrictions 40, 140
  Suppress 40
  Unsuppress 40
Pre aspect 4, 42
Pre'Class aspect 6, 42
precondition 4
  class-wide 45
  specific 42
predicate
  dynamic 56
  static 56
Predicate_Failure aspect 201
Preelaborable_Initialization pragma 40
Preelaborate aspect 40
Preliminary Ada 85
Preliminary Green 85
primitive operations 93
priority 100
Priority aspect 39
procedure
  Ada.Containers.Generic_Array_Sort 187
  Ada.Containers.Generic_Sort 188
  Ada.Unchecked_Deallocate_Subpool 139
profile
  No_Implementation_Extensions 24, 142
Profile pragma 142
Pure aspect 40

Q

qualified expression 80
quantified expression 12, 71, 131

Query_Element procedure 166
queue containers 27, 180

R

raise expression 199
Ravenscar profile 18
Reference function 167
reference type 127
Relative_Deadline aspect 39
renaming of entry 113
Replace_Element procedure 166
requeue 112
reserved words 191
restriction
  No_Access_Parameter_Allocators 24, 140
  No_Anonymous_Allocators 23, 136, 140
  No_Coextensions 24, 140
  No_Implementation_Aspect_Specifications
                                      24, 141
  No_Implementation_Identifiers 24, 141
  No_Implementation_Units 24, 141
  No_Specification_Of_Aspect 24, 141
  No_Standard_Allocators_After_Elaboration
                                      23, 136, 140
  No_Use_Of_Attribute 141
  No_Use_Of_Pragma 141
Restrictions pragma 40, 140
Result attribute 6, 43
Reversible_Iterator interface 124
root directory 152
root node 169
Round_Robin_Within_Priorities 101

S

scheduling 100
Schonberg
  Ed 1
scope
  of revision 1
shared variable 109
sorting 29
SPARK 33
specific invariant 51
specific postcondition 42
specific precondition 42
stand-alone object

of an anonymous access type 133
static conditional expression 70
static predicate 56
Static_Predicate aspect 8, 56
Steelman 84
storage pool 23, 135
Storage_Size aspect 39
streaming 189
subpool 23
    of a storage pool 137
subtype
    CPU 104
subtype predicate 8, 56
Suppress pragma 40
suspension object 19, 101
Synchronization aspect 21, 113
synchronized interface 111
synchronous barrier 19
System.Multiprocessors package 19, 104
System.Multiprocessors.Dispatching_Domains
                    package 19, 105, 203
System.Storage_Pools.Subpools package 137

T

Taft
    Tucker 1
Taft amendment type 90
Tags package 146
task
    priority 100
    scheduling 100
task execution time 108
Task_Dispatching_Policy 100
Task_Identification package 136
time zone 143
Tokar
    Joyce 1

tree container 27
tree node 169
type invariant 6
    class-wide 54
    specific 51
Type_Invariant aspect 7, 51
Type_Invariant'Class aspect 8, 54

U

Unchecked_Union aspect 38
universal quantifier 72
Unsuppress pragma 40
Update_Element procedure 166
use all type clause 17, 94
use clause
    package 93
use type clause 93
UTC_Offset 143
UTF-16 encoding 25, 148
UTF-16BE 148
UTF-16LE 148
UTF-8 encoding 25, 148

V

Value
    environment variables 157
Variable_Indexing aspect 130
volatile 109
Volatile aspect 38, 110
Volatile_Components aspect 38

Y

Yield procedure 18, 101
Yield_To_Higher procedure 18, 101